DISCARD

Black Women in New South Literature and Culture

Studies in American Popular History and Culture

JEROME NADELHAFT, *General Editor*

For a full list of title in this series, please visit www.routledge.com

Women and Comedy in Solo Performance
Phyllis Diller, Lily Tomlin, and Roseanne
Suzanne Lavin

The Literature of Immigration and Racial Formation
Becoming White, Becoming Other, Becoming American in the Late Progressive Era
Linda Joyce Brown

Popular Culture and the Enduring Myth of Chicago, 1871–1968
Lisa Krissoff Boehm

America's Fight over Water
The Environmental and Political Effects of Large-Scale Water Systems
Kevin Wehr

Daughters of Eve
Pregnant Brides and Unwed Mothers in Seventeenth-Century Massachusetts
Else L. Hambleton

Narrative, Political Unconscious, and Racial Violence in Wilmington, North Carolina
Leslie H. Hossfeld

Validating Bachelorhood
Audience, Patriarchy, and Charles Brockden Brown's Editorship of the *Monthly Magazine and American Review*
Scott Slawinski

Children and the Criminal Law in Connecticut, 1635–1855
Changing Perceptions of Childhood
Nancy Hathaway Steenburg

Books and Libraries in American Society during World War II
Weapons in the War of Ideas
Patti Clayton Becker

Mistresses of the Transient Hearth
American Army Officers' Wives and Material Culture, 1840–1880
Robin Dell Campbell

The Farm Press, Reform, and Rural Change, 1895–1920
John J. Fry

State of 'The Union'
Marriage and Free Love in the Late 1800s
Sandra Ellen Schroer

"My Pen and My Soul Have Ever Gone Together"
Thomas Paine and the American Revolution
Vikki J. Vickers

Agents of Wrath, Sowers of Discord
Authority and Dissent in Puritan Massachusetts, 1630-1655
Timothy L. Wood

The Quiet Revolutionaries
How the Grey Nuns Changed the Social Welfare Paradigm of Lewiston, Maine
Susan P. Hudson

Cleaning Up
The Transformation of Domestic
Service in Twentieth Century
New York City
Alana Erickson Coble

Feminist Revolution in Literacy
Women's Bookstores in the
United States
Junko R. Onosaka

**Great Depression and the
Middle Class**
Experts, Collegiate Youth and
Business Ideology, 1929–1941
Mary C. McComb

Labor and Laborers of the Loom
Mechanization and Handloom
Weavers, 1780–1840
Gail Fowler Mohanty

"The First of Causes to Our Sex"
The Female Moral Reform Movement
in the Antebellum Northeast,
1834–1848
Daniel S. Wright

**US Textile Production in Historical
Perspective**
A Case Study from Massachusetts
Susan M. Ouellette

Women Workers on Strike
Narratives of Southern Women
Unionists
Roxanne Newton

Hollywood and Anticommunism
HUAC and the Evolution of the Red
Menace, 1935–1950
John Joseph Gladchuk

**Negotiating Motherhood in
Nineteenth-Century American
Literature**
Mary McCartin Wearn

**The Gay Liberation Youth Movement
in New York**
"An Army of Lovers Cannot Fail"
Stephan L. Cohen

**Gender and the American
Temperance Movement of the
Nineteenth Century**
Holly Berkley Fletcher

**The Struggle For Free Speech in the
United States, 1872–1915**
Edward Bliss Foote, Edward Bond
Foote, and Anti-Comstock Operations
Janice Ruth Wood

The Marketing of Edgar Allan Poe
Jonathan H. Hartmann

**Language, Gender, and Citizenship
in American Literature, 1789–1919**
Amy Dunham Strand

Antebellum Slave Narratives
Cultural and Political
Expressions of Africa
Jermaine O. Archer

**Fictions of Female Education in the
Nineteenth Century**
Jaime Osterman Alves

**John Brown and the Era of Literary
Confrontation**
Michael Stoneham

**Performing American Identity in
Anti-Mormon Melodrama**
Megan Sanborn Jones

**Black Women in New South
Literature and Culture**
Sherita L. Johnson

Black Women in New South Literature and Culture

Sherita L. Johnson

Routledge
Taylor & Francis Group
New York   London

First published 2010
by Routledge
270 Madison Ave, New York, NY 10016

Simultaneously published in the UK
by Routledge
2 Park Square, Milton Park, Abingdon, Oxon OX14 4RN

Routledge is an imprint of the Taylor & Francis Group, an informa business

Typeset in Sabon by IBT Global.
Printed and bound in the United States of America on acid-free paper by IBT Global.

Library of Congress Cataloging in Publication Data
Johnson, Sherita L.
    Black women in new South literature and culture / by Sherita L. Johnson.
        p. cm. — (Studies in American popular history and culture)
    Includes bibliographical references and index.
    1. American literature — Southern States — History and criticism.   2. African Ameri-
can women in literature.   I. Title.
    PS261.J55 2009
    810.9'352996073 — dc22
    2009015478

ISBN10: 0-415-99220-6 (hbk)
ISBN10: 0-203-86785-8 (ebk)

ISBN13: 978-0-415-99220-6 (hbk)
ISBN13: 978-0-203-86785-3 (ebk)

*In memory of my aunts, Anna Louise Strode
and Louvenia "Bay" Ware*

Contents

Acknowledgments   xi

Introduction   1

1   'In the Sunny South': Reconstructing
    Frances Harper as Southern   10

2   Conjuring a New South: Black Women
    Radicals in the Works of Charles
    Chesnutt and George Washington Cable   45

3   New South, New Negro: Anna Julia Cooper's
    A Voice from the South   97

4   'The South *Is* Our Home': Cultural Narratives
    of Place and Displacement   111

Epilogue
    Voices, Bodies, and Texts: Making
    the Black Woman Visible in New South
    Literature and Culture   128

Notes   131
Bibliography   147
Index   159

Acknowledgments

There are many individuals to thank for the support given to me while I worked to complete this book. Among them are mentors and friends, namely Stephanie Foote who is usually enthusiastic about my ideas and always offers firm, concise criticism of my analysis. She has carefully guided me through the process of writing this first book and, though any errors are my own, I appreciate all that she has done to boost my confidence and to keep me focused on my work. Robert Dale Parker, Arlene Torres, and Nancy Castro were also there at the beginning of this project and I hope they recognize their imprints on it. As a fellow in 2002–2003 of the Illinois Program for Research in the Humanities (IPRH) at the University of Illinois at Urbana-Champaign (UIUC), I participated in peer discussions about "the South" in seminars with guest scholars which helped to sharpen my critique of Southernness. The IPRH funding and other resources allowed me to develop the first case study on Frances Harper. My academic life has been full of achievements and disappointments, and I could not have sustained the strength to persevere had it not been for my family: my mother, Pearlie Ware, and siblings—Mary, Barbara, Louise, Shirley, Ann, Donna, and Godfrey—and many other relatives. This extended family also includes good friends like Rychetta, Erika, Faye, Danielle, Vivian, Heidi, Shawn, and Kenyetta as well as members of the True Light Missionary Baptist Church. Finally, the sacrifice of time spent working long days and late nights on this book has only strengthened my relationship with Johnny, who understands my ambition and keeps me laughing when I take myself too seriously.

Introduction

> The colored woman of today occupies, one may say, a unique position in this country. In a period of itself transitional and unsettled, her status seems one of the least ascertainable and definitive of all the forces which make for our civilization. She is confronted by both a woman question and a race problem, and is as yet an unknown or an unacknowledged factor in both.
>
> —Anna Julia Cooper, *A Voice from the South: By a Black Woman of the South*, 1892.

Through the voice of Anna Julia Cooper, I find a black woman interrogating and professing multiple subject positions not in the twenty-first century but at the close of the nineteenth. Industrialization, progressive era politics, and social conflict define the late nineteenth-century America as "transitional and unsettled," it *seemed* that the status of a black woman was not of any real significance. When we think about nationalism in the late-nineteenth century, scholars discount black women, but if we think about the region of the South and the project of reunification, new subjects appear to us. The status of a Southern black woman is more pronounced when juxtaposed to the forces of sexism and racism combined with economic and political problems as well as social movements to "uplift" those in need. Cooper, taken as a case study, was disenfranchised (like most black men and all women) and faced gender discrimination in employment and at educational institutions, yet, as a public intellectual, she is empowered by her perceived marginality to deliver notice to antagonists in *A Voice from the South: By a Black Woman of the South*. She helps scholars today see that social change in the late nineteenth century happened as a result of the most marginalized social actors. Cooper's recognition of how subjective and objective realities of black women can affect how they experience and understand societal changes inspired this book's critique of the South.[1]

Although the South has been an enduring site of criticism in American Studies and in American literary history, this book argues that it is impossible to consider what the "South" and what "Southernness" mean as cultural references without looking at how black women have contributed to and contested any unified definition of this region. I focus on the late nineteenth and early twentieth centuries, a period of intense regional conflict when Southern blacks, especially, witnessed the reassertion of white hegemony. Hence, the dominant Southern ideology and identity become synonymous with "whiteness" as it solidifies in literary and political narratives. *Whiteness also became mostly an unacknowledged component in the region's race problems.* Public debates about these issues often rested on black liberties in a post-slavery society. White Southerners thus identified a regional "problem" without acknowledging the power of white supremacy at its source. African Americans, on the other hand, did not. This book examines the relationship between Southern literature and the South's social history. Specifically, I look at that relationship by focusing on black women, fictional and historical, arguing that they are under-acknowledged agents of cultural change. Though black women were integral to Southern society, they are often invisible in historical accounts of regional politics and culture, especially as *Southern* black women. Black women, likewise, are a largely under-critiqued presence in the regional fiction of the period.[2] However, the way we think about the South changes if we recast black women, looking at the region as organized by and around black women.

Current studies of the South, its cultures and people, have affirmed that regional homogeneity was a fiction based on lost, limited, and often, biased historical memories and records. New perspectives of the "global South," for instance, have opened the field to multiple possibilities of Southern cultural identity.[3] Postcolonial critics have especially contributed to this advancement. Although my work is influenced by such scholarship, it does not fully engage with the disciplinary treatment of the South as internationally situated in a history of oppression. In my analysis, I try to define the subtleties of white-black relations in the South because it was how we identified most "Southerners" in the nineteenth century. White males who fought for the Confederacy and slavery, who later became proponents of the "New South" might have been the self-styled Southerners we have recognized mostly in the century or so since then. They claimed the identity of the South as a victory in defeat. By contesting that construct of Southernness, however, this book renews Southern studies just as it acknowledges its past.[4] It shows how "the" South was both fixed and fluid to broaden the idea of Southern regional and cultural identity and embrace black women as regional figures. If we see the typical nineteenth-century white Southerner as a construct, we can see that hierarchies of race, class, and gender are contested in the South because regional identity and social status are linked by a history of inequality. Whiteness and patriarchy limits the agency of white women and black men though each group benefits some by association with the dominant forces at work in constructing the South. Other groups form a third class, so to speak, comparable to colonized subjects in the power dynamics of colonial states. Thus, I regard the South as a place, a space and cultural region that (re)constructs black womanhood, but I also consider how black womanhood transforms the region of the South.

Like Cooper, I am interested in the nature of regional representation through black women and the experiences of black women as regional representatives. Cooper was a black woman whose Southernness is all but ignored despite her self-identification as a Southerner. This maybe due in part to the overshadowing of her role as an outspoken critic of Southern race relations in comparison to her contemporary and regional icon, Booker T. Washington, whose accommodationist stance authenticates his experience of being Southern in sharp contrast to Cooper's. Both were born prior to the Civil War, but, in coming "up from slavery," she would dismantle hierarchies of race, gender, and class by repositioning her "place" theoretically from the margins to the center in *A Voice from the South*. Cooper's political consciousness, along with the literary and political writings of other Southern black women, and the representations of black female characters in Southern texts construct complex formulations of black womanhood in general and black Southernness in particular. I concentrate on historical black women's self-identification, self-determination, through their sense of place. One of the ways we can see that black women were important agents of change is to see that many writers used them in fiction to do certain cultural and political work. So you can not only see how black women change the 'text' that is the South but also how they were used in all kinds of texts about the South, even those by white men.

Historian Anne Firor Scott asserts that "[f]iction may indeed provide a way to confront issues which the social milieu would prefer to deny" (30). I turn to Southern writers of dissent who critique race relations in the early stages of Jim Crow: Cooper, Frances Ellen Watkins Harper, Charles Waddell Chesnutt, and George Washington Cable. Harper, Chesnutt, and Cable were all outspoken social activists who wrote political treatises as well as radical fiction throughout their careers. Harper's early years as an abolitionist informs her writings during the Reconstruction era when she returned to the South assessing the conditions of freedmen/women. Her "genteel protest" literature then serves as a prelude to the race problem narratives that Chesnutt, Cable, and Cooper wrote at the peak of agitation in the 1880s and 1890s. In their fiction, Harper, Chesnutt, and Cable do not depict the idyllic images of plantation life popular in Southern literature of the late nineteenth century. They are however useful case studies for other writers to show how closely fiction and political rhetoric about the South's racial problems appear in print history. These writers are more concerned with progressive politics and solving the purported "Negro Problem," as it becomes the foundation for Jim Crow policies.

The Negro Problem evolved around issues concerning the huge population of ex-slaves who had remained in the South after the Civil War. Frustrated by the debacle of Reconstruction, which tried to force them to treat all African Americans as equals, white Southerners like Thomas Nelson Page later declared that "the Negro was the Southerner's problem." Some extremist advocated African colonization as a possible solution to the race problem by returning blacks to their "homeland." Ultimately, Southern whites created policies of segregation to reestablish and maintain social order, signaling the birth of Jim Crow that lasted for several decades into the twentieth century. The South as "home" for African Americans remains a multi-layered text of memory, time, and place and it draws on long histories assembled by both the dissenting writers I examine as well as the conservative writers against whom they stood in contrast.

Although I am writing about the role of black women in the texts that made up the South, my analysis draws on social history. As a consequence, I discovered that while investigating the South's race problem of the late nineteenth century, there are two ways of understanding the debate by looking at the *political or legal component* versus the *social component* of the "problem." The legal component relates to the issues of suffrage, disenfranchisement, segregation, and civil rights. While African Americans pushed for racial equality based on these political issues, most Southern whites worked to keep the status quo via black disenfranchisement in particular. For African Americans, suffrage defined their citizenship and signified their desires for freedom.[5] Although only black men were given voting rights as stipulated in the fifteenth amendment, all African Americans were vulnerable to violent threats against their humanity without the right of civic representation and other legal protection. The social component of the Negro Problem then is a concern with improving the appalling condition of race relations without necessarily relying on civil laws but on ethics instead. This social component supports the creation and maintenance of strong communal ties despite racial differences in the South. Hence, it does not support the separate but equal policies instituted by Southern laws.

Each component reinforces prescribed gender roles depending on separate spheres of influence. The legal component is a masculine concept because men, as public figures, were empowered by suffrage and patriarchal systems of dominance. There were also general expectations of American women to be moral exemplars, capable of molding the social behaviors of their families and, by extension, affecting the moral impulse of the nation at large.[6] The social component is thus gendered as feminine because women were disenfranchised and, ideally, women were assigned to the home, but not just to *their own homes*. A large percentage of black women in the South worked as domestics in white households. As such, these women held an intermediary position in Southern society and culture, crossing racial boundaries at the very time when they were being fortified. Education also provided an added advantage to those Southern black women like Cooper who may not have worked as domestics but still managed to intercede in public debates about the race problems and offer their own solutions. In their fiction and political discourse, Harper, Chesnutt, and Cable rely on black women as social actors to address the Negro Problem. Cooper does so in her own right. All of these writers reify black women's experiences in the context of the South and its cultural history. Therefore, fictional black women that go beyond stereotype make notable appearances in their literature. They are community leaders, educated "mammies," and activist housewives among other roles they play in reshaping the South.

These writers are Southern, and understood themselves as Southern even in a culture quickly equating "Southern" and "white." They could therefore expose flawed perceptions of regional identity in their works. Idealized Southern history (based on slavery and Confederate symbolism) projected the dominant perception of the "the" South as "white." Charles Reagan Wilson believes that white Southern identity solidified during the late nineteenth century, a period of modernization, as a way of maintaining a sense of pride and distinctive regional culture. The defeat of the Civil War weakened the South's identity as a nation-state. Thus, the "invention" of traditions made it possible for regional identity to be based on more than a rebellious attempt to dissolve the Union. Southern historical societies, for instance, were organized to preserve Confederate artifacts and perform public rituals (e.g. battle re-enactments, pageantries, erecting monuments, etc.).[7] In the making of a "New South," most white Southerners began manufacturing their distinctive cultural identity with such traditions of the "Old South" in mind. Northern investments in the Southern economy provided the financial backing for the new master class of Southern whites "to restore and then to uphold the most definitively 'southern' ideals of the Old South, especially its racial, political, and class hierarchies" (Cobb 68). With antebellum settings, romantic plantation literature contributed to the further spread of the New South culture by perpetuating mythical images of the South as outlined by Wilson and others.

We can discover central themes in Southern history and literature when we understand how myths are created and evolve, always illustrating what is uniquely "Southern" about the South. For historians, according to George B. Tindall, the study of mythology provides another take on how "reality" of the Southern past creates/enforces various myths that identify the South for outsiders and for native Southerners' claim to distinctiveness. Tindall credits literary scholars for realizing the importance of mythmaking in creating a distinctive Southern identity since various mythical images of the South are portrayed in literature. As it appears in works by John Pendleton Kennedy, Thomas Nelson Page, and Joel Chandler Harris, the "Old South" of plantation fiction is set with white aristocrats, Southern belles, "happy darkies," sprawling estates, and mint juleps. The "Savage South" is inhabited by glorified poor whites and plagued by economic depravity, violence, ignorance, and racial segregation. This is the South of Henry L. Mencken's "The Sahara of the Bozart" (1920), Thomas Dixon's *The Clansman* (1905), and Erskine Caldwell's *Tobacco Road* (1932). William Faulkner, Eudora Welty, Carson McCullers, and other writers of the Southern Renaissance portray the "Changing South," a modern landscape stripped of cultural traditions yet looking backwards toward the very plantation hierarchies installed by late nineteenth-century popular writers like Dixon.

The writers I profile responded to Southern myths by focusing on socio-political problems that certain myths try to ignore. Unlike in the plantation myth of a romantic South, Harper's writings show examples of African Americans participating in the making of the South not just as slave laborers, but also as productive local citizens building communities. In counteracting the "legend of Reconstruction," purportedly the nightmarish movement of radical idealism which granted freedmen equal rights only to punish the South, Chesnutt uses conjuring to offset white Southerners' fears that "Negroes would Africanize the South." Through Uncle Julius (and his conjure tales about Aunt Peggy), for instance, Chesnutt advocates social equality. George Washington Cable, too, was very much apart of what Carl N. Degler calls "the other South," lesser known for its denouncement of slavery and aversion to succession as a legal right of Southern states. Cable was like other white Southerners, a "large minority," who were conservative unionist in the pre-Civil War era and staunch liberalists in the post-bellum era (Degler 126). Cable's role as a social historian and a political activist fuse in his fiction and his non-fictional writings clarify his liberalist principles of racial equality.

Against the façade of the New South, black women tell of their own ways to solve the Negro Problem. Cooper presents her "insider's view" in *A Voice from the South.* Other political autobiographies show ordinary women engaging in a public debate, providing the kind of intimate details that are uncommon in dominate discourses on the topic. These women take a practical approach to presenting the race problem by explaining how their daily lives were affected by systematic white oppression. Breaking taboos, they speak freely about being sexually harassed and the threat of sexual assault by white men. Their testimonies reveal how anti-miscegenation laws and other restrictions to keep the races separate were widely promoted in public forums but were not in practice privately by many white Southerners. The black women's autobiographies on the race problem highlight the similarities not differences between whites and blacks. For instance, they focus on common family values about teaching children Christian morals and on class values about the importance of property ownership.

So far I have been discussing the idea of who counts as a real Southerner. I have chosen to look at the black woman as both trope and social actor in the various texts that comprise the South, which in turn lets me carefully take apart ideas of "really belonging" and of exile, and of the right sort of bodies. In the first chapter, "'In the Sunny South': Reconstructing Frances Harper as Southern," I critique Harper's status as an exiled Southerner and the affect regional displacement had on her life and literature. A native of Baltimore, Maryland, Harper spent her formative years in a city with a sizable free black population, which created a community network of churches, schools, and benevolent societies. When discriminating laws of her home state made it difficult for free blacks like Harper to remain in the South, she left the region and became an official "exile by law." Thereafter,

Harper's struggle with a Southern sense of place kept her in a perpetual liminal state, literally and psychologically. The emphasis on black Southern experiences throughout Harper's political and literary career makes this conflicting attachment to the South more apparent. Notably, Harper represents the unexpected and often overlooked desires of black women after the Civil War. Harper also serves as a case study, for she embodies much of the textual work in which the other writers in this study are engaged. She creates archetypes of fictional black women accomplishing important cultural and political work in the South. These images are based on personal observations of historical black women during Reconstruction and Harper's own experiences of being Southern.

Chapter two, "Conjuring a New South: Black Women Radicals in the Works of Charles Chesnutt and George Washington Cable," interrogates these writers' gendered vision of the South as presented in *The Conjure Woman* (1899) and *The Grandissimes* (1880). Chesnutt's black male characters often overshadow his black female characters in view of the author's preoccupation with the South's Negro Problem. Yet, the construction of Southern identity is realized in the images of his fictional black women; their caste status and modes of self-preservation implicate them in the making of a different kind of South, where their struggles are vindicated and appear universal. The representations of conjure women found in both books are critical to the political arguments in each work. Cable, for instance, features this type of black woman as a participant in the (re-) making of the "new" South, although people of color are excluded from a homogeneous white Southern identity. In this chapter, I show how black women are positioned as displaced Southerners considering the narrative conventions used to construct a regional identity on the basis of white, upper class masculinity and the advocacy of human rights and racial equality. Though they use black women to construct narratives in which the very possibility of pure Southernness is flawed, Cable and Chesnutt also relegate black women to the margins of these narratives. Both men condemn their black female characters to the same fate the authors' shared as regional outcasts. I set Chesnutt and Cable's fiction against their controversial political essays about race relations in the South to indicate the vital role fictional black women play in their community, the narrative structure, and a radical civil rights campaign.

The work of Anna Julia Cooper is best known for critiquing the displacement of Southern black women within regional politics and culture. In the race problem equation, the power of whiteness negates blacks' civil rights. The dynamic figure of the black woman however interrupts the "natural" juxtapositioning of white superiority and black inferiority. She also appears as a gendered other, as Cooper proclaims in *A Voice From the South*. Therefore, in this third chapter, "New South, New Negro: Anna Julia Cooper's *A Voice from the South*," I concentrate on the status of black women, as Cooper frames it, by recognizing what Susan Gillman and Alys Eve Weinbaum call "the politics of juxtaposition." This theory of displacement clarifies how Southern black women, in the context of the Negro Problem, were positioned against "multiple political issues and related world historical movements for social justice as associated, as necessarily juxtaposed, if not fully interlinked, or self-consciously interwoven" (Gillman and Weinbaum 3). When Cooper speculates that the status of black women "seems one of the least ascertainable and definitive of *all the forces which make for our civilization*" (emphasis added), she refers, on the one hand, to the political, economical, and social changes taking place in late nineteenth-century America. It is also clear that the other "forces" upon which the status of black women depends include their juxtaposition to black men, white men and women, and other ethnic minorities. In this chapter about Cooper's life and text, I discuss how the figure of the black woman affects social policy as an intermediary and, as writer-activists, how black women like Cooper challenged the racist status quo while remaining connected to the region.

Since writings by and about Southern black women can be rare discoveries, in the final chapter, "The South *Is* Our Home: Cultural Narratives of Place and Displacement," I focus on a series of autobiographies written by Southern women in response to the Negro Problem at the start of the twentieth century. Some Southern black women struggled to shape and maintain their own autonomy, proclaimed their Southern legitimacy, and worked within the region for radical change. I argue that these black women wrote political autobiographies as cultural narratives about the South to challenge a constructed Southernness based on white supremacy. I focus on how these women position themselves in a chaotic historical moment—during the early days of Jim Crow and American modernization—that not only threatened their physical wellbeing but also undermined their ability to identify with Southernness, a group affiliation whose importance we have only begun to recognize. These women wrote against racial injustices while exposing the potential erasure of their cultural identities. I close with historical, Southern black women and their work to provide comparative evidence of the black woman's "place" in Southern society and culture, which helps to historicize the literary portrayals of black women.

This book takes part in the critical efforts to bring Southern black women into focus with their regional identities intact. It challenges the homogeneity of a "white" South and Southern cultural identity by recognizing how fictional and historical black women are positioned as under-acknowledged agents of cultural change, when dissenting writers recreate and respond to racial discrimination, segregation, and violence. As a displaced Southerner, Frances Harper's progressive politics target the South especially. Charles Chesnutt's personal and professional writings about the South also focus on distinctive cultural traits. Many readers maybe more familiar with his fiction than with his non-fiction. Yet, the irony in his "simple tales" about slavery and his sentimental romances are balanced by the persuasive rhetoric in his essays and speeches about securing African Americans' civil rights. I have always been intrigued by this nearly white, fair-complexioned "black" man's poised stance on the color line. Likewise, I am drawn to George Washington Cable's culturally diverse world in his novels and short stories about Creoles, Africans, and European immigrants in Louisiana. Such hybridity marks the "New South" in Cable's fiction as a place recognizable to us in the twenty-first century, one populated by multilingual individuals, practicing various religions and customs, and producing their own brand of Southernness. That he finds a unique place for black women in this exotic milieu during the nineteenth century captures the imagination and suggests ways of understanding their reality. From her own perspective, for instance, Anna Julia Cooper delivers a scathing critique of the South that juxtaposes black women to multiple political issues and social problems. She deconstructs racism and sexism to reveal black patriarchy and interracial conflicts among black and white women. It is her voice that we hear in a chorus of others whistling "Dixie" though to her own tune. Cooper recognizes the subordinate "place" designated for her (and other black women) in America and the South, but she also understands that as one of "the forces which make for our civilization" black women help to construct and reconstruct society especially when it is "transitional and unsettled." Focusing on black women lets me chart a much different trajectory for Southern identity because I bring regional history and regional literature together from the perspective of central, but ignored, social actors.

1 'In the Sunny South'
Reconstructing Frances Harper as Southern

Frances Ellen Watkins Harper's travels in the South are historic, mapping geographical space and her own sense of "place" as a Southerner. From about 1867 to 1871, she was busy with the work of Reconstruction, volunteering to assess the socioeconomic conditions in the region and to assist freed populations. She visited almost all the Confederate states except Texas and Arkansas, with stops in remote towns and urban areas. She spoke before audiences of black and white Southerners—including former slaves and "Rebs," conducted smaller seminars for local black women, and shared her message of racial progress and regional politics with Northern readers of the liberal press. Harper's assignment was similar to other black women like Sojourner Truth, Harriet Jacobs, Elizabeth Keckley, and Charlotte Forten (later Grimké): "they had to confront racism [and sexism] . . . that influenced their assignments, and that regularly allocated them less salary and their projects smaller budgets" (*Brighter* 121). Former slaves Truth and Jacobs worked with communities in Virginia and, with her daughter Louisa, Jacobs also traveled to Savannah, Georgia. Forten, whose relatives were among the leading black abolitionists, bravely volunteered for the "Port Royal experiment" of Northern educators dispatched to South Carolina. When the Union army captured Port Royal harbor in 1861, many slaveholders abandoned their plantations and slaves. The federal government and Northern abolitionists seized the opportunity to domesticate the contrabands and make them self-sufficient. Historians view this project as one of a few "rehearsals" for Reconstruction.[1] Forten documents her Sea Island experiences in diary entries from 1862 to 1864, revealing that the Port Royal mission was twofold: it was an early social experiment to uplift the masses and, for a naïve, passionate young woman the "journey south was a physical displacement that, while forging a public exposure of the body, also enabled the discovery of a site of self-authorization" (Peterson 190). Harper went south under much different circumstances than Forten though their trips yielded similar results. The older lecturer and poet returned to local sites under reconstruction, in the guise of a familiar public persona—that of a human rights activist—and reclaims the South as "home" in multiple texts.

Political history, gender studies, and literary criticism place Harper as central within the sphere in which her radical contemporaries also served. She worked along with other black women like Mary Ann Shadd Cary "to move beyond both local racial uplift programs and the national antislavery movement to participate in the work of national institutions that focused on broad questions of social and political economy" (Peterson 230). So to identify Harper as *Southern* might appear to relegate her to the margins of national discourses, isolating her own reconstructive cultural work to the region and local African American communities. But "Southernness," I argue, drawing from the experience of Harper, is a pervasive ideology within U.S. culture, politics, and literature of the late-nineteenth century. It extends beyond geographical specificity and, in its most critical form, it enforces white supremacy as national policy with severe local consequences. Thus, I draw attention to Harper's involvement in national as well as regional politics and social reform. The South, in turn, is a text that she constructs for broad audiences in her poetry, fiction, and prose using Southern black women as agents to accomplish her nationalistic goals of civil equality and racial progress.

Today Frances Harper (1825–1911) is recognized more as a literary foremother of African American women writers than as a Southern writer. Harper's collected works remain essential reading as the canon expands to include the lost work of her lesser-known contemporaries. One might even argue that the continual efforts to recover Harper's once discarded legacy have led to the search for others'. Most recently, Henry L. Gates Jr. and William L. Andrews have separately discovered nineteenth-century black women narratives which have familiar Southern settings, themes, and characters. Racial and gender studies are foundational for our understanding of early African American women writers and the world in which they lived. Archival recovery of Hannah Crafts' *The Bondswoman Narrative* (2002) and Julia C. Collins' *The Curse of Caste; or The Slave Bride* (2006) helps the project of Southern textual analysis necessary to (re)evaluate black women's subjective and objective realities, agency and authorship.

Frances Harper is an important Southern writer at a moment, during the nineteenth century and today, when Southernness was/is constructed and reconstructed to locate its cultural specificity *and* diversity. Her black male and white contemporaries have received more attention as regional writers when Southern cultural history mark the region as patriarchal, white, and limited by slavery. Harper's *Southernness* is often overlooked while William Wells Brown, Frederick Douglass (a fellow Marylander), Harriet Jacobs, and Charles Chesnutt are often included in literary anthologies of the American South. Harper only recently appears in Carolyn Perry and Mary Louise Weaks' *The History of Southern Women's Literature* (2002). Harper's absence in Southern literary history is not an unsolvable mystery when canonicity is determined by publishing budgets and editorial premises to re-present the South to succeeding generations. Consider, for instance, what we learn about the South and the burgeoning field of Southern studies in W.W. Norton's *The Literature of the American South* (1998). Henry L. Gates Jr.'s childhood experiences in the Allegheny Mountains, as chronicled in *Colored People* (1994), warrant his inclusion in this anthology, to which the memoir "broadens our understanding of black experiences on southern soil" beyond the Black Belt and slavery finally (1053). True, the editors cite common characteristics of racial prejudice, class distinctions, and caste systems recorded in Gates' book as a representative Southern text. I think Gates' inclusion in the anthology underscores Harper's exclusion when he is mostly responsible for the recovery of early black women's writing, especially in the Schomburg Library nineteenth century series. Gates' Southernness, however, like Harper's, is usually unacknowledged and so the Norton editors seek to redefine black Southern identity in the twenty-first century with more emphasis on cultural hybridity. If Michael Kreyling is correct, such re-inventions are likely to continue. Nineteenth-century black writers, along with the Plantation School of white Southerners and other local colorists, produced foundational texts of early Southern literature. Harper's original creations of folk figures and the black middle class predate Chesnutt's works by decades. However, the omission of Harper's depictions of black Southerners after slavery and before the Great Migration leaves a void in this early phase of Southern literature and American literature in general. My point is that while we know how to think about an expanded notion of Southernness and race now, we have not yet learned to see that conjunction historically, even though historical actors like Harper are responsible for it.

This chapter examines how Frances Harper's regional displacement contributes to several innovations she makes to Southern writing and the contests over the definition of Southernness that is now so critical to scholars. That is, how she connects race, gender, *and* region in her letters, poems, speeches, and other prose writings. Specifically, I argue that Harper respond to prevailing attitudes and ideas about the South by manipulating static characteristics of regional identity. In the volume of poetry *Sketches of Southern Life* (1872), she represents the unexpected and often overlooked desires of black women reconstructing their identities, their lives and communities. This narrative theme appears also in her periodical fiction about black domestic relations, which should be examined in a more comprehensive study of her Reconstruction literature. Though Harper remained active—in politics and publishing—during the twenty years between her post-bellum tour of the South and the birth of Jim Crow at the close of the century, I focus on these two historical moments as critical signposts in the making of the New South and defining Harper as Southern. She accentuates cultural flaws of the region in *Iola Leroy* (1892), for instance, when many white Southerners presented in their literary and political narratives a uniform vision of the South. Thus, this chapter reveals how Harper's expressions of "Southernness" go against the grain, making it possible for her to reclaim and reconstruct not just a region but a regional identity as part of her cultural identity and literary legacy.

"IN MY OWN SOUTHERN HOME": LOCATING FRANCES HARPER IN SOUTHERN HISTORY

When she ventured South after the Civil War, Frances Harper did so to experience "a brighter coming day" for black freedmen and women. She was no longer the agent of an anti-slavery society touring the North on an exhaustive lecture circuit, but, during the post-bellum Southern mission, she was just as overworked and, at times, optimistic of racial equality and progress for African Americans after centuries of enslavement and degradation. Hers was also a journey of a Southern exile returning home.

Harper was born into a family of free blacks on September 24, 1825 in Baltimore, Maryland, which was then a slave state. She was orphaned at three (her mother dead and father unknown) and raised by her uncle the Rev. William Watkins and his wife Henrietta. When literacy was illegal for slaves and unavailable for most other African Americans, Harper attended the William Watkins Academy for Negro Youth, the strict, Methodist-based school her uncle established in Baltimore. She remained enrolled at the school until about the age of thirteen when she began working as a domestic in the city. Harper continued her studies, reading at her leisure when not serving as a nurse-maid and seamstress for her employers. She also began writing poetry during this time (though this material has not been recovered, especially her first collection *Forest Leaves*). When the Fugitive Slave Law and other provisions curtailed the rights of free blacks in the South, Harper left her home state of Maryland around 1851 to teach in Ohio and Pennsylvania. Later, as "an exile by law" (Still 758), she spent over a decade lecturing on the abolitionists' and women's rights circuit throughout the Northeast and Midwest.[2]

Despite the support provided by the mentoring relationship Harper had with abolitionist William Still (1821–1902), the success of her writing and oratorical career, and the growth of her new family (she married Fenton Harper in 1860 and had a daughter named Mary), the effects of being uprooted from the South lingered. Still refers to her as being "a young and homeless maiden" after her move to Philadelphia in the early 1850s where she was not immediately embraced by the close circle of anti-slavery activists in the city. Harper did find refuge while living with Still's family and working on the Underground Railroad. Still was a pillar of black society in antebellum Philadelphia, a member of the Philadelphia Vigilance Committee before leading the Pennsylvania Abolition Society by 1851. Born free in New Jersey to parents who had secured their own freedom through escape and self-purchase, Still later documented the plight of other such fugitive slaves. For over fourteen years, he risked his safety and that of his black and white cohorts. His narrative collection is a rare historical record of slavery in its broad scope; it includes hundreds of short "sketches" of average fugitives' escapes and brief biographies of "conductors" of the Underground Railroad. His intents were to preserve the records as genealogical history for ex-slaves who searched for their relatives.[3] Still's heroism also inspired Harper's activism. She began to publish in religious and abolitionist newspapers like *The Christian Recorder*, the *Aliened American*, *Frederick Douglass' Paper*, and *The Liberator* (Foster 10–11). In the Pre-Civil War era, Harper engaged in cultural and political work like middle-class white women in the North. Using moralistic rhetoric, images, poetry, and fiction, they addressed the high stake dissolution of the Union and, collectively, these women used their public writing to enter the political sphere as concerned citizens though with gender circumscriptions (Cullen Sizer 4–8). Northern publishers in Boston and Philadelphia released several editions of Harper's poetry as her profile increased on the abolitionist circuit. *Poems on Miscellaneous Subjects* (1854 and 1857) sold more than 10,000 copies (Foster 14). Harper was among few American women writers, with a broad-based audience, who could parlay her political celebrity into a successful writing career, which included several books of poetry appearing between 1857 and 1901, many released in multiple editions and a few she published on her own by hiring local printers (Foster, "Introduction" 35).[4]

In becoming a popular writer-activist, Harper remained committed to helping blacks enslaved throughout the South, while painfully aware of her own regional displacement: "'I have lived in the midst of oppression and wrong, and I am saddened by every captured fugitive in the North; a blow has been struck at my freedom, in every hunted and down-trodden slave in the South'" (Still 763). Harper also recalled the struggles of free black Southerners in Baltimore trying to create and sustain communities. She worked tirelessly on behalf of the enslaved, fugitives, and "nominally free" like herself with thoughts of returning home: "'I might be so glad if it was only so that I could go home among my own kindred and people, but slavery comes up like a dark shadow between me and the home of my childhood. Well, perhaps it is my lot to die from home and be buried among strangers; and yet I do not regret that I have espoused this cause'" (Still 763). Harper was around twenty-five years old when she left Maryland in the 1850s. Thus, she grew to adulthood as a Southerner and expressed her Southernness in contrast to dominant ideologies of cultural and political identities of being a Southern woman. Her own "fugitive" status marks her as a displaced Southerner, juxtaposed to the slaves whom she helped to escape bondage as well as the free blacks who were marginalized by slavery. About sixteen years had passed when Harper finally returns *home* to the South during Reconstruction.[5]

Once exiled from the South, Frances Harper is inspired to activism and returns home again and again in her written and spoken texts. William Still recalls her being "sorely oppressed with the thought of the condition of her people in Maryland" while teaching in Little York, Pennsylvania (756). She pledged her commitment to the anti-slavery cause upon learning of a free black man's unlawful entry into Maryland, where he was imprisoned and sold into slavery. Harper's poem "Be Active", published in *Frederick Douglass' Paper* on January 11, 1856, reminds others that the struggle begins "Where the Southern roses blossom, / Weary lives go out in pain; / Dragging to death's shadowy portals, / Slavery's heavy galling chain" (ll.25–28).[6] Delivering a fervent address to the New York City Anti-Slavery Society on May 13, 1857, Harper goads her audience to "Ask Maryland, with her tens of thousands of slaves, if she is not prepared for freedom and hear her answer: 'I help supply the cofflegangs of the South'" (*Brighter* 100). Finally, in keeping her vow not to be buried in "a land of slaves," Harper's bittersweet return home during Reconstruction is documented in her letters and reimagined in *Sketches of Southern Life* and *Iola Leroy*. In the series of "Aunt Chloe poems," from *Sketches*, Harper critiques the political and economic transition the South and African Americans experienced through slavery, the Civil War, and Reconstruction. An underlying theme in these works is the plight of black Southerners, like Harper, as regional outcasts.

When so little is known about the day-to-day circumstances of Frances Harper's early life, we can fortunately examine the historical record to understand what possibly compelled her to leave home. Maryland during the nineteenth century was on "the middle ground" with its mixed-moderate political affairs and, quite literally, geographical location. It held the unique distinction among other border-states for having the largest amount of free blacks and, with its dual labor system, slave and free black populations by 1850 divided the state into "two Marylands."[7] Such bifurcation is illustrated on a regional state map, which looks like a wishbone with the Northern counties, particularly Baltimore, at the pressure point. The tobacco industry—and its slave labor operations—separated the state into three sub-regions distinguished by economic systems, demography, and social histories: the Northern free soil, the Eastern Shore, and the Southern slave territory. The Northern region operated mostly on white and free labor once tobacco's dominance was replaced by more industrialized productions. "Free" blacks, native born and fugitives, congregated in the cities of Northern Maryland where relative anonymity and safety was more secure. By mid-century, sixteen percent of this region's population was black and only five percent were slaves (Fields 6). Southern Maryland had an agricultural-based economy and boasted a black population of almost fifty percent, the majority of whom were slaves. The Eastern Shore was an agricultural society too, mostly cereal production instead of tobacco. This region's oddity mirrored that of the state at large; its intermediate position made it less distinguishable by race and class compared to the extremes within the other regions. Barbara Jeanne Fields interprets the subtleties of a state located on the Northern border of freedom and Southern reaches of slavery and unable to negotiate internal complications. Slavery was practiced throughout Maryland, with concentrations in the Southern and Eastern Shore regions, where Frederick Douglass was enslaved in Talbot County. White Marylanders fought to preserve the "peculiar institution" or the semblance thereof in their vulnerable region of the country. "Black residents knew the middle ground inch by inch from a perspective that white people could not share," however, "for the peculiarities of border-state slavery added bitter occasions for suffering to those that accompanied slavery everywhere" (Fields xii).

Frances Harper's activism is traceable to the antebellum conditions in Northern Maryland. She advocated for "free labor" when Baltimore had a symbiotic relationship with slavery in the southernmost parts of the state and the rest of the South. The growth of the city's economy relied on slave labor to provide raw materials for manufacturing, marketing, and other services. Factories in Baltimore especially made cigars from tobacco and processed cotton to earn profitable gains for the city and state. Baltimore's market economy was driven by the exportation of agricultural goods in general (Fields 7–17). Harper understood the commercial foundation of slavery well and tried to dismantle it even in small measures:

> I have reason to be thankful that I am able to give a little more for a Free Labor dress, if it is coarser. I can thank God that upon its warp and woof I see no stain of blood and tears; that to procure a little finer muslin for my limbs no crushed and broken heart went out in sighs; and that from the field where it was raised went up no wild and startling cry unto the throne of God to witness there in language deep and strong, that in demanding that cotton I was nerving oppression's hand for deeds of guilt and crime. (*Brighter* 45)

She spoke about free produce only three months into her career as an abolitionist lecturer in 1854. Later, she presents the same values in "Free Labor," published in her 1857 poetry collection. Harper's beliefs were backed by her actions and infused her writing. Wearing "an easy garment" not made by a "toiling slave" was a moral sacrifice and poetic expression with economic consequences.

In Northern Maryland, free labor was predominately white by comparison to other areas in the state. Thousands of foreigners immigrated to the urban manufacturing centers drastically increasing the white population by sixty-nine percent in 1850. Baltimore, as a port city, attracted German and Irish immigrants as well as out-of-state migrants (Fields 12–14). Thus, the South is not uniformly "white" for Harper; the concentration of ethnic foreigners in close contact with blacks, free and slaves, creates a mixed culture. Northern Maryland, much like the rest of the antebellum South, was however controlled by white slaveholders in the Southern and Eastern Shore regions despite their small numbers. The landed aristocracy wielded control over state and local politics by virtue of their accumulated wealth and caste status, even if the industrial urban areas were at an economic advantage with larger, diverse populations.

The imbalance of power in Northern Maryland affected free blacks tenfold. Historical accounts of Southern cities record surprising discrepancies in statistical data that suggests the vitality of free black populations in contrast to cities in the Northeast. Between 1800 and 1850, for example, communities of free blacks thrived in Charleston, New Orleans, Louisville, St. Louis, Washington, and Baltimore: "The national free black population grew to almost 435,000 in 1850, well over half of which (54.41 percent) were southern" (Curry, "Free Blacks" 36). Universal suffrage was prohibited in these cities with such large free black communities. Even though slavery prevailed, free blacks lived relatively "free" with limited occupations, owned real estate, established schools—especially those affiliated with churches—and formed benevolent societies. These conditions were especially precarious in Baltimore, Harper's hometown. It hosted one of the largest populations of free blacks in the state (more than 10,000, "roughly a sixth" of the city), most of whom were natives of Maryland. While some Southern cities implemented employment restrictions for free blacks—"largely designed to prevent giving assistance to the urban slaves or to lead to any weakening of white control over slaves," Baltimore by far had fewer such prohibitions or, if at all, they were often "violated and ignored" (Curry, "Free Blacks" 36–37).

However, certain regulations were characteristic of the state's "middle ground" politics and culture. In addition to vagrancy laws to restrict their mobility and wages, free blacks' freedom could not resemble that of white Southerners in Maryland:

> Free black persons could not own dogs or firearms or purchase liquor or ammunition without a special license. They could not sell bacon, pork, beef, mutton, corn, wheat, tobacco, rye, or oats without written certification from a justice of the peace or three 'respectable persons' of their neighborhood that they had acquired the goods honestly. They could not operate boats except under the supervision of a white person. Some counties forbade them to enter a tavern or shop between sunrise and sunset and some denied altogether their right to hold peddlers licenses or operate boats ... After 1858 they could be sold upon being convicted of crimes for which whites would be punished by imprisonment. (Fields 35)

White Marylanders were concerned about the relative stability of the state's dual caste system, which was threatened by the sizable free black population. Maryland's demography was comparable to New Orleans and slave societies in the Caribbean and Latin America, but the social status of free black people were not similar. Privileged free people of color constituted a third category, a "buffer" class in Jamaica, Curaçao, Brazil, and Cuba where they outnumbered whites. They created a "petite bourgeoisie—of artisans, shopkeepers, clerks, and small-holding farmers—of which slave society could make use for minor but necessary economic, administrative, and even peacekeeping functions that the white population could not have carried unassisted" (Fields 3). This was not so in Maryland. Whites in the state were still the majority and free blacks were only "nominally free" occupying equal space with slaves. Policing free blacks was necessary to maintain the ideological basis for slave societies. Thus, white Maryland- ers worked to the extent of the law to settle the "free black question" as the state and nation prepared for the impending Civil War crisis. Con- stitutional conventions in Baltimore were organized to create ordinances regulating the manumission of slaves and capture of fugitives and the expa- triation or enslavement of free blacks that did not comply with local and state policies. The debates were divided by region, among slaveholders and non-slaveholders, who were generally more moderate fearing the potential free black labor shortage if stringent measures were instituted. In 1861, the Committee on Colored Populations, led by C.W. Jacobs, an Eastern Shore slaveholder, battled against public opinion while determined to "'termi- nate freenegroism in Maryland . . . on the most advantageous terms to our white population'"(Fields 75). Illustrating its mixed-moderate politics and culture, the state's legislators (pressured by civil protest waged in the press) dissolved most of Jacobs' proposals and the policing of free blacks was left to the daily interactions of the people.

Considering that they were "[f]orced out of the 'whole society' by preju- dice and discrimination, urban blacks [in Maryland] early found that they could wholly rely on themselves and could wholly trust only themselves. Thus, there emerged sub-societies [i.e. segregated communities] and from them, in turn, slender filaments of connectivity that gave a more affirmative cast to the imposed commonality of subordination and oppression" (Curry, "Free Blacks" 49). Black churches were at the core providing moral uplift, building schools, and creating benevolent societies. The latter was designed to support the less fortunate in comparison to "beneficial societies" that sup- ported only dues-paying members at times of need. In Baltimore alone, about forty benevolent societies were formed between 1830 and 1835, the earli- est was the Woolman Benevolent Society existing since 1821. Black women were principal organizers of urban welfare programs. Two female-centered organizations (or with dominant female leadership) were Baltimore's Female Wesleyan Association and the Daughters of Bethel. Almost half in the city were established by black women (Curry, "Free Blacks" 47–48).

Baltimore also had the most active congregations of black denominations that established schools from as early as 1810 until the 1850s. Compared to national educational trends in the antebellum era, Leonard P. Curry asserts that indeed opportunities for free black children in the South were rare: "black literacy would seem to many southern whites to strike at the very roots of the slave system. Such literacy would make it possible for blacks to read abolitionist tracts and transmit those ideas to slaves, and forge passes for would-be-run-away slaves" ("Free Blacks" 45). Frederick Douglass substantiated such claims when he was hired out to his master's relatives (Hugh and Sophia Auld) in Baltimore. His new mistress began teaching Douglass the alphabets before her husband forced her to stop the instruction altogether. Douglass later received impromptu reading and writing lessons from young white boys by playing the trickster. Frances Harper, by comparison, attended the William Watkins Academy for free black youths. It was likely affiliated with the African American Methodist Episcopal (AME) Church since her uncle was a clergy and community activist who promoted the spiritual and political agenda of the congregation at Sharp Street Methodist Church (Boyd 36–37). The entire free black community supported these schools. Harper remembers the sacrifices of women in particular: "Public and private schools accommodate our children; and in my own southern home, I see women, whose lot is unremitted labor, saving a pittance from their scanty wages to defray the expense of learning to read" (*Brighter* 100). Other educational outlets included bible societies for moral reform and literary societies such as the Young Men's Mental Improvement Society and the Phoenix Society founded during the 1840s in Baltimore (Curry, "Free Blacks" 48–49).[8] The East Baltimore Mental Improvement Society was another prominent literary society for free blacks. Anna Murray Douglass, Frederick Douglass' first wife, was an "illiterate" though active member of this organization when she met her husband.[9]

Frederick Douglass spent several years in the city during the 1820/30s, but he does not provide in his 1845 autobiography detailed descriptions of free black Baltimoreans, especially those among whom he lived and worked. Anna Murray, for instance, was a free black domestic when they met and she also helped him to escape to freedom. Their relationship illustrates the bifurcated "two Marylands" of the antebellum era. To be sure, this border-state provided unstable ground of differences for slaves and free blacks, white slaveholders and non-slaveholders, it also served as a site for self-authorization. Frederick Douglass' transcends ideological bondage upon his arrival to Baltimore: "Going to live [in the city] laid the foundation, and opened the gateway, to all my subsequent prosperity" (56). A large free black population, labor diversity, vital industries, and moderate politics made Baltimore a Southern anomaly in the nineteenth century. So too was Frances Harper. She was an exceptionally literate, free born Southerner that threatened the ideological and material structures of a slave society:

> Not that we have not a right to breathe the air as freely as anybody else here [in Baltimore], but we are treated worse than aliens among a people whose language we speak, whose religion we profess, and whose blood flows and mingles in our veins . . . Homeless in the land of our birth and worse off than strangers in the home of our nativity. (Still 757)

The juxtaposition of slavery and freedom in Maryland—the "middle ground"—presents an ideal way to read intermediary Southern texts and the South. Reading Frederick Douglass—his body and autobiographical writing—we recognize him as a Southerner inscribed by his slave experiences. He ran away from "home" and it remained fixed in his imagination as a hostile site; it was not because he "love[d] Maryland less, but freedom more" that he would not return there ("Letter" 137). But contrast him to Harper, whose expectations, if not sense of home and belonging, were shaped by a similar world. *Frances Harper experienced regional detachment while she yet remained in the South since she was both "free" and "black" in a slave society.* Like Douglass, the region is geographically situated in Harper's consciousness as "home" and not home. It has familiar features—physical landscape, communal relations, family ties, dwellings, and material possessions—but not a welcoming environment. Harper was indeed bound by legal restrictions and societal mores (dictated by racial and class prejudice) similar to her enslaved counterparts: "Homeless in the land of our birth and worse off than strangers in the home of our nativity." Harper's ironic "homelessness" refracts Southernness: it alters the appearance of "Southerners" by understanding cultural identity through a different medium. Frances Harper, a free black woman, represents the South and claims Southernness from any position inside or outside the region. Harper was made to feel like she did not belong in the larger South, Maryland, or Baltimore. While there, she—and other free blacks—understood their "place" but often did not remain it. When viewed from the position of a free black Southerner like Harper, the Fugitive Slave Law and other black codes equate Southern with whiteness and freedom; however, these laws were flawed in a state like Maryland where Southern identity was undermined by geography rather than fixed by it. The frustration and alienation Frances Harper experienced as a freeborn, black Southerner is presented in her written and spoken texts just as it is inscribed on her body.

(RE-)CONSTRUCTIONS OF A SOUTHERN SELF

Feminist critics examine the ways in which Frances Harper's race, gender, and sometimes even class status have influenced her career as a writer and political activist. By focusing on issues of authorship, authentic representations of social life, and female agency, their main concern has been to recover and restore Harper as a notable American writer and architect of the tradition of African American women's literature. Her position is more secure than others considering the diversity and length of her career as well as the sheer volume of materials now available for study thanks to Frances Smith Foster's recovery efforts. Hazel Carby, Carla L. Peterson, Shirley Wilson Logan, and others have provided an important context for such recovery projects by directing our attention to generations of black female novelists, poets, orators, and public intellectuals of the nineteenth century. Because scholars like Foster, Carby, Peterson, and Logan have made it possible to study the development of Harper's career, I expand their modes of inquiry, adding the political and cultural category of region to present Frances Harper's (re)constructions of a Southern self.

This is an important historical task, for it allows a history of the current global South as one that has always been racialized. Harper's middle class background and freeborn status have caused many scholars to mislabel her as a Northerner. To them, Harper appears to be an indifferent though empathetic "outsider" merely observing the conditions of Southern black life.[10] Foster describes her as a "free southerner by birth," she forgoes any detailed analysis of Harper's life and work that would interrogate this positioning. She concludes that Harper "did not restrict her notion of 'self'" but instead "she pragmatically chose to emphasize one aspect of her identity over another" depending on the political cause ("Introduction" 20). Harper's evasive nature, as recognized by Foster, perhaps has caused many scholars to overlook or minimize the significance of her connections to the South. As a native Southerner, and more importantly, *as a self-described native Southerner*, Harper had a supportive personal and professional network of colleagues and friends that included other Southern black women like Ida B. Wells-Barnett, Anna Julia Cooper, Harriet Jacobs, and Mary Church Terrell, all of whom also claim their Southernness. A crucial link between these women and the South is that their regional experiences informed their writing, shaped their political views, and/or incited their activism.[11]

To clarify Harper's Southern status further, we can examine the relationship between regionalism and representations of blackness in addition to gender politics. Thadious M. Davis has refuted the way the South was traditionally defined by a white-black binary when blackness should weigh equally into this equation of Southern cultural identity. In labeling "Southerners," Davis contends, whiteness is most often overlooked as a racial concept and any mention of "race" refers to blacks in the South but not as *a part of* the South. Davis nonetheless claims that the culture and history of the region, "though fraught with pain and difficulty," provides " a major grounding for [black] identity," especially for black migrants in recent decades, and, in literature at least, it offers a greater understanding of "'the regionality of the black self'" ("Expanding" 6–7). Jon Smith and Deborah Cohn insist further that even Davis' conception of a monolithic "black South," or rather, "black southerness needs to be treated as skeptically as any other nativist attempt to imagine community" (4). For all of these reasons, I find Harper's positioning on "the middle ground," separate from and next to other free blacks (in various parts of the South), black slaves, freedmen and women, and other Southerners, pivotal to understanding Southernness as it was constructed by white hegemony.

When we think of the white South in the nineteenth century, a black woman like Frances Harper appears as a marginal social actor in the project of reunification after the Civil War. Most historians—notably Eric Foner—now view the era as a prolonged struggle over the labor, racial caste, and a political system that replaced slavery, lasting well into the twentieth century. "Unreconstructed" white Southerners lost some political power under new federal regulations. However, white Northerners—with the exception of a few "radical Republicans"—were more lenient on Southern dissenters than expected. Many Confederates quickly regained their confiscated property and their military leaders, who had been captured, only served brief imprisonment (Foner 110). Businessmen were eager to restore the Southern economy for the benefit of both regions. Black men were also starring actors in the Reconstruction social drama: they gained voting rights and held public offices (local and state) in unprecedented numbers for the first time in American history. White female suffragists prepared for their supporting roles as emancipated citizens eligible for equal rights like freedmen; when their appeals failed, these women dissolved their alliances and remain empowered by whiteness. Black women, also disenfranchised, at times supported and contested the leadership of black men as delegates for the family. In total, this governmental experiment failed when Andrew Johnson's policies did not take into account leading white Southerners inability "to accept the twin realities of Confederate defeat and slave emancipation," which jeopardized their Southernness (Foner 111). Like free blacks in the antebellum era, freedmen and women worked to create a place within the South's geographical boundaries and ideological concept of identity as Southerners. Their Southernness would be based on their past and reconstructed present lives: communal relations, economic prosperity, and civil equality.

In my analysis of Frances Harper as Southern, then, I use the term "reconstruction," as Henry L. Gates Jr. conceives it, to signify the historical moment and as a metaphor for the transformation of regional and personal identity. This type of reconstruction helps us to understand how blacks represent antithetical images of blackness as compared to the dominant white and racist public view. This "trope of reconstruction," as presented in the figure of the "New Negro," appears throughout African American discourses from 1895–1925, according to Gates. Black intellectuals constructed the image of a "New Negro" against the degenerate, iconic Sambo, or "Old Negro," then prominent in American popular culture, particularly black face minstrels. This dichotomy of the New Negro versus an Old Negro cuts across generations, classes, and, as I see it, geographical boundaries: free citizens versus slaves, educated elite versus illiterate masses, urban versus rural, and the North versus the South. If the "Old Negro" derives from a slave past in the South, as assumed in Gates' essay, the "New Negro's" response to this figure is largely directed towards Southern life and culture. But Gates does not consider the cultural origins of the New Negro, that is, the possibility of the "regionality of a black self" as manifested in the New Negro, whose image is rooted in blacks' Southern experiences. Actually, his utopian theory about the development of a cultural product—the "New

Negro"—dismisses the culture that produces it—the South. Or, just maybe the producers (i.e. black intellectuals) have a bad case of amnesia; while striving for upward mobility, they no longer have a sense of place and therefore create this "rhetorical figure, . . . a black person who lives no place . . . at no time" (Gates 132). Interestingly enough, Booker T. Washington and Anna Julia Cooper, among others who embodied the image, were New Negroes themselves from various parts of the South.

As a writer and political activist, Frances Harper merges the divide between the "Old Negro" and the "New Negro." Her past *is* rooted in slavery (or, a rebellion against it) though she was not a slave and her writing and activism always project a progressive future for African Americans. Moreover, Harper's career spans the evolution of the "Old South" to the "New South." We can explore ways in which and reasons why Frances Harper's contact with the South reverberates throughout her writing; how her close association with fugitive slaves and black freedmen and women aggravate her own status as an exiled Southerner; as a writer and public figure, how she intercedes in debates about the South.

In part we can do this because Frances Smith Foster has made archival materials for Harper more readily available. The critical reader, *A Brighter Coming Day* (1990), is a career-spanning collection of Harper's letters, poetry, fiction, speeches, and essays. Consequently, without a published autobiography or even an interpretative "literary biography," Foster maintains that we must look to Harper's literature as "her presentation of self" ("Introduction" 23). The complexity of this task however lies in the many *selves* Harper presents in the fragmented biographical details found in her writings, especially her letters to William Still during her tour of the Reconstruction South, from 1867 to 1871. In these condensed episodes, Harper's various self-perceptions as a freeborn, black southerner, an adopted Yankee/sometime Northerner/southern expatriate, and a "race woman" in America appear. These overlapping representations can sometimes appear in a single text. The time, place, and format in which her letters were composed can help us to understand Harper's hybridity.

As a politicized genre, Harper's correspondences are subject to cultural (re-)historization. First, we can situate these epistles in the tradition of private women's writing, for most of her letters were not intended for publication. They therefore expose the personal and feminine interiority of the writer. Most of the letters I examine were written to Still, her mentor and friend, who later appended them to his collection of slave narratives and other materials in *The Underground Railroad* (1872). This volume is a multi-vocal documentation of the experiences of ex-slaves and "conductors" who maintained the subversive network to freedom for years. Harper's biographical sketch—written by Still and supplemented by her letters to him along with public notices of her lectures—is included in the book as evidence of her contributions to the abolitionist movement and civil rights activism thereafter. Private correspondences like the Harper/

Still exchange were commonly made public in such ways during the nineteenth century; the self-consciousness of the writer then is expected and often revealed in conventional ways (Decker 95). In the absence of Still's responses to Harper's letters, we concentrate on her identity as a public figure—famed writer-activist—but, it is also important to recognize Harper's own awareness of self-exposure within the generic epistolary form. During the nineteenth century, professional writers of letters, as William Merrill Decker explains, were aware of "the self-conscious use of language that the vocational writer brings to the task and the ability of the writer to see the epistolary exchange as exemplary of the destiny of language in general. For these authors as for others of comparable sophistication, the sending and receiving of letters becomes a trope for the linguistic act" (94–95). What I find most interesting is how we can read these texts (and their purpose) as hybrid representations of the self, not just in terms of race, gender, and class—but with regional distinctions too.

Harper wrote indeed to inform her friend of her travels as she witnessed the South under reconstruction. Narratives about the radical changes in the region would appeal to Northerners desiring national reconciliation. Her letters also survey the South as a new "home" for her and other African Americans. Harper like other black Southerners imagined a place and role for blacks in a *reconstructed* South (a South rehabilitated from the wounds of the Civil War), even as they dealt with the social, economic, and political chaos of the war's aftermath.[12] In many ways, Harper's tour is similar to Mary Ann Shadd Cary's. The latter was an outspoken journalist who went in search of free land for blacks in Canada. Cary had become frustrated with the racial atmosphere during the 1850s that became increasingly bleak for African Americans. "[B]y deconstructing home as a place of origin and a primary point of reference, by remaining ever aware of her own geographic and social displacement, and by conceptualizing home as a working out of relationships subject to change rather than as a natural and fixed entity," Cary advocated in her *Provincial Freeman* newspaper emigration to Windsor ("Canada West"), a province near Detroit, Michigan (Peterson 105). Before heading South during Reconstruction, Harper went in search for a "free state" on her own.

Harper's letters show that while exiled from the region, she was constantly in contact with the South as a psychic space, an entity beyond geographical specificity. Her first adopted home was Ohio, just on the northern frontier of slavery, "a kind of Negro hunting ground," and it did not provide enough comfort and safety (Still 762). When Harper made a lateral move to Pennsylvania, to her dismay, she discovered once again that "the shadow of slavery" prevailed in areas beyond the Mason-Dixon line (*Brighter* 46–47). She was constantly insulted, for instance, for trying to board trains and sometimes not permitted to enter the railroad cars. However, Harper's frequent encounters in Philadelphia with fugitive slaves while living at a station of the Underground Railroad (likely William Still's home) did inspire her to persevere (Still 758). From Ohio to Philadelphia, the development of Harper's career reflects the evolution of her character and self-determination. While abiding in these liminal territories, Harper was uncertain about her future and her identity seemed in flux as well. She was unable to form another community-based identity like she had before as a freeborn black Southerner, "though fraught with pain and difficulty," in Baltimore. Traumatized more by her community disconnect, she searches continually for a more tolerable environment. In 1854, she arrived in New England. There, a more confident Harper emerged as she began her career as a lecturer and official representative of the State Anti-Slavery Society of Maine.

The symbolism of New England marks a stark contrast to the previous areas where Harper lived. First, it was further north and hence geographically set apart from constructions of the South as a place as defined by slavery. No doubt New England's proximity to Canada made it a perfect "asylum for the oppressed," as it was known within abolitionist circles. New England had an integrated population of abolitionists. It is no wonder then that Harper became a "Yankee" upon her arrival to New Bedford, Maine, "the hot-bed of fugitives" and their staunch supporters. After her first speaking engagement in August 1854, Harper wrote to a friend that her new home in New Bedford was "[p]erhaps as intellectual a place as any I was ever at of its size" (*Brighter* 44). The following month she described her relationship with a white colleague:

> The agent of the State Anti-Slavery Society of Maine travels with me, and she is a pleasant, dear, sweet lady. I do like her so. We travel together, eat together, and sleep together. (She is a white woman.) In fact I have not been in one colored person's house since I left Massachusetts; but I have a pleasant time. My life reminds me of a beautiful dream. (*Brighter* 44)

Harper's dream-like existence within a community distinguished by intellectual activity, social intimacy, and racial tolerance is much different from the memories of her Southern past. She is relieved to have escaped the nightmarish conditions back home in Baltimore. In her view from exile, Harper feels more secure in the company of white Northerners who recognize her humanity. She later proclaims as much in a letter published in the abolitionist paper *The Liberator* on April 23, 1858:

> Oh, how I miss New England,—the sunshine of its homes and the freedom of its hills! When I return again, I shall perhaps love it more dearly than ever. Do you know that two of the brightest, most sunshiny (is not that tautology?) years of my life, since I have reached womanhood, were spent in New England? Dear old New England! It was there kindness encompassed my path; it was there kind voices made their music

in my ear. The home of my childhood, the burial-place of my kindred, is not as dear to me as New England. (*Brighter* 46)

Harper wrote this letter while visiting Pennsylvania (on her lecture circuit) and after experiencing racial harassment, "the shadow of slavery, oh how drearily it hangs!" (*Brighter* 47). Apparently, New England freed her from the burden of a Southern past, but her blissful exclamations barely conceal a residual pain of slavery's influence on Northern mores. New England offers only temporary relief.

When she returns to the Reconstruction South, Harper's identity as a Northerner appears stable as she tries to objectify Southern culture in correspondences with William Still. The letters I examine were sent from only three states: Alabama, Georgia, and South Carolina.[13] Therefore, her experiences with Southerners from different classes, races, and economic status in these states are representative but do not present the South as a monolith. Harper's reports from the "Deep South" contrast sharply with her own experiences in the border-state of Maryland. Her travels throughout the Midwest and Northeast provide additional contrast to Harper's geographical (re-)positioning:

> You see by this that I am in the sunny South . . . I here read and see human nature under new lights and phases . . . I am glad that the colored man gets his freedom and suffrage together; that he is not forced to go through the same conditions of things here, that has inclined him so much to apathy, isolation, and indifference, in the North. (*Brighter* 123–124)

The "sunny" South is both physically and psychologically set apart from "the North;" it is an idea manifested by the experiences of a weary traveler returning "home." Harper constructs a regional self by justifying the North/South binary in this letter from Darlington, South Carolina compared to the one published in *The Liberator* almost ten years prior. In both, she is *not* at home in the North and she is indifferent to the South after years of exile. This leaves her still "on the middle ground" as in Baltimore. Symbolic characteristics are thus transposed and thinly veiled by Harper's "sunny" disposition in both locations: warm homes and freedom in New England awaits her escape from the South initially but she is welcomed back to the South not by the warm weather alone but by retreating from tepid social relations in the North. As Decker notes, "[o]ne of the first places one might look for evidence of [epistolary] self-consciousness . . . is in the handling of the genre's stock gestures . . . The most extraordinary communications are frequently prefaced, and thus made possible, by the most commonplace beginnings" (Decker 95). Harper, for instance, gives her locations in the opening of her travel letters as the form dictates and each greeting is followed by a description of extraordinary people and events to symbolize social climate changes. In both letters above, Harper describes her unexpected encounters in the North *and* South: the antebellum North is not the land of the "free" for African Americans and the Reconstruction South shows few signs of progress for them.

A month after her arrival, Harper was still optimistic about the freedmen's fate in the South. She predicted that "[t]he South is to be a great theatre for the colored man's development and progress." This moved her even further to claim allegiance to South Carolina: "No state in the Union as far as colored people are concerned, do I like better—the land of warm welcomes and friendly hearts" (Still 768–769). Harper visited numerous cities, small towns, and other "out-of-the-way" places in her travels; each encounter with the local folk brings greater insight about interactions between black and white Southerners. Her (re)positioning within these situations also reveals a self-awareness of *othering* as a strategy of trying to be in one's place in multiple ways as she tries to understand freedom in abstract and concrete terms. How can freedmen be empowered by the vote if they face intimidation at the polls? How can black communities create schools with meager resources? How can black men and women suffer abuses— beatings, rapes, and murders—within the limits of Southern laws? Harper's enthusiasm thus is short-lived when reporting from Wilmington, South Carolina on July 26, 1867 that "[t]he South is a sad place, it is so rife with mournful memories and sad revelations of the past . . . We [blacks] have had a mournful past in this country, enslaved in the South and proscribed in the North" (*Brighter* 124). We are not told what caused her foreboding, but Harper can not even conceive of America as a home for African Americans. (She does not support African colonization or other efforts to remove blacks from the country.) In this same letter, Harper reveals her growing concern with not only Southern blacks but also the poor white "cracker class." This shows how the caste hierarchy in the Old South, based on slavery, was still evident in the development of the New South. Or, it becomes clear who would claim the distinct Southernness we readily recognize in the post-bellum era. Nonetheless, Harper continued lecturing on behalf of the oppressed to the oppressors. Her observations as a travel writer (like Alexis de Tocqueville's vision of democracy) map the South as monolithic only if by showing how injustice pervades it.

While reporting on race relations, Frances Harper deconstructs the "sunny South" that is shaded by black advancement and, in response, white oppression. Black suffrage, land ownership, and schools, which create community, identity, and purpose, were obvious signs of change. These activities were closely monitored as Harper witnessed them. She lectured to mixed audiences of both races and so her messages were scrutinized by the media, "rebel" newspapers in particular: she spoke of hope and possibilities for African Americans as white Southerners listened for insurrection cues. She observed that "there [was] a sensitiveness on this subject [of politics], a dread, it may be, that some one will 'put the devil in the nigger's head'."

"[I]n conversation with a former slave dealer," Harper "had rather an exciting time" (*Brighter* 123). The social contradictions she experiences make it clear that the reference to a "sunny South" is an optimistic and despairing moniker. During Reconstruction, many black Southerners purchased land, built homes, could vote, held public office, received an education, and prospered in general, but they also faced racial discrimination and violence. Such circumstances accentuate Harper's own status as a regional outcast returning "home."

Throughout her travels in the South, Harper did not assume a fixed cultural identity in her letters instead she takes advantage of her border state heritage at will. That is, though she has adopted the North, her association with it does not prohibit her from re-aligning herself with the South when possible. In the process, we witness Harper's literal and figurative border crossings. Her abolitionist past compelled her to remain loyal to the Union in principle at least. "Victory was perched on our banner," she writes when referring to the arrival of Union soldiers in Darlington, South Carolina, but claiming Yankees was a complicated matter. When Harper describes the relationship between Union soldiers and Southern blacks, she pictures the soldiers as emancipators of the ex-slaves. Generally, "unreconstructed" white Southerners were suspicious of Union soldiers as their enemies, who were posted throughout the South in the aftermath of the Civil War. Harper learns that she too was perceived as an interloper by freedmen/women:

> One woman here [in Montgomery, Alabama] has been expressing her mind very freely to me about some of our Northerners, and we are not all considered here as saints and angels, and of course in their minds I get associated with some of all the humbugs that have been before me. (*Brighter* 130)

According to Foster, "Harper braved the suspicion of southern blacks who were wary of fast-talking Yankees of any hue and of southern whites whose methods of dealing with outside agitators were not softened if that agitator happened to be a woman" ("Introduction" 19). Speech signifies Harper's regional status as a "fast-talking Yankee" and class status, her urbane manners in contrast to assumable dialect-speaking blacks in the rural South.

Public perception is key to understanding Frances Harper's paradoxical Southernness. As she often wrote open letters for Northern newspapers to expose the reality of Southern black fugitives and free blacks everywhere, the press in turn easily manipulated her image. While in Mobile, Alabama, Harper wrote of "strange truths" she discovered during her stay there in July 1871. In her encounters with an enterprising black family of former slaves, she noticed that the women especially contributed to the success of the trading and farming business on a revitalized plantation. Her biggest shock however was when a white "rebel" editor of a local newspaper praised one of her public performances. Despite having being exiled from her home state and living elsewhere for years, she was introduced that night as "Mrs. F.E.W. Harper, from Maryland." The editorial contains a detailed critique of her speech: "it was very apparent that it was not a cut and dried speech, for she was as fluent and as felicitous in her allusions to circumstances immediately around her as she was when she rose to a more exalted pitch of laudation of the 'Union,'" or of execration of the old slavery system" (Still 775). The editor noted her "remarkable" voice and articulation especially. He was also satisfied with Harper's advocacy of domesticity and morality: "She urged the cultivation of the 'home life,' the sanctity of the marriage state (a happy contrast to her strong-minded, free-love, white sisters of the North), and the duties of mothers to their daughters" (Still 776). The Southern editor describes Harper in relation to white feminists (or Northern suffragists), middle-class gentility signified by refined ethics and domestic virtue and, thus, marks Harper as a "true" woman—a Northern-based ideology of womanhood—though no Southern belle. The editor admits that "[t]here were parts of the lecturer's discourse that grated a little on a white southern ear, but it was lost and forgiven in the genuine earnestness and profound good sense with which the woman spoke to her kind in words of sound advice."[14] Even as a Southern expatriate, Harper successfully appealed to her audience and made a lasting impression. She stood bold in her convictions, and yet was not threatened while in the midst of enemies. The "Rebs," on the other hand, accepted Harper as a prodigal daughter at best.

We learn from Frances Harper's letters that Southerness could be reconstructed metaphorically as black and white, of any class, from anywhere in the region. James C. Cobb describes Southern identity formation as individual groups in opposition forging a unique Southern ethnicity: white Southerners "made their racial supremacy the cornerstone of their regional identity" while, "[w]hen emancipation came, African Americans' celebrations of their freedom and heritage served notice of their determination to offer an alternative version of southern identity" (Cobb 5). How each group perceived the other also defines their own Southernness:

> Identity may, of course, be grounded in verifiable fact, but as the case of the South demonstrates all too well, it is often a mixture of the unvarnished and the varnished of even the whitewashed truth. The matter of perception versus reality is compounded by the fact that, historically, identities have not existed in isolation, but always in relation to other perceived oppositional identities against which they are defined. (Cobb 6)

White paternalism versus black accommodationism, for instance, is a common perception of racialized Southern identity. But, these images of white and black Southerners do not hold standard. Likewise, rural life and impoverished conditions define the black masses in opposition to Harper's experiences of being Southern—urbane and middle class. Her "regionality of a black self" is exposed as oppositional to both black and white Southerners whose identities are fixed by geographical location and/or social histories.

VOICES OF THE SOUTH

Frances Harper's ultimate contribution to regional identity is her ability to include blacks' participation in the development of the South and its fictions about itself and its "authentic" inhabitants. Her emphasis on black communities surviving under dire conditions during the rise of Jim Crow undermines popular literary tastes of the late nineteenth century while still exploiting the features of more conventional Southern regional fiction. Thomas Nelson Page and Joel Chandler Harris, among others of the "Plantation School" of Southern writers, often portrayed docile blacks in idyllic antebellum settings. These writers rarely depict black Southerners as productive citizens and therefore we see a South defined primarily by white (male) authority. In Harper's *Sketches of a Southern Life*, however, we get images of various black communities that are absent from the traditional canon of Southern literature. Details of the South's social history authenticate the narrative as an original work written within realist conventions.

In *Sketches,* slavery is de-mythologized; concrete representations of the practice, slaveholders, and the slaves themselves are depicted instead. The economic history of slavery—the exchange rate of human flesh to support local and state economies—is also explicit. No "happy darkies" and benevolent masters/mistresses reside in Harper's depiction of the Old South. Patricia Hill points out how Harper corrects black stereotypes (especially of the mammy figure) and how the poet credits the destruction of the black family to slavery, a feature *not* found in plantation romance literature (407–408). Moreover, Harper illustrates the reality of the Reconstruction South as she witnessed it: "[I]n her connected series of Aunt Chloe poems, Harper offers us a portrait of the declining socio-economic order of the feudal South. . . . the Aunt Chloe series is Harper's poetic dramatization of the Southern blacks' struggle for liberation and equality" (Hill 404–405). Stabilized black communities and blacks' prosperity as well as antagonistic post-Civil War race relations and political corruption complete Harper's portrait of the "New South."

The realism in Harper's works is not merely a literary technique but a consequence of her commitment to servicing black communities throughout the South. For seven years, Harper maintained a rigorous schedule of public lectures. She stood before mixed crowds of blacks and whites, men and women, in rural and urban areas. At times, her feminist agenda took charge of her full race commitment. Harper conducted exclusive seminars for black women that addressed their roles within the family. By starting with their own homes, Harper predicted that the socioeconomic conditions of all blacks could be improved. Her intentions were clear: "I am going to talk with them about their daughters, and about things connected with the welfare of the race. Now is the time for our women to begin to try to lift up their heads and plant the roots of progress under the hearthstone" (qtd. in *Brighter* 127). During these intimate sessions, Harper obtained details about average living conditions and the home life of her audience members. What she did not get from the lectures, she gathered from her boarding experiences. Writing from somewhere in rural Alabama in 1871, Harper laments that "[t]he condition of the women is not very enviable in some cases. They have had some of them a terribly hard time in Slavery, and their subjection has not ceased in freedom. . . . One man said of some women, that a man must leave them or whip them" (qtd. in *Brighter* 133–134).

Good marital relations were essential for rebuilding black families and communities in the Reconstruction South. It was a way ex-slaves illustrated their autonomy from white control and paternalism. Many ex-slave couples wanted to legalize the bonds formed during slavery while others searched for partners sold off in order to remarry them. Performing such ceremonies, or acting as marriage counselors, was among the many tasks of the Freedmen's Bureau. By 1870, record numbers of African Americans were living in two-parent households according to census reports (Foner 83–84). In the poem "The Deliverance," Frances Harper devotes several stanzas to the power relations in many black marriages to illustrate how, as Glenda Elizabeth Gilmore describes it, "marriage itself was political." Black male voters were expected to act as "family delegates to the electoral sphere" (Gilmore 18). They could represent their wives' interests as well as their own when women were disenfranchised. To Harper, more was at stake than "the political side of the question." She believed:

> the colored man needs something more than a vote in his hand; he needs to know the value of a home life; to rightly appreciate and value the marriage relation; to know how and to be incited to leave behind him the old shards and shells of slavery and to rise in the scale of character, wealth, and influence. . . . A man landless, ignorant and poor may use the vote against his interests; but with intelligence and land he holds in his hand the basis of power and elements of strength. (Still 770)

Black women of the post-Reconstruction generation were more than just housewives and mothers, but they also partnered with their spouses to strengthen their marriage for the good of the entire race. For instance, the marriage between Sarah Dudley Petty and Charles Calvin Pettey was one of equals. He was a prominent bishop and community leader with her at his side, lecturing on women's equality and writing about such political matters in local papers in New Bern, North Carolina (Gilmore 16–18).

African Americans committed to racial uplift, like Harper, understood that suffrage was important to acquire and maintain American citizenship. But, even with the vote, they considered other ways for improving their caste status. As a disenfranchised black woman, Harper was convinced that education and property ownership made civil equality more attainable than a flawed voting system. The former were proven methods of survival used by many African Americans striving for upward social mobility during the late nineteenth century.

Harper's poetry dramatizes black domesticity in this new era and the narrator, Chloe Fleet, becomes her "mouthpiece" (Hill 408). Nineteenth-century white Southerners might have recognized "Aunt Chloe" as one of many black mammies who worked on plantations, but Aunt Chloe is much more. She is an ex-slave intent on being completely "delivered" from her oppressors. In many ways, Aunt Chloe is an amalgam of the black woman Harper encountered in her Southern journey. Like them, Aunt Chloe restores her family and work to rebuild the community, using education, social reform, and politics. Despite being disenfranchised themselves, black women were active (if not equal) participants in political affairs: they attended rallies/parades, endorsed speakers, wore election paraphernalia, and, occasionally, voted locally in mass meetings. They supported black male leaders who were committed to racial uplift and black women felt betrayed by those who appeared as race traitors, especially black Democrats. (Brown, "Catch the Vision" 133–136). In an era of political corruption, selling of the black vote in support of the Democratic Party was akin to treason for the majority black Republicans, members of "the party of Lincoln." Thus, Aunt Chloe is critical of black male leadership in the public sphere and at home:

> You'd laughed to seen Lucinda Grange
> Upon her husband's track;
> When he sold his vote for rations
> She made him take 'em back.
>
> Day after day did Milly Green
> Just follow after Joe,
> And told him if he voted wrong
> To take his rags and go. ("Deliverance," ll. 213–220)

In her tirade, Aunt Chloe presents stereotypical public perceptions of black men's incompetence during Reconstruction, but she is also aware of her (white) audience's voyeurism. As Gilmore contends, the progress of African Americans—as illustrated by efficient marriages—was carefully monitored by white Southerners, peering "through domesticity, searching for degeneracy" (18). Though Aunt Chloe is critical of black male leadership, she addresses potential white readers directly by taking a stand for racial solidarity:

And yet I would not have you think
That all our men are shabby;
But 'tis said in every flock of sheep
There will be one that's scabby. ("Deliverance," ll.225–228)

Aunt Chloe juxtaposes respectable models of manhood against degenerate prototypes to provide a broader view of black males.[15] There were those after all

Who know their freedom cost too much
Of blood and pain and treasure,
For them to fool away their votes
For profit or for pleasure. ("Deliverance," ll. 237–240)

Though she uses folk characters, the marital model Harper depicts mim-
ics the spousal partnerships common among middle-class blacks (e.g.
the Dudley-Petty marriage). This transference of values shows that class
can influence how women express feminism, and, therefore, it illustrates
Harper's crusade for gender equality for all black women. Describing progressive African American women as "women radicals" (herself included),
Aunt Chloe perhaps exaggerates the role of women to exemplify how "the
women as a class [were] quite equal to the men in energy and executive ability," as Harper closely observed in her travels throughout the South (qtd.
in *Brighter* 271).

Indeed Aunt Chloe is a central figure in the slave community but also
implicitly in the context of regional fiction. Inspired by her numerous
encounters with hard working, resourceful black women in the South to
whose struggles she was a witness, Harper creates Aunt Chloe almost as
if to pay homage to her muses. Like the women Harper met, Aunt Chloe
acquires property, values education, and is an active member of her community. Though a fictionalized character, Aunt Chloe has a multi-dimensional
personality that complements other realist elements of the work. She is
strong-willed yet vulnerable at times. She is insightful and discerning. Even
as a house servant, she is more liberated than expected of traditional black
domestics in plantation fiction. She observes her white owners' behaviors
and mocks them:

Mister Thomas wrote to Mistus,
Telling 'bout the Bull's Run fight,
That his troops had whipped the Yankees
And put them all to flight.

Mistus' eyes did fairly glisten;
She laughed and praised the South,
But I thought some day she'd laugh
On tother side her mouth. ("Deliverance," ll. 85–92)

Despite the subservient role she must play to her owners, Aunt Chloe is a free thinker. She is aware of the ideologies and policies meant to separate her from her owners. She speaks "on tother side of her mouth" to avoid violent repercussions and she remains invisible to white slave owners except for her role as a servant. Using this invisibility to her advantage, Aunt Chloe scrutinizes their actions and does not align herself with their cultural identity. During the raging battles of the Civil War, Aunt Chloe takes sides:

> Mistus prayed up in the parlor,
> That the Secesh all might win;
> We [the slaves] were praying in the cabins,
> Wanting freedom to begin. ("The Deliverance," ll.81–84)

Her familiarity with her white owners allows her to make adept observations about their behavior and yet clarify her own self-identity in comparison:

> I used to watch old Mistus' face,
> And when it looked quite long
> I would say to Cousin Milly,
> The battle's going wrong;
> Not for us, but for the Rebels.— ("The Deliverance," ll.93–97).

Aunt Chloe's opposition to the "Secesh"/"Rebels" contrasts her regional identity (and black Southerners in general) to traditional Southern cultural representatives. Harper uses this vexed coupling to show how, though antebellum black and white Southerners' experiences were different from each other, they were so intertwined that both groups are "quintessentially [S]outhern" (Boles 213). While white Southerners rely on the battles of the Civil War (and later defeat) to establish Southern cultural identity, the collective slave past informs many black Southerners' regional identity.

In *Sketches*, Frances Harper challenges the ways the South and Southernness are defined by overturning the hierarchical structure of the social order. Black women are brought to the forefront in this poetic historical narrative to provide insights about their own existence in the South. Aunt Chloe and the women who inspired Harper accomplish important work of reconstructing the South by being involved in regional politics and social reform. Their grassroots activism starts in their homes and extends to their community to affect national policies. At least this appears to have been Harper's vision of reconstruction. What is central to this analysis of *Sketches of Southern Life* is how black women are ideally situated at an advantage to create change. We read their experiences not as separate from but apart of a more inclusive Southern narrative of reconstructed lives. The life of Chloe Fleet—from slavery to freedom—illustrates a continuum of marginal social actors in the making of the South. Frances Harper presents a more diverse cast in *Iola Leroy*, a longer Southern narrative, to critique the "white South's" purified image in transition.

HARPER AS SOUTHERN NOVELIST

It would be impossible to fully understand Harper's understanding of the joint commitment to race, gender and region without looking at the novel for which she is arguably best remembered. Published in 1892, *Iola Leroy, or Shadows Uplifted* covers crucial moments in the evolution of African Americans' social status, from slaves to freedmen to second-class citizens in the post-Reconstruction era. In particular, it chronicles the life of Iola Leroy, a mixed-race Southern woman, daughter of a Creole planter and his mulatto mistress. Once she finds out the truth about her black heritage, Iola endures years of physical endangerment and emotional turmoil. Eventually, she reunites with the rest of her family, which is torn apart by slavery. The typical tragic mulatto plot involves mixed-race characters who usually "pass" for "white" either by choice or because they are unaware of their whole heritage. Once those who do not already know learn of their "black" ancestry, they eventually succumb to a tragic end partly due to an inability to fit in either the black or white world. Harper's novel includes a racial miscegenation theme but it does not adhere to the classic tragic mulatto plot. In Harper's story, mixed-race characters assume a distinct black identity and lead successful lives as "race men and women." Harper maps the South through characters and settings. Most of the action takes place in Southern towns and cities, inland and along coastal areas. Yet, Harper nullifies regional boundaries to present flawed Southerners, produced by mired and varied interactions between different cultural regions (real and imagined).

In the binary North/South relations in nineteenth century Southern literature, the line is drawn between industrial progress and materialism vs. traditional agrarian values; cold, sterile settings vs. sunny, lush climates; moral depravity vs. religious fervor; individualism vs. concerns for family and community. Last but not least, the antagonism between Northern abolitionists versus Southern slaveholders made both of these groups iconic representatives of entire regions. With the passing of the Fugitive Slave Law, Frances Harper, like other blacks at the time, knew firsthand that no real distinctions held between the North and the South. Harper made more distinctions between the U.S. and Canada. When she first arrived in Canada in 1856 to visit black fugitives, she was astonished to "gaze for the first time upon Free Land" (Still 760). (Her uncle and cousins had migrated to the area also around this time given the conditions at home in Maryland.) Here, Canada, the extreme "North," is compared to all of the U.S. as "the South." "Southernness" then is still determined by geography, but also cultural and political differences (i.e. slavery vs. freedom). The Fugitive Slave Law makes the boundaries of the South permeable, allowing the capture of slaves and spread of cultural ideas. "Ohio," Harper declared, had "become a kind of Negro hunting ground" for fugitives (Still 762). During her travels in "every New England state, in New York, Canada, and Ohio," she counted Pennsylvania as "about the meanest of all, as far as the treatment of colored people is concerned" (*Brighter* 46). Ohio, Pennsylvania, and Maryland (as previously discussed) all figure as liminal states in Harper's critique of Southern culture and its pervasiveness. These were all places that Harper lived as a young adult and, excluding Maryland, as a Southern exile. In her indictments of the practice of upholding slavery to the extent of the law within these states, Harper erases the ideological and geographical boundaries separating "the North" and "the South," which the Fugitive Slave Law also undermined.

Specifically, the Fugitive Slave Law stipulated that the courts could "enlarge the number of Commissioners . . . to reclaim fugitives from labor" (Still 344). These officials were then "authorized and empowered . . . to appoint . . . any one or more suitable persons . . . to execute all such warrants" for the arrests and even to "summon and call to their aid the bystanders or *posse comitatus*." Moreover, "all good citizens" were "commanded to aid and assist in the prompt and efficient execution of this law whenever their services may be required . . ." (Fugitive 321–322). The captors were licensed "to use such reasonable force and restraint as may be necessary" to seize the fugitives. The law also decreed that even suspected fugitives could by "rescued by force" (Fugitive 322). The Fugitive Slave Law was controversial for reasons of morality, but also the law revealed the U.S. government's corrupted policies. Those authorized to capture "fugitives" became U.S. government employees with benefits. Financial reward aided the effectiveness of this law. The deputies were "paid out of the treasury" accordingly, since their duties were considered equivalent to "the transportation of criminals" (Still 347). Black slaves were considered property and thereby the loss of a valuable commodity constituted theft in the minds of Southern slaveholders. With the passing of the Fugitive Slave Law, the North was "charged" with the crime of harboring escaped slaves unless they could be legally confiscated as the property of Southern slaveholders. Consequently, black slaves were really the spades in the political card game played out between the North and a developing Confederacy, as Southern slaveholders and their political allies pressured the federal government to support the expansion of slavery into new U.S. territories in the West. The passage of this law proved that slavery extended beyond regional boundaries. (Harper alludes to this metaphorically in the title of her poem, "To the Union Savers of Cleveland," with a play on words, "Union Savers" instead of Union "slavers.")

After the defeat of the Confederacy and the debacle of Reconstruction, the New South's economy recovers because of partnerships between Northern investors in Southern resources. By the 1890s, when Jim Crow restrictions were created, the cultural ties between the two regions were increasingly visible. African Americans were not included in the South's revitalization project (except as a cheap labor source) but considered "a problem" instead in the New South. Even optimists like Harper realized that the New South was one with considerable cultural imperfections.

Hence, individuals not readily identified as "Southern" populate Harper's fiction. Described with the same rhetoric as "true" Southerners, by reason of birthplace and/or allegiance to the region, flawed Southerners do not fully subscribe to the tenets of Southern society and culture, which are predicated on race, gender, and caste hierarchies. In *Iola Leroy*, such cultural differences are coded in the language of racial amalgamation. By the same logic that stipulated blackness in the one-drop equation of racial purity, Frances Harper creates *flaws* in her portraits of white Southerners that in turn undermine the cultural labeling of "Southernness."

She achieves this most effectively, I think, in the reversal of the tragic mulatto theme in the portrayals of Eugene Leroy and Alfred Lorraine. Both men are Creoles or the products of cultural mixing. Her use of Creole characters as flawed Southerners draws attention to Louisiana's miscegenated cultural heritage. The French, Spanish, and Africans were all apart of an ethnic gumbo (especially in New Orleans) since the state's colonial history. During the nineteenth century, white Creole identity hence was undermined by the very suspicion that they were a "mixed breed" (Tregle 173). Harper's Creoles' biological impurities are indicative of their not belonging to "the South." Eugene (Iola's father) was orphaned as a child and grows to maturity under the guidance of distant relatives and as he attends school in the North. As it relates specifically to Eugene (and other characters I will discuss later), Northern education contributes to the development of flawed Southerness. It makes some of these Southerners have liberal views about race relations, hence making them "unfit" for Southern life:

> Leroy, although in the midst of slavery did not believe in the rightfulness of the institution. He was in favor of gradual emancipation. . . . But so strong was the force of habit, combined with the feebleness of his moral resistance and the nature of his environment, that instead of being an athlete, armed for a glorious strife, he had learned to drift where he should have steered, to float with the current instead of nobly breasting the tide. He conducted his plantation with as much lenity as it was possible. . . . (86)

Although Eugene is "brave" enough to marry his mulatto slave, he does not stand by his political convictions that by chance conflict with his Southern heritage. His weak disposition makes him an impotent Southerner and ultimately contributes to Eugene's tragic downfall. He dies from yellow fever while trying to escape the plague, an omen of the coming devastation to Southern life caused by the Civil War.

Alfred Lorraine (Eugene's cousin) succumbs under similar circumstances after being drafted into the Confederate army. His tragic death seems predestined by miscegenated imperfections, "the warmth of [his] Southern temperament had been modified by an infusion of Northern blood" (62). Lorraine is a flawed Southerner literally and metaphorically produced by North/South relations. His "mixed" heritage includes not only an educated mother from the North, but also Lorraine had benefited from a Northern education. Unlike Eugene Leroy, Lorraine is not liberal-minded; he is determined to destroy his cousin's "black" family after Eugene dies. Lorraine's bigotry is due to a more complex cultural equation. Lorraine's father, whom he describes as too "easy and indulgent with his servants" (like Eugene), married a Northern schoolteacher. Lorraine's mother eventually adapts to Southern living by getting "bravely over her Northern ideas" (64). She becomes a domineering plantation mistress in spite of her husband's shortcomings. Details of Lorraine's lineage initially support the North/South cultural dichotomy of good versus evil. But Harper also uses his background to show how both regions were equally influenced by slavery. Lorraine's mother becomes an adopted Southerner who conforms to plantation society instead of opposing it like a Northern transplant.

Against the tragedies of two white Southerners, Harper presents the triumph of black Southerners. In the characterizations of Harry and Iola Leroy, she implicates race in the making of regional identity as well as personal identity. In the letter Iola writes to her brother Harry away at school in Maine explaining the family's misfortune after the death of their father, she advises him three times to forgo any plans of returning home (122). Harry is so shocked by the disclosure of his true racial identity as a "black" man that he suffers a nervous breakdown that leaves him incapacitated for months. This would appear to be a conventional way to eliminate a mulatto character but Harper keeps Harry to complicate the narrative further. Once he recovers, the details of his situation are fully explained to him—the confines of his new reality depend on both race and region. The *black mother clause* of legalized slavery in this country stipulated that the children followed the conditions of the mother, whether slave or free.[16] Without the protection of his white father, Harry like the rest of his family would be reprimanded to slavery. The greater loss is not his financial inheritance, but more so the patriarchal legitimacy of white Southernness.

Harry's new outsider status is the story of the black Southern exile. The South is both home and *not* home for him. As with Harper, Harry's physical detachment from the region is caused by slavery and forces to sustain a static social order. Their return to the South could be life threatening. Unlike Harper who yearns to reunite with her "kindred and people," Harry's homecoming would be more bittersweet. Both he and Iola were reared in isolation from their surrounding community in Natchez, Mississippi.[17] None of their fathers' relatives (except his treacherous cousin Lorraine) ever visited their home, and neither did any of their neighbors. As Iola explains the conditions of their childhood to Dr. Gresham, "the white population was very sparse . . . [and there were] no young white girls with whom I ever played in my childhood; but never having enjoyed such companionship, I was unconscious of any sense of privation. . . . Our home was so happy. . . . At home we had books, papers, and magazines to beguile our time. . . . " (113). Consequently, Iola's racial identity is formed in the absence of "pure" whiteness; their plantation home was an amalgam of Creole culture and black slaves. With the exception of occasional trips to New Orleans—which likely re-enforced their miscegenated heritage—and the devotion of their slaves, the Leroys were isolated from the surrounding community and insulated by the comforts of their own plantation.

There are striking comparisons between the Leroys and Charles Chesnutt's Waldens in *The House Behind the Cedars* (1900). John and his family were veiled in secrecy within the shadows of the cedar trees that set up the physical barrier between them and other blacks in the community. Notwithstanding, the mulatto Waldens assume superiority based on their blood connections to "an old race." The Leroy plantation works in reverse to contain the tainted offspring within its boundaries. As John absorbs the adventure tales and chivalrous romances in Sir Walter Scott's novels—"the literary idol of the South"—as well as other classic writers, Harry likewise find his Southern birthright in the books and periodicals he browsed as a child. Harper does not mention the titles by name, but Chesnutt provides a full description of the volumes contained in the ancient walnut bookcase in the Waldens' home and other cultural artifacts (like 'Godey's Lady's Book' and Confederate bank-notes) that incubate his Southern characters. Harry's self-perception (and Iola's) as Southerners are influenced in several ways due to their isolation from the surrounding community and the contact with others within their immediate reach.

By the time he returns south, Harry has become a Southern gentleman well nurtured by his Northern relations. The allowance received before his father's death afforded him a life of leisure among the elite set similar to his father's experience abroad as a young man. As with Iola, Harry is recognizably "Southern" due to the influences of slavery on his character, notably the prejudice of caste. As Thadious M. Davis explains, "'[s]lavery and a 'slave-based economy' historically provided a primary means for cultural outsiders to define the region, and for cultural insiders to justify both self-perception and social order" ("Expanding" 4). When given the choice to enlist with either a white or black regiment in the Union army, Harry's indecisiveness pivots on his bigotry: "On one side were strength, courage, enterprise, power of achievement, and *memories of a wonderful past.* On the other side were weakness, ignorance, poverty, and the proud world's social scorn. *He knew nothing of colored people except as slaves, and his whole soul shrank from equalizing himself with them*" (125, emphasis added). What exactly are Harry's "memories of a wonderful past?" Harper takes license here to re-imagine Harry's isolated childhood within the collective memory of an idyllic antebellum South. When he does enlist as "a colored man" in order to find his family, Harry eventually returns to the South as part of Gen. Grants' siege of the Mississippi near Vicksburg. In a striking paradox, it is a vengeful return of the exile to his "home."

The native displacement Iola experiences also reveals the complexity of being "black" and "Southern" when the South is constructed as white. Once rescued by the Union army and stationed as a nurse in the battle-fields, Iola tries to explain her situation to Dr. Gresham: "[I have] no home but this in the South. I am homeless and alone" (60). Unlike Harry who is an exile by law, Iola remains in the South as a slave and former Southern belle. Her black lineage causes the change in social status and, by the same means, race revokes her claims to "Southernness." Even if the practice of miscegenation was widespread, for Iola, the binary split between "black" slave and "white" woman denotes distinctly separate categories in the context of Southern society and culture during the nineteenth century. As Davis asserts, "[p]resumption of racial affinity, commonality in the dominant view of the South as a region has meant that difference, not diversity, is at issue. One result has been curious: whites in the South became simply 'Southerners' without a racial designation, but blacks in the South became simply 'blacks' without a regional designation" (4). As a former heir to her father's fortune, Iola goes from owning property to becoming part of the estimated value of the estate itself. She becomes the *illegitimate* daughter of a white Southern planter. The financial loss notwithstanding, she must now adjust to her new social status in the South at large. It is difficult for her to re-affirm her self-identity grounded in her previous understanding of the connections between race, place, and regionalism.

At the height of the local color movement of the 1870s and 1880s, it was common for Southern writers to depict reconciliation scenes between the North and the South. Marriage between a former Union soldier and a Southern belle was a popular trope used in the plantation tradition especially. Harper complicates this scenario by initially pairing Iola with Dr. Gresham. He is smitten by her modest demeanor as a devoted, bedside Union army nurse and mystified by her personality. He observes that

> Her accent is slightly Southern, but her manner is Northern. She is self-respecting without being supercilious; quiet, without being dull. Her voice is low and sweet, yet at times there are tones of such passionate tenderness. . . . I cannot understand how a Southern lady, whose education and manners stamp her as a woman of fine culture and good breeding, could consent to occupy the position she so faithfully holds. (57)

Dr. Gresham views Iola as a defenseless Southern belle like the ones in plantation fiction that was popular with Northern readers. But, Iola seems to be a cultural paradox. She is well educated because she went to a Northern boarding school and, while living on her isolated plantation, she read books and periodicals to break the monotony. In general, there were better educational institutions in the North than in South during the latter half of the nineteenth century. As depicted in the novel, white Southerners that could afford to educate their children sent them to Northern schools.

Harper uses Northern education to complicate claims to Southern distinctiveness as it is represented at other times in the text. It even seems to serve as her solution for the South's "Negro problem." Educational opportunities would improve the lives of African Americans, and Harper wants to spread this message to white Southerners. In the chapter "Open Questions," she issues this resolve in the conversation between educated blacks, liberal whites, and a conservative white Southerner. The masking of an educated young "white" doctor, Dr. Latimer, defies the white Southerner's racist perceptions of blacks' innate inferiority. Dr. Latimer is a Southerner by birth, but refuses to inherit a Southern aristocracy that dismisses his black heritage. Like the league of other flawed Southerners, black and white, Dr. Latimer was educated at Northern institutions. He later decides to join the ranks of "race men and women" when he returns to his Southern home.

Both Iola and Harry also return to the South committed to building black communities that were dispersed after the war. Despite Dr. Gresham's last efforts to convince Iola to marry him and stay in the North, asserting that her "education has made her unfit" for living among other Southern blacks, Iola thinks otherwise: "It was, replied Iola, through their unrequited toil that I was educated, while they were compelled to live in ignorance. I am indebted to them for the power I have to serve them. I wish other Southern women felt as I do" (235). This proclamation sounds like Harper's own commitment to blacks and the South. Iola's gratitude is in reverence to her grandmother and thus to the racial ties to other blacks that survived the struggles from slavery to freedom. Harry, likewise, renews his connections to the region. Consequently to his previous state of exile, "[h]is Northern education and later experience had done much toward adapting him to the work of the new era which had dawned upon the South" (201). Unlike Eugene Leroy and Alfred Lorraine, Harry and Iola's cultural imperfections make them more suitable for living in the "New South." As a Southern novelist and progressive activist, Harper acknowledges the value of cooperative efforts to rebuild the region at the turn-of-the-century. Her solution is the combination of Northern resources, namely cultural institutions, with Southern opportunities. In *Iola Leroy*, she envisions a "new" Negro for the New South, offering both as improvements on the past.

A woman of words and might, with poetic sensibilities, "enlightened" intelligence, and professional savvy, Frances Ellen Watkins Harper rarely recorded personal reflections of her life and career. She was a popular writer and political activist as well as a devoted wife and mother. Though she had few close relatives, she operated within a supportive network of prominent nineteenth-century African Americans like abolitionists William Still and Frederick Douglass, the evangelist Francis J. Grimké and his wife, the poet Charlotte Forten Grimké, and journalist Ida B. Wells-Barnett. This rich historical context has both its advantages and disadvantages. These references can provide clues about the circumstances of Harper's own life in light of her contemporaries. They often lived in the same areas (or visited each other), participated in the same political organizations, and/or attended the same social events. Yet, such important details about Harper's life uncollected make writing a full-length critical biography a necessary though unfinished project to date.[18] Harper's travel in the Reconstruction South inspired perhaps her most autobiographical writing. Her letters, poetry, and essays/speeches also reveal how the South is constructed as "pure" though with considerable flaws; we can recognize these imperfections in comparison to dominant perceptions of the region unified by white hegemony. Harper's own life is proof of such contradictions: a freeborn, black Southerner from the border state of Maryland who became a Southern exile only to return home to the South.

Considering the literary and social history, Frances Harper had an unlimited opportunity to write as a Southerner during the late nineteenth century. Richard Brodhead interprets authorship in the nineteenth century by explaining the many "literary-cultural situations" that influenced and ultimately shaped creative expression and the literary market of the period. Regionalism emerged when North/South antagonism dissolved after the Civil War, and, in re-building the nation, literary interests in provincial sectionalism increased. The Northern bourgeois reading audience in particular was curious about the South and its varied local color scenes. Hence, regionalism, or the local color movement, according to Brodhead, provided many writers "access" to authorship by requiring mainly local knowledge or having personal experience: "[I]t made the experiences of the socially marginalized into a literary asset, so made marginality itself a positive authorial advantage" (Brodhead 116). Furthermore, "[a]uthors 'made' themselves authors of different sorts by the way they accepted or resisted the values constellated around this form" (Brodhead 116). That is, they tended to respond to different forces and mechanisms (like the publishing industry and factors of race and class, as Brodhead sees it), which were relevant to their own literary-cultural background (Brodhead 174). William L. Andrews claims that post-bellum writers of the South, in particular, sought new ways of presenting regional literature that both incorporated elements of the Old South but from new critical perspectives. These texts were usually experimental in form, but written with a firm sense of authoritative knowledge of the culture.[19] Frances Harper experimented with a combination of fact and fiction. In her Southern texts, this experimental form was useful to challenge previous depictions of Southernness, which minimize Southern black life and place more emphasis on white identity and culture. Both Andrew's and Brodhead's critiques are helpful to explain how and why certain 'voices' may have been heard in American literature and others not (or at least not as loudly). That is, by focusing on "literary-cultural situations," as Brodhead does, it is easier to understand the limited space African American writers occupied and, more importantly, the position held by black women writers.

Frances Harper could take advantage of her authorial situation by relying on her Southern heritage, the ambiguity of this regional status, and the prevailing national caste hierarchy. She fulfilled her desire to write "a purpose novel" in *Iola Leroy* by responding to the "Negro question." In effect, she provides an outlet for the voice of displaced Southern blacks within this public debate that ignored their humanity, their motivation to speak on their own behalf. Along with Harper, other black Southern men and women, most notably Anna Julia Cooper and white Southerners like Thomas Nelson Page, George Washington Cable, and Thomas E. Watson contributed to the dominant discourses about the Negro Problem. As a "local colorist," Harper observed the black communities in transition during Reconstruction and preserved material for her literary depictions. Her images are a mixture perhaps of all the areas she visited from the Carolinas to Mississippi, which affects her role as a local colorist as defined by conventional standards. However, this style is characteristic of her experimental writing: mixing politics, poetics, social history, and race theory. The popularity of regionalism provided Harper an opportunity to cast her own impressions. She chose to correct stereotypical images of blacks prevalent in the white literary imagination when she created Aunt Chloe (in *Sketches*) as an unconventional mammy figure and allowed Iola Leroy to escape a potentially tragic fate. Harper's feminist perspective was perhaps influenced by the historical objectification of black women in slavery, but also by her own experiences that culminated in the "Black Woman's Era" at the turn of the century. In her writing, she was able to claim yet alter the images of the most dominant representations of black womanhood at the time. Always concerned with "uplifting the race," Frances Ellen Watkins Harper, as a black female and Southerner nonetheless, would achieve this goal literally from the bottom up.

Frances Harper's Southern life is indicative of others who appear as marginal actors in the (re)making of the South by the late nineteenth century. They all were caught between the fray of racial politics, modern economics, and rigid social customs. The "New South" emerged with Jim Crow legislation, sharecropping (as a replacement for slave labor), and resistance to social equality among blacks and whites. Within this milieu, Harper, a representative Southern black woman, operates as an agent of change, manipulating static characteristics of the region (while still in its transitional stages) to reveal flaws in a predominate white and patriarchal culture. Throughout her life and in her literary works, Harper reveals how fluid geographical margins, mixed-race people, and the agency of gendered minorities undermine white hegemony as a hallmark of the South, especially as it is constructed by the late nineteenth century. Harper can serve, therefore, as a historical model for our present methods of (re)defining Southernness on the basis of cultural hybridity, geographic location(s), and social histories. Harper's project remains unfinished as we have only begun to seek ways of reading various Southern texts in plural contexts. Houston

A. Baker Jr., Kathryn McKee, Annette Trefzer, Jon Smith, and Deborah Cohn, among others, reason that "new" Southern Studies must attend to the border crossings, figurative and literal, of different people in local and global spaces marked as "Southern" by political history, economic trade, and social interactions in general. The results are multiple "Souths" and less conventional Southerners. I introduce Frances Harper as one such case study. Next, turning to other black female figures (literary and historical), I will continue to make connections between race, gender, and region by examining the actions and experiences of conjure women at the margins yet central to Southern culture and communities. The hemispheric South, extending to Latin America, is mapped onto their bodies and interrogated in their speech. Thus, writer-activists like Charles W. Chesnutt and George Washington Cable use the figure of the conjure woman in convincing ventriloquist acts to contest racial injustice in America.

2 Conjuring a New South
Black Women Radicals in the Works of Charles Chesnutt and George Washington Cable

Charles Waddell Chesnutt (1858–1932) and George Washington Cable (1844–1925) were dissenting Southerners whose personal friendship, literary relationship, and political alliance congealed in their passionate rebuttals to the "silent South." They called for immediate changes in the racist status quo to grant African Americans civil (if not social) equality. In his essay collections *The Silent South* (1885) and *The Negro Question* (1890), Cable underscores the critical need to solve the South's race problems that had only worsened after slavery and the Civil War. His passion for reform also manifested in his popular fiction featuring Louisiana Creoles and bigotry as part of local color. Cable met Chesnutt in 1888, learned that he was "a colored man," and recognized immediately the contributions the latter could make to public debates of "the Negro problem" from "an insider's view." White supremacists and liberal dissenters like Cable argued about the causes, extent, and viable solutions to racial discord in the South. Chesnutt by the late nineteenth century was a young writer anxious for an opportunity to advance his career with Cable's assistance.

Surviving correspondence between the two men from 1888 to 1891 show Cable's influence on his protégé. Having garnered praise for his early short stories, Chesnutt nevertheless sought Cable's advice about publishing in mainstream periodicals with hopes of becoming financially dependent on his writing and not so much his stenographic services.[1] Cable critiqued early drafts of the "Rena" manuscript, which developed later into Chesnutt's first racial problem novel *The House Behind the Cedars* (1900). However, Cable encouraged his protégé to write polemic rather than fiction.

Cable himself had forgone much of his own fiction while writing controversial articles and delivering speeches throughout the South. He lectured and wrote about such topics as the convict lease system, segregation in public accommodations and in schools, and the biased judicial system, all which discriminated against African Americans. Cable's overarching social liberalism developed around these issues. In his published works as well as at public appearances, Cable made candid observations about the unjust treatment of black Southerners (often citing alarming statistics of abuses) and advocated immediate changes for improvement. He challenged the silent South to acknowledge a shared humanity, to grant African Americans their civil rights without violent repercussions or without fear that this decree would ultimately dictate social relations too. His motto being "Social *choice*, civil *rights*," Cable understood that white Southerners would not tolerate inter-racial relationships (*Negro Question* 84), even though such social taboos were evident by the large mulatto population in the South.

So light in appearance that he could pass for white, Charles Chesnutt, in 1858, was born in Cleveland, Ohio into a middle class family of free blacks with a mixed racial heritage. The family had migrated from the South two years prior to his birth to escape persecution and prejudice. Chesnutt showed no physical traces of his black lineage, but he relied on it as an art-ist. As a young man, he boasted of being able to "write a far better book about the South" than Northern white authors Albion Tourgee and Harriet Beecher Stowe. Chesnutt's reaction to the success of Tourgee's *A Fool's Errand* (1879) and Stowe' *Uncle Tom's Cabin* (1852) reveals his ambition for a successful writing career as a native black Southerner, considering how these outsiders presented their perceptive of Southern race relations (*Journals* 124–125). Chesnutt grew up in the post-Reconstruction South when his family moved back to Fayetteville, North Carolina in 1866. For seventeen years, until he was twenty-five, Chesnutt spent his "apprentice-ship years of life" there (Mason 77–78). His memories of the folk culture and experiences with segregation and racism would continue to influence his life and writing after he left the region in 1883. He moved his wife and children to Cleveland where he continued working as a stenographer and anticipated his future of becoming an author. Like his parents before him, Chesnutt wanted to take advantage of Northern opportunities and did not want his children to suffer the burden of racial discrimination while grow-ing up in the South.

George Washington Cable knew well the caste system in the South and the experiences of those positioned at its disadvantage. In 1844, he was born into a slaveholding family in New Orleans, whose members were ardent supporters of the Confederacy. Cable defied their expectations when he began to question the conservative South's racial politics. Though he became a Confederate soldier, shortly after the Civil War, Cable argued against the cause for secession, the support of slavery, and even racial seg-regation. He formed his new convictions on the basis of historical research into civil law and developed a moral stance against racial inequality. In the 1870s, Cable began writing short stories about the Creole culture he remembered while growing up in New Orleans. Initially serialized in magazines, his first collection, *Old Creole Days*, was published in 1879. These early short stories became the foundation for later works in which he defined the South by focusing on marginalized groups like Creoles, foreign immigrants (especially Caribbean refugees), free blacks, and slaves.[2] Cable began to express his liberal views about the rights of citizenship early on in these sketches. He knew that New Orleans' cultural diversity was unique, but its class issues were universal to the region. The rapid transformation of the racial caste system in colonial New Orleans, for instance, indicated similar changes that would occur in the post-bellum South. The Creoles were French and Spanish descendents who reluctantly became American citizens after the Louisiana Purchase and so did former Confederates who were bitter about losing the Civil War. Cable discovered that though some white Southerners approved of gradual changes for granting blacks their civil rights, they feared radical changes. These white Southerners passively advocated 'evolution rather than revolution' (*Negro Question* 113). Thus, Cable used New Orleans to cast a shadow over the rest of the South, which had mainly remained silent to the abuses against African Americans.

At the height of his career as a popular fiction writer and public intellectual, Cable participated in the most controversial debates about the South's "Negro Problem." As a major sociological concern, the Negro Problem indicates the systematic oppression of African Americans under the tenets of white supremacy as it is presented in legal documents, journalistic articles, photographic images, and political essays / speeches. Black disfranchisement, lynch law / mob rule, "peonage slavery," and the creation of Black Codes to enforce this systematic oppression all signified the loss of political advantages African Americans had gained during Reconstruction especially in the South. These problematic race relations captured the public's attention, bringing what most Americans considered to be a regional issue into a national focus. In 1888, Cable formed the Open Letter Club as a forum for analyzing race problems among a select group of peers, all of whom were sympathetic to racial discrimination against African Americans. The membership included college professors and presidents, lawyers, doctors, clergy, and politicians, mostly white male Southerners.[3] Chesnutt, the only African American, joined the group soon after meeting Cable. The members distributed drafts of essays to review prior to submitting for publication in the broad press. One such symposium on Southern race problems appeared in *The Independent* in 1889 featuring the education of African Americans as partial solution to many of the problems plaguing the South. Chesnutt did not contribute an article to it nor to the second and final forum planned by the Open Letter Club that was never published. However, he did work as a research assistant to Cable, gathering statistical data for relevant topics and compiling a list of potential black subscribers to future Open Letter pamphlets. Chesnutt eventually became involved in the debates to address the race problems on a national scale like his mentor publishing essays and delivering speeches. Such works were recently compiled as a documentary collection in *Charles W. Chesnutt: Essays and Speeches* (1999). Although Cable convinced Chesnutt that focusing on civil rights was a greater calling than creative writing, he insisted that Chesnutt's literary sketches should reflect his beliefs and be "truthful" to his subject matter. For both men, their political discourses bolster their realist Southern fiction.

This chapter examines Charles Chesnutt's and George Cable's vision of the South as presented in *The Conjure Woman* (1899) and *The Grandissimes* (1880), respectively. These books present arguments for civil equality and social justice in satirical racial dramas of the Jim Crow South. Chesnutt's collection of conjure tales proved entertaining while exposing the inhumanity of slavery and Cable's novel also shows how the then contemporary Southern race problems were traceable to the past. The representations of conjure women found in their books are critical to the political arguments that reconstruct the South in each work. Chesnutt's black male characters often overshadow his black female characters in view of the author's preoccupation with the South's Negro Problem; in this case, black male leadership for change is underscored. Yet, the construction of Southern identity is realized in the images of his conjure women; their caste status and modes of self-preservation implicate them in the making of a different kind of South, where their struggles are vindicated and appear universal. Cable also features this type of black woman as a participant in the (re-) making of the "new" South, although people of color are excluded from a homogeneous white Southern identity. In this chapter, I show how such black women are positioned as displaced Southerners by considering the narrative conventions used to construct (and to contest) a regional identity formed on the basis of white, upper class masculinity and the advocacy of human rights and racial equality. I set Chesnutt and Cable's fiction against their political rhetoric about race relations to indicate the vital role fictional black women play in Southern communities, the narrative structure, and a radical civil rights campaign.

NOTES ON CONJURE WOMEN, CONJURATION, COMMUNITY, AND NARRATIVE DISCOURSE

"Trickster disrupts . . . [t]his disruption is normal," begins Elizabeth Ammons in a description of narrative discourses that seek to reinterpret communities of differences. In *Tricksterism in Turn-of-the-Century American Literature: A Multicultural Perspective* (1994), Ammons introduces the trickster figure as one who makes "trouble—messing up the order—is part of the order" (vii). Tricksters appear in various cultures and times whether in written or oral traditions as the essay contributors to the volume makes clear. Such is the case, theorizing the trickster is a standard approach in African American literary criticism, particularly in Henry L. Gates, Jr.'s *The Signifying Monkey* (1988). Ammons' multicultural analysis (which builds on Gates') of the trickster as unruly yet with justifiably disruptive actions frames my reading of the conjure woman in works by Chesnutt and Cable. Conjuration is a featured folk tradition in both settings—rural "Patesville" (Fayetteville), North Carolina and the colonial city of New Orleans—and it appears as a result of cultural mixing within the American South: African and Caribbean spiritualism and Native American rituals, superstitions, and folklore. The conjure women characters these writers create are troublesome, partly responsible for disrupting social order if only to undermine hegemonic powers by staking claim to their "normal" roles (read as rights) within their communities. Moreover, though they appear to exist only at the margins of society, these women play a central role in the narratives. We learn about them in framed folk tales or they are introduced in public gossip in the stories; these characterizations represent marginalized people who might appear voiceless. They live on the outskirts of plantations or within the city's shadows and appear as esoteric deviants even. However, they engage in master-slave disputes and high society scandals—messing up the order of things—well within public view. So I contend that both Chesnutt and Cable's works includes disruptive "trickster energy" in the plots and/or feature conjure women as "tricksters" involved in domestic relations, penetrating the boundaries of segregation to (re)produce a miscegenated culture in the South.

Charles W. Chesnutt's vision of the South would undoubtedly be incomplete without his black female characters in *The Conjure Woman*. His collection of folktales depicts black Southerners surviving before and after the Civil War under an oppressive social regime while Aunt Peggy, the legendary voodoo priestess, which the book owes its title, governs the lives of slaves and white masters alike with her magical powers. In these conjure tales, her presence captivates readers, turning skeptics into believers. She exists in the world within the tales told by Uncle Julius and John and this marginal displacement within the narrative is a plot device worth examining in terms of gender and social history in the South. I will discuss this topic at length shortly, but, to summarize, I contend that her world is the reality that Chesnutt tries to control at a time when African American men suffered a loss of authority and control especially of their familial and political lives. In this reading, Aunt Peggy (and other conjure women) might appear to emasculate Uncle Julius and other black males. Chesnutt however creates these characters in a white-controlled world whose authority he undermines in the guise of a white voice. Chesnutt then is the ultimate trickster as many scholars acknowledge. It is this "trick" of storytelling that makes subversive interpretations possible:

> Trickster offers a different plot [compared to the basic "individual-against-society plot"] . . . [E]mbodied in trickster and trickster energy is a principle of human rebellion and resistances that exists both within a protagonist/antagonist framework *and* within a totally different context, one in which the disruly—the transgressive—is accepted as part of the community's life. Individual desire and group authority cohabit within a network or web of relations; the dynamic is one of interaction rather than dominance and submission. (Ammons ix)

Chesnutt appeals to white audiences successfully through Julius' stories as told by John. The protagonist/antagonist relationship between John and Julius is expected given the set-up for the stories: a white Northern-transplant and his wife, Annie, moves to the South for better health conditions and economic opportunism to encounter an ex-slave's own claims to the land and resources. The most "disruly" or "transgressive" element in this narrative is the conjure woman not Julius (an impotent antagonist); she lives freely beyond white authority, "'mongs' de free niggers on de Wim'l'ton Road" (36), and therefore she is in a better position to challenge it. This freedom to cast spells, to intercede in social problems, makes her a vital appendage to the community. Julius, on the other hand, tells stories about powerful conjure women (and a few men) to gain favor with his new employers, but his ability to pose a serious threat is not fully realized in the folk tales. As Eric Selinger argues, Julius, an enterprising entrepreneur, is a more threatening figure to the Post-Reconstruction caste system in the beginning rather than by the end of the book. He seems "castrated," for instance, when he fails to captivate his listeners' empathetic response to his story, "The Gray Wolf's Ha'nt," with interest and compassion as with earlier stories. This story illustrates intraracial conflicts, particularly the competition between a conjure woman and conjure man to resolve matters, and so it does not influence either John or Annie to support Julius' usual trickery. Selinger's focus is genre and black men and though he and others do not consider Chesnutt's role as trickster reconstructing regional identity, his work is useful for such a cultural analysis of literature. Thus, I argue that Chesnutt best accomplishes this task by allowing conjure women to act within a "web of relations" (in the antebellum South and Post-Reconstruction setting of the framed narrative) to change "the dynamic . . . [to] . . . one of interaction rather than dominance and submission" when his narrator Julius cannot.

A crucial link between Chesnutt's preoccupation with gender and gender expectations and his political passion and creativity becomes visible only when we emphasize regional factors that were important to him. My interpretation of Chesnutt's vision of the South therefore centers on conjuration, or "goopher," based on his own understanding of the craft:

> The origin of this curious superstition itself is perhaps more easily traceable . . . [to] African fetishism which was brought over from the dark continent along with the dark people. Certain features, too, suggest a distant affinity with Voodooism, or snake worship, a cult which seems to have been indigenous to tropical America. (*Essays and Speeches* 155)

Writing about collecting folklore, Chesnutt admits that conjuring ignited his imagination of childhood memories of conjurers. Conjurers were not mere oddities but held significant roles in their communities. An "old Aunt This and Uncle That" were among a select few conjurers Chesnutt interviewed to substantiate the strange antics of goophering. Chesnutt creates such literary figures, which are recognizably regional, to present solutions to the Negro Problem to audiences throughout the U.S. Cable, likewise, presents a voodoo priestess and her assistant in a multiracial, multi-caste society.

When Chesnutt and Cable present an image like the conjure woman, it is a useful narrative technique and it serves as a historical reference for understanding the construction of cultural identity, especially when considering the diasporic spread of conjuring among black folk in the states and abroad. My concern then is not just with fictional conjure women or the act of conjuring itself. I am also interested in the kind of character who signifies in a local way to influence a national social conscience. Even if the names "Aunt Peggy," "Tenie," (*'po' Sandy's'* wife), and "Viney" or, in Cable's fiction, "Palmyre" and "Clemence" are not familiar to most readers, the arduous circumstances that determine their survival in the South as slaves and free women are better known.

Chesnutt's and Cable's strategic use of black women in their fiction is complicated as well as clarified by the South's social history. Industrialization and urbanization ushered in a new modern age with tense race relations and class struggles that also created an identity crisis for white Southerners during the waning decades of the nineteenth century. The "grounds of difference" once distinct in a slave society between blacks and whites had become fluid following the Civil War and were reconfigured by the Post-Reconstruction era. The emancipation of slaves to become citizens and the dismantling of the Confederacy to reinstate rebels into the nation changed the social and political landscape of the South. The one constant was race: blackness made visible by scientific racism, constitutional law, and by laws of segregation also made whiteness visible in opposition. Modernity forced individuals to redefine the self in regard to the instability of societal changes. So, according to Grace Elizabeth Hale, the "New South" became a united white space in order to stabilize the "ruptures of modernity" and white Southerners reclaimed power in the visibility of their status to dominate. Still holding on the promises of Reconstruction, downtrodden African Americans became "New Negroes" to escape their dismal reality as second-class citizens. Black men identified with their gender to achieve patriarchal status in their communities and household though perceptions of black inferiority held by whites kept them in close ranks with the common masses. Black women were in the most ambiguous states of existence: they knew "the doubled oppression of the doubled self" (Hall 33). The irony of their dilemma is made apparent in the segregated public restrooms at train depots marked "FOR LADIES" AND "FOR COLORED PEOPLE" during Jim Crow. This scene of ambiguously drawn color and gender lines indicates more the fluidity than rigidity of the culture of segregation when black women are prepared to transgress boundaries. Those who remember having to make the decision to chose which door to enter did so with the understanding that breaking social taboos and laws were repercussions they regularly faced in the South. Despite the changes in Southern society, racist and sexist views about black women remained constant in light of historical oppression.[4] The infamous attack of white journalist James Jacks, for instance, on black women's character—labeling them as stereotypical prostitutes and thieves—ignited a movement of black women in defense of themselves during the 1890s club movement. Black women turned to practical solutions to resolve racial problems and deal with issues concerning their gender identity; class values weighed on their constructed selves and, not the least, on their regional identities and roles since Southern attitudes about black women were the most stringent. African American women's record of leadership on the grassroots and national levels defied expectations and fulfilled the promises of enfranchisement even without obtaining this privilege themselves. Though they were denigrated in public as salacious "wenches," black women committed to reform work through organizations to improve educational opportunities and social conditions for all African Americans, especially in Southern communities.[5] They also formed interracial coalitions with white women (when possible) for various political and social reform issues. In doing so, Southern black women tried to change public perceptions of their womanhood to reflect pride in their race and to rebuild the region and the nation.

Based on my understanding of the black woman's role in social history, I view Chesnutt's and George Cable's fictional worlds as a complicated reflection of then contemporary society, where men appear to dominate in order to compensate for the threat against black masculinity and patriarchy in general. Considering how much he had at stake in his writing (his accreditation as an author and racial pride), Chesnutt's concern with the Negro problem is conveyed in his gender characterizations, especially with his black male characters operating as representative citizens. Indeed, many critics place emphasis on Chesnutt's male characters usually against the backdrop of a gender-biased historical perspective on lynching and the "race question" in the South when black women were also involved in both of these issues.[6] Black women equally participated in the reconstruction of the South though apparently on their own terms. Disenfranchised and disrespected by white society, black women nevertheless became spokeswomen of their race and the region. Anna Julia Cooper was joined by Mary Church Terrell, Ida B. Wells-Barnett and members of The Colored Women's League of Washington, D.C. and The Tuskegee Women's Club in their nation-building efforts that began in their homes quite literally at times. In Chesnutt's fiction, black female characters have similar cultural experiences and societal roles as did historical black women.

Likewise, George Washington Cable presents black women as an index for racial and gender problems in the South. His story of an aristocratic Creole family includes two conjure women in *The Grandissimes* that are binary opposites in New Orleans Creole culture and society. Palmyre la Philosophe is a free, beautiful quadroon with a commanding presence. Behind her calm and regal façade lies a "concealed cunning and noiseless but visible strength of will" (60). Even as a young slave-maid, she was "the ruling spirit" over her white mistress, Aurore Nancanou. After she is freed, Palmyre secures herself a position in the community as a voodoo priestess. Clemence, "the marchande des calas," is an enslaved, itinerant cake vendor. She is discerning (like Palmyre), yet boisterous and talkative. Their verbal and non-verbal modes of communication are essential to their means of survival and my critique of their characterizations as a *non*-"tragic mulatto" (Palmyre) and an anarchistic mammy figure (Clemence). Both women gain private access into white society through the public services they provide: Palmyre is entrusted with her clients' innermost secrets when she is solicited for her mystic powers, and Clemence, as well, obtains privileged information through her daily contacts. She also assists Palmyre in her voodoo services. These women nevertheless are disposable members of their community despite the services they provide. Cable sacrifices Clemence and Palmyre in the narrative seemingly to justify his resolutions for the Negro Problem, as I will argue, *without* addressing the racialized problem of gender for black women, for instance, as he does for his white heroines. In the novel, white and black women differ on the basis of working to survive, the need for a male protector, and depictions of their sexuality (i.e. erotic primitivism vs. Victorian values of feminine virtue).

In this chapter's analysis, black women in fiction by Chesnutt and Cable convey cultural messages about actual regional conditions. These characters appear subversive, but I intend to show how both authors use the figure of the conjure woman (or conjuration) to emphasize the interconnections between race, gender, and regional identity as these factors pertain to the construction of Southernness. Their "trickster strategies," therefore, "are not just a way to get 'in' or 'back at' the dominant culture. Tricksters and trickster energy articulate a whole other, independent, cultural reality and positive way of negotiating multiple cultural systems" (Ammons xi). Thus, my reading challenges the historical characterization of the South as a figurative space of whiteness by interrogating the subject positions that Cable allows black women to occupy in the text. The narrative conventions that construct a place-based regional identity, on the basis of white upper class masculinity, and the advocacy of human rights and racial equality position both Palmyre and Clemence as displaced Southerners. First, I examine representations of the conjure woman in Chesnutt's popular short stories to illustrate how their caste status and modes of self-preservation implicate black women in the making of an inclusive South. I find that Chesnutt relies on black women to promote a political agenda for African Americans' civil rights and equality not only in the South but also in the nation at large. When circumstances worsen, he finally looks further south to Latin America for solutions to the Negro Problem in the U.S.—signifying on Cable's earlier fiction and encompassing a symbolic return to conjuration.

"RACE MAN": THE VIEW FROM INSIDE THE NEGRO PROBLEM

To understand the marginalization of black women in Charles Chesnutt's fiction, as in society at the time, we should consider the definitions of black manhood in light of American social history at the end of the nineteenth century and at the dawn of the twentieth. By constitutional decree, black males were bestowed rights and privileges not to be taken for granted as leaders of a rising race. The fourteenth and fifteenth amendments stipulate their rights as citizens and insure the privilege to exercise their rights of representation by voting. Many African American men of this generation had endured slavery in the South and injustice throughout the nation. These constitutional amendments added broader dimensions for black manhood: patriotism, civil responsibility, and patriarchal power. Consequently, these elements were foundational for "Best Men" to take the reins of leadership. White racial privilege and validation provide the stimulus for this developing middle class among African American men; especially in the South, those that wanted to secure political power conformed to a white ideology of merit. "According to this paradigm, only the Best Men should hold office, the men who, by faith and by works, exhibited benevolence, fair-mindedness, and gentility" (Gilmore 62). White Southerners used this model to limit the number of black male voters and office holders during Reconstruction and only those favored by whites could achieve the worthy distinction. Educated African Americans who wanted to show how quickly the race could progress embraced this ideology too. For them, a social pedigree was essential: "[t]he Best Man pursed higher education, married a pious woman, and fathered accomplished children. He participated in religious activities, embraced prohibition, and extended benevolence to the less fortunate. He could collaborate on social issues across racial lines . . . [and] hold a modest number of political offices" (Gilmore 62). These conditions were not unlike those for "race men," a black-oriented ideology akin to white standards of black masculinity in purpose and preparation for leadership. For both, elitism is essential to the race man's commitment to "uplifting" the black masses (as Kevin Gaines and others recognize) and the same may be true for Best Men. The latter may lead an exemplary life and still be condemned by white disapproval of any African American compared to those deemed exceptional. Race men had to align themselves with the masses knowing that the progress of one depends on the other.

In the aftermath of Reconstruction, Chesnutt fulfilled his leadership role by speaking out against the nullification of blacks' civil rights that were once protected by law. Throughout his career as a political activist, public orator, and protest writer, he composed many essays and delivered speeches that heralded his concern for African Americans in the South, the rights of the individual, and national identity. He wrote and spoke as a "black" man, a Southerner (in exile), and an American citizen. He presented before his peers and foes alike his case for the protection of blacks' civil liberties. Quite simply, Chesnutt was a well-educated, outspoken race man with which white Southerners had to contend. To understand the transference of his political rhetoric to his politically charged fiction, to see how black males are poised as national figures, mediators of the race and region, I look closely at representative works from Chesnutt's non-fictional writings. The clarity of purpose and political desires expressed in these essays and speeches are typical of most of Chesnutt's non-fictional writings on the race problem.

On January 10, 1889, Chesnutt drafted "An Inside View of the Negro Question," solicited for publication by his new mentor Cable. Chesnutt's premise challenges the common belief among white Southerners about blacks' inferiority and contentment: blacks supposedly were satisfied with the status quo and were not capable of challenging proponents of this sociopolitical view. Chesnutt's intelligence and successful writing career undermines this claim. Furthermore, he carefully notes the educational progress of African Americans since Reconstruction. The most important point Chesnutt makes is how differently whites and blacks respond to the "Negro question." It's all a matter of perception. For whites, he asserts, it was left to one's discretion to decide whether or not blacks deserve equal political rights and if, in turn, this correlated with social equality, or "admission to private white society" (*Essays and Speeches* 59). Indeed, the "Negro problem" had a legal component that was also used by whites as an indicator of dire social consequences. Chesnutt addresses both issues in his essay about black rights, which were nullified by many states' constitutional guidelines and unspoken prejudices. In the South especially, whites, according to Chesnutt, were "afraid that Southern society" would become "Africanized"; they equated racial equality with the unlawful "sin" of miscegenation (*Essays and Speeches* 59). Furthermore, Chesnutt speculates, did Northern whites even see themselves—as "bigots"—contributing to the problem? Or, were Northern whites also implicated in finding a solution to the "Negro Problem" with so much emphasis on race relations in the South? It was all a matter of personal assessment for the white conscience (*Essays and Speeches* 57).

As for the need for a *black* explanation for the problem of race in America, Chesnutt contemplates: "It is to him [the Negro] the question of life itself" (*Essays and Speeches* 58). Blacks viewed the problem in terms of their whole existence, their past with slavery, the Jim Crow experience, and even their future—the fulfillment of their freedom dream. *The 'problem' persists in their writing; it determines their sense of identity.* As a spokesman for his people, Chesnutt describes the facts and fictions of the controversy. Blacks' desire for fair and equal treatment under the law was their main focus in the campaign for civil rights. Suffrage was the primary way to obtain equality and an effective tool to fight against white supremacy. Social equality would be a way to co-exist with whites without the fear of violence. All of these measures would help resolve the "problem" more than segregation or colonization. In Chesnutt's view, the fact that public discussion had pushed the "race question" to the forefront of America's consciousness was a good indication of progress (*Essays and Speeches* 59–68).

The distinctions Chesnutt makes between rights and responsibilities and social propriety are key to any discussion about the "Negro problem." For blacks, the rights of the individual, as an U.S. citizen and a human being, were at stake. To consider blacks as either one was nearly impossible for most whites. Nevertheless, Chesnutt relies on the humanitarian guidelines established by the Constitution in his defense, but he is fully aware of the catch-22 created by its liberal principles of equality. He knows that human behavior is never completely dictated by law, which is why the fourteenth and fifteenth amendments were being ignored. Balancing legal rights with social mores on the justice scale would never be easy in the court of public opinion. It would be a messy affair to force change among people with such a complicated history of racial prejudice and discrimination. Yet, Chesnutt believed in the possibility of doing so without separating the races.

Bringing immediate attention to the problem with practical solutions was necessary for the progress of the region and nation. Chesnutt believed that the South was the best laboratory for this sociological experiment. We find this message in his fiction over and over again as he depicts characters with an ambiguous racial status (like John Walden in *House Behind the Cedars*) or scenarios that pair blacks and whites as enemies and friends in the South (as in *The Conjure Woman*). The racial experiment imagined in his early fiction is presented again with statistical data in his 1916 speech "A Solution for the Race Problem." The U.S. had invaded Haiti as a prelude to entering World War I when Chesnutt delivered his speech calling for global solutions to America's race problem inland.[7] So Chesnutt looks a little further south to Latin American countries for viable solutions. He catalogs the development of "harmonious" race relations in Cuba, Puerto Rico, Martinique, Guadaloupe, Jamaica, Barbados, and Brazil after decades of slavery and colonization. The exception being Haiti and San Domingo, ruled by black and mulatto governments after successful revolutions, illustrates just the opposite of solving America's race problem. The Haitian revolt led by Toussaint L'Ouverture in 1804 inflamed white Southerners with fears of "Negro domination" even decades later during Reconstruction. Chesnutt finds in other countries governed by the French, Spanish, Portuguese, and English more ideal models for dealing with their black populations: class outweighs race, less policing of the color line, equal rights, education, justice, and mutual respect. At least, blacks and whites must learn to consider "theoretical equality and refusing to accept race as a ground for denying practical equality" (*Essays and Speeches* 391). Racial harmony would not be achieved as Chesnutt rationalized in the early twentieth century, as it was not even conceivable in the closing decade of the nineteenth.

Despite its urgency, Chesnutt's "The Negro's Answer to the Negro Question," the revised version of the "Insider's View," was never accepted for publication by any major periodical. William Sanders Scarborough, a prominent black educator and scholar, had written a similar essay scheduled for publication in *The Forum* in March 1889.[8] Cable assured Chesnutt that this was the reason his "Negro's Answer" was denied by the same magazine. After several other rejections, Cable declared that all the attention drawn to the issues in the South by numerous others was more important than personal success at the moment. Cable's concern for his protégé here ignores the artist in favor of the politician. Chesnutt nevertheless insisted that his view of the race problem was different from Scarborough's: the latter's lacked enough "fervor" and Chesnutt disagreed with Scarborough's suggestions that blacks emigrate to the West to escape the conditions of the South. *The Century* also rejected the "Negro's Answer," accusing Chesnutt of being "so partisan." Chesnutt finally resolved that his essay was constantly rejected because of his relative obscurity as a writer and public persona.[9]

The optimism he displays in the "Insider's View" waned by 1903 when Chesnutt presents the case of "The Disfranchisement of the Negro" in *The Negro Problem: A Series of Articles by Representative American Negroes of Today.* Chesnutt's essay appears with others by race men Booker T. Washington, W.E.B. DuBois, Paul Laurence Dunbar, T. Thomas Fortune, H.T. Kealing, and Wilford H. Smith in the collective symposium. The volume appeared only months after DuBois' pivotal *The Souls of Black Folk.* Together, these works present black male leadership as absolute. In *The Negro Problem,* each contributor confronts the dim reality of African Americans at the "nadir" with little protection against unjust laws and racial prejudice as well as little relief from Jim Crow social customs. Although he opens his address by citing the guarantee of constitutional rights for representation via suffrage, Chesnutt's diatribe is one of a nearly defeated populace. Beneath the passion of his rhetoric, the fear of the inevitable dissolution of African Americans' humanity is perceptible:

> Now, what is the effect of this wholesale disfranchisement of colored men, upon their citizenship? The value of food to the human organism is not measured by the pains of an occasional surfeit, but by the effect of its entire deprivation. Whether a class of citizens should vote, even if not always wisely—what class does?—may best be determined by considering their condition when they are without the right to vote. (*Essays and Speeches* 181)

Chesnutt surveys the limitations placed on the black man's voting privileges throughout the South: requirements of property ownership, military service, employment, poll taxes, and circumstantial proof of literacy. The latter two requirements in addition to the "the grandfather clause"—the inherited right to vote of a "descendent of any person who had the right to vote on January 1, 1867"—were practiced in Chesnutt's home state of North Carolina (*Essays and Speeches* 180–181). His argument rests heavily on the paradox of blacks' lack of political representation due to disfranchisement when blacks *were* included in population statistics used to determine Southern delegations to Congress, where the rights of blacks were in turn denied (*Essays and Speeches* 183). In this case, an apple rotten at its core ruins the whole fruit.

In his political essays, Chesnutt posits that there were national consequences for the disfranchisement of African Americans. The lack of respect for laws anywhere in the U.S., as illustrated in the Jim Crow South, threatens the democratic principles of the nation and infringes on the rights of all Americans (*Essays and Speeches* 184). A nation is not free when any individual may be denied their inalienable rights—such tyranny corrupts national identity. At the moment, the Supreme Court, according to Chesnutt, had already failed to uphold the Constitution, giving way to states' legislation unchecked political power by the end of the nineteenth century (*Essays and Speeches* 182). Many state governments in the South had passed infamous "Black Codes," which severely limited the rights of freedmen. As far as he was concerned, America was certainly doomed: "Contempt for law is death to a republic, and this one has developed alarming symptoms of the disease" (*Essays and Speeches* 184). In the end, Chesnutt falters on the possibility of improvement. In the South, black men had lost a battle. Their Northern counterparts had a better chance of winning the war, while their rights to free speech remain intact without fear of intimidation or violence (*Essays and Speeches* 191). Over a decade since providing an "insider's view" of the factors that threatened the livelihood of black Southerners then and at the start of the twentieth century, Chesnutt in "The Disfranchisement of the Negro" turned once again to the court of public opinion, a dim beacon of hope for change.

As the conditions in the South worsened, Chesnutt modified his views slightly to encourage northern migration for blacks to build better alliances with white liberals and to sustain enough political power there to pressure the federal government to act.[10] He compared this strategy to the passing of the Fugitive Slave Law in 1850 when white Southerners pressured the federal government to support their claims to slave property once they escaped to the North. Chesnutt hoped to turn the tide of public opinion in favor of black Southerners' claim to freedom accordingly. When his options were even more limited, Chesnutt's persuasive methods became similar to those used during the abolitionist campaign; he would emphasize moral responsibility on behalf of African Americans. He tried to appeal to different audiences for this purpose. In 1904, before an assembly of mostly white Northern women, Chesnutt pleaded the case of the race problem yet again, though the tone and approach of his performance differs from the previous tracts discussed. In "The Race Problem," he reiterated the importance of "a wholesome public opinion which will demand political action" (*Essays and Speeches* 201). This time he solicited the aid of white women in particular asking them to wield their powers of influence on their male relatives to correct the unlawful record of racial discrimination, segregation, and violence.[11] As Christians, these women were in a position to uphold their moral responsibility, Chesnutt argued. These were women like Annie in *The Conjure Woman*, and Chesnutt, the "trickster," also played on their sympathy. He wanted to gain support for his political campaign like Uncle Julius receives gifts and certain privileges for spinning his tales. Unlike in the previous two lectures/essays, in "The Race Problem," morality is a distinctly feminine quality. His persuasive arguments reveal Chesnutt's desperation for building alliances. He had to prove that Northerners had as much at stake in this issue as Southerners. Reports of lynchings in Ohio and Illinois were proof enough that the race question was not just a Southerner's problem—it was a national controversy in which women must participate.[12]

A focus on race and gender is explicit in Chesnutt's non-fictional writings as far as the legal component of the "Negro problem" is concerned. Men, with full rights of citizenship, were authorized agents of potential change. Though they had temporary rights, black males were recognized as part of the official governing body politic. Chesnutt's emphasis on a "wholesome public opinion" and sentiment, however, signals a shift from the masculine to the feminine sphere of influence (albeit white women). Coincidentally, the early women's rights movement had reached a climax by the turn of the twentieth century. As domestic subjects if not legal ones, women had long been considered a force to reckoned with when it came to so-called matters of the heart. The literary market catered to this belief since women were the leading consumers for novels, especially melodramatic ones like those that Chesnutt wrote.[13] As a political activist and novelist, he was in a unique position to boost his career in both areas. It's no surprise then to see how much Chesnutt turns from writing mostly political tracts directed, it seems, at men, to concentrating more on novels. The women at the political rallies were also potential readers of Chesnutt's politically charged fiction. Even without the ballot, women had freedom of speech, which helped them gain support for their campaign for women's rights when they had few other options.[14]

Throughout his career, Chesnutt also emphasized the freedom of speech as a tool—especially for blacks—to help resolve the race problem:

> The colored people can speak out for themselves, and ought to whenever they can safely do so. The right of free speech is as sacred to a freeman as any other right, for through it he sets in motion the agencies which secure his liberty. Whether or not he can exercise his rights is not the point, he should nevertheless assert them. . . . [A] just self-respect requires that [blacks] should let the world know that they are not 'dumb, driven cattle,' but that they know, and know better than any one else can, the extent to which they are oppressed and outraged. (*Essays and Speeches* 83)

Chesnutt's focus here on voice and representation is common in his non-fictional writings. He develops similar themes about African Americans' right of free speech and humanity in his fiction, especially on the topic of black manhood. Consider, for instance, in "Dave's Neckliss," the slave's predicament when he is criminalized and vindicated only after he loses his sense of identity—he believes he's turned into a ham and no longer a man empowered by his voice—Dave was a literate preacher, leader among slaves on a plantation. Essentially, Dave is a castrated race man. To compensate for the threat against African Americans' civil rights, Chesnutt tries to accomplish in his fictional world what had been lost in the South. The fourteenth and fifteenth amendments were never repealed, but no Southern state recognized their legality by the end of the nineteenth century (not to mention the subsequent decades into the twentieth century). All the legal factors of the "Negro Problem"—disenfranchisement, in particular, are revealed in characterizations of black men trying to navigate the political struggles transitioning from slavery to freedom.[15]

When African Americans' collective identity is narrowed to a single sex (and sometimes class of individuals) as often the case appeared in the Negro Problem debates, there lies an opportunity to challenge biased historical perspectives and interpret the cultural influence of literature. Maybe the gender-specific language in Chesnutt's essays and speeches is simply due to linguistics, but his emphasis on black masculinity is a way of also identifying only black males as ideal leaders despite black women's activism.[16] He closes his 1916 speech, for instance, with Rudyard Kipling's poem "If," apparently as a political and social etiquette manual for race men (*excerpted here*):

If you can keep your head when all about you
Are losing theirs and blaming it on you;
If you can trust yourself when all men doubt you, .
But make allowance for their doubting too;
If you can wait and not be tired by waiting,
Or, being lied about, don't deal in lies,
Or, being hated, don't give way to hating,
And yet don't look too good or talk too wise; (ll. 1–8)

If you can talk with crows and keep your virtue,
Or walk with kings—nor lose the common touch,
If neither foes nor loving friends can hurt you;
If all men count with you, but none too much;
If you can fill the unforgiving minute
With sixty seconds' worth of distance run
Yours is the earth, and everything that's in it,
And—which is more—you'll be a Man my son! (ll. 25–32)

Glenda Elizabeth Gilmore cites this same poem to illustrate how white Southern men—"educated, urban, and bourgeois"—read Kipling's poetry to distinguish themselves from their father's generation and ideas of manhood. The concept of "Best Men" is credited to Southern white men who forged fickle alliances with black male leaders in Populist/Republican coalitions during Reconstruction. The younger generation of "New White Men," according to Gilmore, judged this as a moral flaw and impotent white supremacy. The modern era thus held promise and risks for New White Men who constructed a new regional identity (and public space) partly on the foundation of antebellum social history, against a generation of failed white masculinity of the Civil War and Reconstruction era, and in defeat of racial minorities. As the "ideal southern man," Thomas Dixon, Jr.—in his then popular white power fiction—perpetuates the fantasy of a purified white South governed by his generation of New White Men (Gilmore 66–67). These white males organized to regain their authority by distancing themselves from black men altogether and disenfranchising black men was their legitimate right as architects and heirs of the New South power structure (Gilmore 61–64).[17] Ironically, if such white men appreciated the self-restraint of Kipling's model of manhood, race men like Chesnutt also found it appealing to counter attacks on black masculinity.[18]

Black women were more than capable of supporting black male leadership but compromises were also necessary. As previously noted in the first chapter, black women took advantage of black men's voting privilege by influencing their electoral decisions. In effect, black men became "delegates" for their families in many cases (Gilmore 17–18). In *Sketches of a Southern Life* (1872), Frances Harper's depiction of relationships between black men and women after Reconstruction replicate the political compromises they made for the sake of the entire family. Aunt Chloe, in "The Deliverance," illustrates how black women promoted domesticity as a subversive political strategy in the making of a unified black body politic.

Similarly, as in Chesnutt's fiction, black women were effective agents in the political equation and as regional subjects within the public sphere. They formed local, state, and national organizations to assume race leadership and forge alliances, when possible, with white Southerners. They had often relied precisely on their freedom of speech—their ability to "speak truth to power"—to create changes for themselves and their communities. Orators and activists Mary Church Terrell, Anna Julia Cooper, Victoria Earle Matthews, Josephine Ruffin, among others, were leaders of the club movement that coalesced under the auspices of the National Association of Colored Women (NACW). The NACW formed to "uplift" the race at the "nadir." Ideologies of uplift mandated self-sufficiency and education in general.[19] Race women saw the problems affecting black women as "race problems." They therefore organized food banks, taught sewing and cooking, established nurseries, patrolled neighborhoods, and performed any duties deemed necessary for the protection and rebuilding of their communities. These race women believed action was more effective than the talk of race men held at numerous conferences and councils on the race problem (White, *To Heavy a Load* 37). Those women like Cooper who were disheartened by the loss of the vote especially blamed Southern black men for being incompetent. If the NACW was the "first step in nation-building" for black women, it empowered them as race leaders and citizens. Most believed that "'[i]t is the Afro-American that the world looks for the solution to the race problem . . . the first step has been the banding of ourselves together . . . putting our heads together, taking counsel of one another.'" Fannie Barrier Williams stood firm in her belief, "'the Negro is learning that the things that our women are doing come first in the lessons of citizenship'" (qtd. in White, *To Heavy a Load* 36). No greater field of service and commitment then was the divided South. Chesnutt's fiction illustrates the gender wars of race leadership as well as the problems among blacks and whites. While the male characters are useful to understand the legal aspect of the "problem," the women, especially black women, work on another part of the equation, the social component. They help alleviate racial tension in the South caused by the "Negro problem" in light of black disenfranchisement, violence, and segregation.

CONJURING TO COMMUNICATE: GENDER CONSTRUCTIONS

As a part of the "New Negro Literary Movement," Chesnutt was motivated to "'give the character of beauty and power to the literary utterance of the race'" (qtd. in Gates 144).[20] Along with colleagues like Paul Laurence Dunbar and W.E.B. Du Bois, Chesnutt used what Henry Louis Gates Jr. calls the "trope of reconstruction" to correct stereotypical images of blacks embedded in the public white conscience. This antithetical image of blackness was christened "the New Negro" and it appeared as professional men and women, primarily of the black bourgeoisie, with cultural capital. (Those not in this category were encouraged to emulate the prototypes.) With a new name and appearance, the "New Negro" had to acquire a new voice as well:

> [B]lack intellectuals seemed to feel that nothing less than a full face-lift and a complete break with the enslaved past could ameliorate the social conditions of the modern black person. While this concern with features could imply a visual or facial priority of concern, it was, rather the precise structure and resonance of the black *voice* by which the very face of the race would be known and fundamentally reconstructed. (Gates 143)

As a man of his generation, Chesnutt responded to these literary and cultural imperatives in his writings about the South. In addressing the Negro

Problem, blacks' racial identity and sense of regional identity was at stake. For this reason, I find speech and visual representation to be so important to Chesnutt's depictions of black women. They may be as beautiful and vulnerable as Rena and Molly Walden in *The House Behind the Cedars* or as outspoken and powerful as Aunt Peggy and other conjure women. Many of them even appear silent with invisible scars; for instance, as a mutilated slave, in "The Dumb Witness," Viney's rebellion to her white abuser is neither spoken nor heard but she survives to undermine his authority in the end. With such intense social pressures to reconstruct the race, these black female characters bear the burden in Chesnutt's narratives as did black women during the club movement. Thus, their creed—"lifting as we climb"—linked the destiny of the people to the progress of women.

Consider black female characters' language use and identities in Chesnutt's fiction as compared to the rhetoric used in his non-fictional pieces and the construction of black male identity. Chesnutt tries to prove in his essays that the black man as Southerner was first and foremost an American; therefore the rights he was given, as with any other individual citizen, deserve to be respected by law. Chesnutt's black male characters consistently face the dilemma of property and propriety in the New South. However, I see Chesnutt's presentation of conjure women, for instance, as a better medium to reveal the obstacles blacks faced and their triumphs over them. These characterizations usually appear in third-person narration, which makes them appear less important to the narrative or less threatening to the social status quo than politicized black male characters. Conjure women however speak in markedly different ways through the narratives to communicate the reality of marginalized black Southerners. They do not narrate the stories but do illustrate how perceptions of voicelessness can be undermined (as in Viney's case). Like race women, for instance, female conjurers are often ignored, yet they "speak" in their actions and, when possible, in dialogue with their oppressors.

In Chesnutt's depictions of the oral culture, conjure women often use rural black Southern dialect versus standard English, and silence, an even more effective mode of communication, in some cases. Robert Hemenway interprets the use of folklore in *The Conjure Woman* as a literary product that transitions to a communicative device that advances the plot. He explains how conjure aligns the relationships between Julius and his white employers with Chesnutt and his audience. Conjure also connects the two narratives within the tales. Hemenway authenticates the folklore in the stories. My analysis builds on Hemenway's by focusing more on the symbolism of conjuring, as an act and mode of representation, when conjuring is used to create characters and influence literary and cultural narratives.

In Chesnutt's fiction, conjure women are a product of the South as well as his imagination. Chesnutt imaginatively rewrites historical figures. In using conjuration for its literary value, Chesnutt admits to being influenced by stories "lodged in [his] childish mind by old Aunt This and old Uncle

That." He later interviewed "half a dozen old women, and a genuine 'conjure doctor'" to confirm the authenticity of the tales he'd created (*Essays and Speeches* 156).[21] As I argue, while still pleading his case for the race, the presentation of conjure women in Chesnutt's fiction is also a way of turning attention away from the "Negro problem" by the easiest means possible, diverting attention from the black man (or even elitism). He still addresses the "problem" through these women, but without the pressures of political correctness because he is working on the *social component* of the Negro Problem. Whereas Chesnutt's black male characters represent black citizenship issues in light of national politics, his provincial black female characters are recognizable *regional* figures, conjurers who define and maintain communal race relations in the South. (*See chart below.*) As he did when he lectured to his white female audiences, Chesnutt could use a figure of a Southern black woman to manipulate public opinion.

If Chesnutt sought to spend his creative energies "to shatter stereotypes of the Negro created by plantation romancers and to present his reader with a new point of view—from the bottom of society" (Mixon 25), turning to the black woman was a good place to start. As evidenced in his non-fictional political tracts, Chesnutt knew well that Southern society was based on a system of hierarchies: white/black, men/women, and aristocracy/plain folk. He re-creates the Southern caste system in his fiction.[22] Today, Southern historians and literary critics acknowledge that the dominant Southern ideology is (has long been) based on a domestic-modeled, patriarchal hierarchy established by a system of dichotomies among race, class, and gender that were created by the antebellum slave economy in the South. The "home" is the "site of production" for prescribed gender roles; even later, when New Negroes emulated white standards for domesticity, women ideally were placed there. Susan V. Donaldson and Anne Goodwyn Jones, especially, emphasize gender as an important category of analysis for Southern texts due to the pressures placed on these texts by regional culture. According to Donaldson and Jones, Southern bodies are "haunted" by the cultural designation of hierarchical relationships (1–17). Even slavery's influence manifested in the New South with former white masters ruling (still) over black sharecroppers in a form of

Table 2.1   Characterizations in Chesnutt's Fiction

Figures	Used to Illustrate	Iconic Representations	Dominant Characteristic Trait(s)
Black males	political problems	As national citizens	Individualism
Black females	Social concerns	As regional subjects	Concern with Community, Emotional ties

"peonage slavery." [23] If blacks were facing a representational crisis as Chesnutt's career as a political spokesman suggests, the portraits of black culture in his fiction certainly reflect this threatening social climate. Enter Uncle Julius to center stage. He is the main character and ex-slave narrator in Chesnutt's *The Conjure Woman*, a collection of folk tales about blacks' survival in the post-Reconstruction South.

Like most critics, Sylvia Lyons Render considers Julius to be a "stereotype plus": he appears content and acts as a subordinate to whites, but in going beyond the stereotype, he is manipulative and harbors bitter, vengeful recollections (62–64). Although Julius is based on images of servile black "uncles" by Thomas Nelson Page and Joel Chandler Harris, Chesnutt achieves a greater degree of realism with Julius because he highlights the inhumanity of slave life in Julius' simple tales. [24] Uncle Julius is credited as the trickster that cons his white employers since he is handsomely rewarded for his entertaining stories. Through Julius, Chesnutt, as a kind of trickster figure himself, spreads his moral message of racial tolerance to an audience of primarily white readers. While Julius and Chesnutt validate black masculinity in light of historical oppression and ensure the survival of the race (Dixon 187–188), the real magic of conjure women escapes detection.

The figure of the conjure woman is a complex representation of black women in regional literature. She synthesizes rural backwardness with professional sophistication, vulnerability with strength, and, yet, in some ways, she is as an unorthodox a stereotype as Julius (Render 65). [25] The aim of my analysis is to expand the definition of a conjure woman to explain apparent contradictions in this characterization. In addition to her magical powers, the conjure woman's cunning ability to provide any illusion to suit her own purpose as a survival mechanism bears consideration. Her very actions may defy the expectations of subordinate gender roles. In Chesnutt's tales, the conjure woman's outsider status complicates her role in the community and in the narrative structure: she is a narrative prop in the "story within the story," though Robert Stepto recognizes Annie, one of Julius' white employers, more for her role as the reliable listener in the tales. Whether as Aunt Peggy, Tenie, Viney, or Phillis, Chesnutt's conjure women define the South and Southernness in their own experiences. Viney's story, in "The Dumb Witness," is perhaps a universal depiction of the status of blacks in the South; she has biological ties to the region and claims the place as home despite her past experience with slavery.

Viney is technically *not* a sorcerer, but she uses silence in the way the conjurers use spells to their own advantage (so does Phillis in "The Marked Tree"). Without speaking, Viney uses body language to express her deviance: she would "stiffen" and the "slumbrous fire" in her eyes signals her displeasure with her former master's commands (160). Viney keeps the location of his inheritance a secret as revenge for his brutality against her. Malcolm Murchison had mutilated her tongue to keep her from "telling tales" about him. (You might imagine Julius mocking his own white employers for not being able to control his tongue since he easily manipulates them with his stories.) Despite Murchison's attempts to educate her, it is Viney's reticence that is key to her survival. After Murchison dies, she reveals the location of the papers to his heir. Viney could talk all along, "ef she'd had a min'ter," Julius explains (171). Actually, Viney uses her disability, or mute pretense, as a conjuring illusion. The loss of speech is a typical spell in the conjure tales. When subjects are turned into inanimate objects or animals, they usually can not speak out to prevent harm or danger when their own lives are at stake. Viney's mute pretense, however, helps to protect her.[26]

The revision Chesnutt made to this tale is just as startling as the resolution. In "The Dumb Witness," we first hear Viney speak when John asks Viney if her new employer was home, and she replies, 'Yas, suh, . . . I'll call 'im' (171). In an earlier version, Chesnutt had Viney respond to John's greeting in standard English: "Yes, sir, I'll call him."[27] Does this linguistic switch suggest that Chesnutt did not want to show how Viney did or could have benefited from her tutor's literacy lessons? Would this acquired education have made her a better actress/narrative prop, but a less convincing regional figure? More importantly, does the change from standard English to black dialect suggest Chesnutt's motives for retaining the authenticity of Viney's cultural background and thus limit her literary characterization to illustrate social concerns and not political problems? Viney's silence serves as a better disguise for her intelligence in keeping with subordinate gender standards and expectations for New Negroes to remain in their "place." Thus, she becomes a more convincing (and likable) character for local color and sentimental fiction. Keeping in mind the New Negro philosophy (or, in this case, Gates' "trope of reconstruction"), however, speech could be more important than visual representation when used to promote racial progress. Viney's bold verbal and non-verbal communication is evidence of this reconstructive process. What I am also suggesting here is that in this "non-conjure tale" Viney's status as a (non-)tragic mulatto promotes Chesnutt's political agenda for improving race relations in the South. Realizing the complexity of Viney's characterization as a "conjure" woman—her role in Chesnutt's fictional, sociopolitical world—makes it easier to understand the ideological burdens that conventional figures like Aunt Peggy also bear as conjure women.

Chesnutt seems to model his other conjure women after Aunt Peggy. All of the conjure women struggle with their adversaries, but Aunt Peggy is more resourceful than the others.[28] In *The Conjure Woman*, Aunt Peggy is an important character in most of the stories, as a member of the fictional black community, and as a narrative figure for the entire collection. She is the means by which other characters achieve goals, and she ignites the action of the narrative.[29] In the "frame story," Julius' recollections of slavery usually focus on Aunt Peggy's relationship with slaves and white slave owners. Through her experiences, however, Julius is empowered. On the one hand, she's a ventriloquist puppet for his performance as storyteller.

But we cannot confuse her image with Julius'; her survival tactics depend on her race, gender, and her ability to speak forthrightly. Conjuring gives her a respected status in the black and white community since everyone is afraid of her powers. Working a "monst'us powerful goopher" is a profitable business, which provides financial support, but also affords her luxuries that define her freedom. Aunt Peggy is rarely paid money when slaves (her best customers) could mainly provide common items of food (e.g. rations of corn, pigs, chickens, hams, and peas) and scraps of clothing. She consistently reminds them though that "you can't 'spec' me ter was'e my time diggin' roots en wukkin' cunj'ation fer nuffin'" (87). She is confident in her abilities, for her labor is her livelihood; it "frees" her from conventional servitude and allows her to live independently and maintain a strong connection to the South. In "Tobe's Tribulations," for instance, Aunt Peggy compares her freedom to the desires of a runaway slave:

"'W'at you wanter be free fer?' sez Aun' Peggy. 'Doan you git ernuff ter eat?'"

"'Yas, I gits ernuff ter eat, but I'll hab better vittles w'en I's free.'"

"'Doan you git ernuff sleep?'"

"'Yas, but I'll sleep mo' w'en I's free.'"

"'Does you wuk too ha'd?'"

"'No, I doan wuk too ha'd fer a slabe nigger, but ef I wuz free I wouldn' wuk a-tall 'less'n I felt lak it.'"

"Aun' Peggy shuck her head. 'I dunno, nigger,' sez she, 'whuther you gwine ter fin' w'at you er huntin' fer er no. But w'at is it you wants me ter do fer you?'"

"'I wants you ter tell me de bes' en easies' way fer ter git ter de Norf en be free.'"

"'Well,' sez Aun' Peggy, 'I's feared dey ain' no easy way." (187)

Human dignity and individual liberty are implicit in this dialogue about regional and self-identity. It reflects the social circumstances of blacks in the South during the early days of Jim Crow that paralleled slavery. Aunt Peggy takes advantage of both privileges and claims the South as her home despite the obstacles in the slave's limited perspective. She is free to practice conjuring and, in turn, it frees her from societal restrictions of the "white South." To Aunt Peggy, freedom is an inherent quality of life and not a civil law. She provides an escape route for the slave, though her concept of freedom does not depend on a specific geographical location.

Aunt Peggy lives independently in a cabin "on 'de Wim'l'ton Road." It is not clear whether she is an actual member (or not) of the free black population there. Sometimes Aunt Peggy is described as "de *free-nigger* conjuh 'oman down by de Wim'l'ton Road" (59), as "a conjuh 'oman *livin' down 'mongs' de free niggers* on de Wim'l'ton Road" (36), and once as being simply "a free 'oman" (116).[30] Against the backdrop of a free black community,

Aunt Peggy's characterization as a Southern woman thus appears to depend on geographical specificity, but this various narrative descriptions about location makes her an exceptional figure. Her residence on the outskirts of the plantation community seems to label her as an outsider despite her involvement with the slaves. Symbolically, however, Aunt Peggy's marginal status determines her Southernness. That is, in Chesnutt's fiction, the plantation serves as a source for a place-based Southern identity for most blacks; this is the case with Viney in "The Dumb Witness" and especially with Uncle Julius, who "had attached himself to the old plantation, of which he seemed to consider himself an appurtenance" (55). Aunt Peggy's metaphorical connections to the South more so than the literal connections define her as a regional subject. The "regions" she inhabits include "the Patesville community, the past, and the 'world' of storytelling," according to Stepto's analysis of Chesnutt's reality-based fictional world (36). Stepto discusses the setting(s) in *The Conjure Woman* as a site for blacks' identity construction; the characters are defined by their connections to a plantation and a master. This master/slave relationship arranges the black community in the stories by caste and makes Southern identity exclusive to those with power considering the confines of this ideological perspective and locale. Thus, on the one hand, it allows us to see people like Aunt Peggy or Uncle Jube, a conjure man, as outsiders. Actually, they are a part of the South as "free" Southern blacks unlike black slaves in the South; social caste and regional designations distinguishes the two groups. While conjure marks Aunt Peggy as "Other," this concept of identity does not explain Tenie's role, as a conjurer woman within the boundaries of the plantation in the story "Po' Sandy," considering conjuring is a way to exclude individuals from a group identity and "free" them from slavery.[31]

At a glance, Aunt Peggy may still appear in exile since she is only acknowledged when her services are needed. But conjuring does more than provide a stable income for Aunt Peggy; it empowers her as a Southern black woman. First of all, it is not clear whether or not Aunt Peggy is "a free 'oman" by law or by social circumstance. We know that she rules by fear, "fer she wuz a witch 'sides bein' a cunjuh 'oman" (36), and she proclaims that "you'll fin' me wusser 'n de patteroles" for the slaves (64). Fear also prevents whites from punishing Aunt Peggy when she is capable of using her powers against them and for their slaves without their owners' permission. Hence, Aunt Peggy is above the law and "could be free en lib lack w'ite folks," a wish unfulfilled by Tenie. References to Aunt Peggy's freedom link her to the South but place her against the dominant southern ideology based on hierarchical relationships of race, class, and gender.

Aunt Peggy's significance to Chesnutt's literary legacy, his vision of the South, is immeasurable. Compared to the abstract black male in his political essays, Chesnutt uses Aunt Peggy to manipulate the divide between blacks and whites and the juxtaposition of private versus public spheres in his fiction. Although she is as cunning and enterprising as Julius, Aunt Peggy is the metaphorical subject of his narration and poses less of a threat to his captive dual audience; she's twice removed (in slavery and Julius' narrative) from their own reality. Aunt Peggy is a valued member of her community when her services are needed and an indisposable nuisance when she interferes with whites' private affairs. Some critics could argue that this is also the case with Julius, but Chesnutt uses sentimentality to preserve Julius as narrator and as John's employee. Similar techniques do not always apply to Aunt Peggy. The other conjure women (Tenie, Viney, and Phillis) are more sympathetic figures than Aunt Peggy. She inspires courage and evokes fear though readers may not fall directly under her spell in the homespun tales. Aunt Peggy is replaced in the narrative by Uncle Jube, by other conjure women, and, in the case of his "non-conjure stories," Chesnutt exchanges mysticism for realism as we see in "Dave's Neckliss."

Nevertheless, Aunt Peggy is the nineteenth-century response to the "woman's question" if not the immediate solution to the race problem. Aunt Peggy works at home, not as a domestic, but as an entrepreneur. Conjuring is a vocation and not just an avocation for her. The labor practices of Southern women are studied as an indicator of their caste status and feminine virtue.[32] The conclusion of studies that focus mainly on white women, labor, and Southern womanhood shows how much black women are excluded from categorical regional distinctions.[33] Yet, it is precisely Aunt Peggy's laboring, as I have argued, which exemplifies her Southern identity. In fact, conjuring allows her to "work" through the "race problem" due to her contact with others, especially whites. After helping to restore one white man's inheritance, Aunt Peggy secures her own retirement: "'he tol' Aun' Peggy he wuz much bleedzd ter her, en ef she got ti'ed cunj'in' en wanter res' en lib easy, she could hab a cabin on his plantation en a stool by his kitchen fiah, en all de chick'n en wheat-bread she wanter eat, en all de terbacker she wanter smoke ez long ez she mought stay in dis worl' er sin en sorrer'" (182). Indeed, Aunt Peggy's life differs from that of bourgeois blacks in the North and urban areas in the South, those concerned with racial progress. But in his depiction of her, Chesnutt places the "voice" of the New Negro in an Old Negro's body. All the work that Aunt Peggy does, her symbolic "labor," may not produce progeny, but she gives birth to hope for a new generation of blacks.

Marjorie Pryse places Aunt Peggy firmly in the development of African American women's literary tradition. She believes that Aunt Peggy represents the oral culture that created slave narratives and autobiographies during the nineteenth century that would evolve into fictional writing by black women. Whereas Chesnutt used conjure folklore (realistically depicted via Aunt Peggy) as *only* a subject matter for black writing, according to Pryse, Zora Neale Hurston would transform it into a medium for writing about black life, especially for expressing the desires of black women and illuminating their lives.[34] To Pryse (and to Hortense J. Spillers and other contributors to their collection), conjuring is the ability to channel the spirit of foremothers for modern black women writers. While I do not agree with Pryse's assessment of Chesnutt's singular use of conjuring as a topic and not also as a literary device, her acknowledgement of the significance of Chesnutt's Aunt Peggy to the achievement of his literary goals sustains my argument: "Although Aunt Peggy does not either tell the tales or write the fiction . . . , Chesnutt offers her and the actual conjure women who served him as models as a source of power that makes his own fiction possible" (11). To suit his literary purposes and achieve his political goals within his fiction, Chesnutt harnessed the power of conjuration to create a characterization of a black woman who did represent the South but *did not* represent the South's race problem.

VICTIMS OF CIRCUMSTANCE?

In the previous section, I discussed how Charles Chesnutt's modern vision of the South is complicated by historical and cultural influences in regards to the Negro Problem. To improve race relations, Chesnutt argued for black suffrage and emphasized the right to free speech in his non-fictional political writings. He tries to promote these civil rights issues and racial progress also in his fiction. In *The Conjure Woman,* he uses slavery as a cultural backdrop to place the "New Negro" in disguise as an "Old Negro." In these stories, conjuring is used as a literary device and as a metaphor to convey societal conditions. Although he does not make "a complete break with the enslaved past" as mandated in the New Negro philosophy, Chesnutt uses Aunt Peggy to clarify the status of black Southerners. Black women as regional figures and conjuring as a literary device sometimes cannot support Chesnutt's representational strategies completely. Some of his black female characters like Viney and Tenie, for instance, appear as victims of sociopolitical circumstances because of their cultural connections to the South. Instead of being empowered by their communal ties, these black female characters appear as societal outcasts because of their race, class, and gender. They suffer the abuses of white power, loss of relatives and sanity as a result. Therefore, they are not useful for promoting Chesnutt's political agenda to resolve the Negro Problem as I outlined earlier, but they remind us of the social injustice done to black Southerners in general.

Chesnutt's mentor and friend George Washington Cable achieves his goals more effectively in his depictions of black women as radicals in his fiction. They are positioned as victims of circumstance, an illegitimate mulatto and abused slave, in his novel *The Grandissimes* (1880), but, in their vulnerability, we witness their strength. "It seems to be one of the self-punitive characteristics of tyranny, whether the tyrant be a man, a community, or a caste, to have a pusillanimous fear of its victim" (315). In his novel, Cable combines his political passions with his historical and literary interests. *The Grandissimes* created more controversy about the South's race problem—black oppression in light of the systematic enforcement of white supremacy—than Cable had anticipated, and he felt compelled to defend his work:

> It was impossible that a novel written by me then should escape being a study of the fierce struggle going on around me, ... I meant to make *The Grandissimes* as truly a political work as it ever has been called. . . . I was still very slowly and painfully guessing out the riddle of our Southern question. . . . But I did not intend to offend [white Southerners]. I wrote as near to truth and justice as I knew how, upon questions that I saw must be settled by calm debate and cannot be settled by force or silence; questions that will have to be settled thus by the Southern white man in his own conscience before ever the North and South can finally settle it between them. This was part of my politics and as a citizen I wrote. (*Negro Question* 14)[35]

Since it appeared in a market saturated by sentimental plantation images of the antebellum era, Cable's realistic treatment of "Negroes" in *The Grandissimes* is now closely associated with the modernist turn in Southern fiction.[36] Cable uses most of his black characters as a medium to expose racial inequality in the South. The deteriorating legal and social status of black Southerners is realized in the portraits of Honoré, f.m.c. ("free man of color"), Bras Coupé, and, most unexpectedly, black women characters.

A major part of the South's race problem stemmed from granting the black vote and revoking it later. Technically, black men *not* black women were disenfranchised during the post-Reconstruction era, but black women remained actively involved in politics. For instance, at public debates, black women in Richmond, Virginia "assumed as equal a right to be present and participate as the delegates themselves." Elsa Barkley Brown thus annotates the history of Southern black women's participation in Reconstruction-era politics. She explains just how black male delegates' voting decisions were influenced by the overwhelming presence of black women at constitutional conventions, rallies, parades, and other forums. These Southern black women were determined to be involved in the political process as "the community made plans for freedom" (Brown, "Catch the Vision" 129). Even if they do not have the judicial power to overturn discriminatory laws, Cable's radical black women confront an oppressive regime in an unmatched aggression by the black male characters. The enslaved Bras Coupé is a heroic figure though his story entertains audiences more than it frightens them.[37] Thus, black female characters achieve a sense of freedom that black men never quite experience in the novel. The black female characters participate in the making of an inclusive "new" South despite the racist status quo. Through their tireless struggle, Cable re-interprets the racial core of the South's "Negro Problem," the issue being whites' assumed privileges *not* blacks' innate disadvantages. In Cable's fiction, the action of black women characters underscores this sociopolitical imbalance.

The Grandissimes has a twofold plot about political discontentment that links the post-Reconstruction era in the South with the hysteria surrounding the Louisiana Purchase in 1803. The disenfranchisement of blacks and the granting of American citizenship to Spanish and French colonists thematically coincide to reveal the ironic discrepancies in the nations' liberal principles of equality. As Cable introduces readers to life among the early Creoles in New Orleans, we learn about their values, customs, speech, religion, and, most importantly, their history. The question of assimilation is inevitable for these Creoles though it is not a practical solution to the race problems of Cable's own time. His depiction of Creoles represents white Southerners as a whole; remove the exotic birthright of the Grandissimes and a Southern aristocracy remains, privileged by its inherited wealth and racial superiority. Elite Creole society—particularly the dominant French portion—is symbolic of white rule throughout the South especially when *unreconstructed* white Southerners held steadfast to their belief in a unified Confederate South despite the spread of U.S. nationalism. In both cases, members of the local body politic feared the ability of a national government to seize control over a local community's laws and transform its culture. This anxiety appears throughout *The Grandissimes*. Barbara Ladd aligns the Creole with the Southerner, but interestingly, she also chooses the black insurrectionist (in this case, Bras-Coupé, an African slave-prince) as a sympathetic reflection of the Southerner dealing with "the pressing issue of his or her own capacity for, and resistance to, assimilation to a national ideal" (80). Led by the "white" Honoré, the Grandissime clan is forced to accept their new American citizenship and must work to improve race relations in the South. The noble Honoré is faced with the dilemma of choosing to preserve his family's fortune and reputation and/or to fulfill moral obligations to those victimized by his family, including his older mulatto brother, Honoré, f.m.c.

Situated in a global South, Cable's *The Grandissimes* maps Creole elite society, African, German, Irish, and Caribbean cultural mixtures within the U.S. and beyond its geographical borders. The novel's setting is fertile ground for the ethnic diversity of the colonial era, late-19th century, and early modern New Orleans as set apart from "the South":

> New Orleans thus defies a fixed location in the geographical imaginary: it evades the frames of U.S. nationalism, as well as their affiliated divisions into regional characteristics, more powerfully than perhaps any other major city. Instead, it serves instead as a kind of conduit point—not only between Gulf and River, North and South, East and West, but also between polarized characterizations of Self and Other; it can be made to figure both as the epitome of southern difference and as an exceptional case within it. (Gruesz 53)

The heightened sensitivity to a white-black dichotomy might be the basis of the broader South's race problem, but Cable senses correctly that "race" and "Southernness" should not be narrowly defined by an U.S. nationalist imaginary of the mainland. Discussions of the Negro problem all too often turn to American slavery and Reconstruction without referencing U.S. expansionism to the West, imperialist interests in the Caribbean and the Philippines, or annexation of Cuba. (Chesnutt theorizes in his 1916 speech that solutions to the American South's race problems are evident in Latin American countries; he draws comparisons between African Americans and their "Negro cousins" in other colonized nations.) Cable's choice of setting is deliberate to expose the multilayered race problems of New Orleans as "a contested borderland, a '*transfrontera* contact zone' of different vectors of cultural, political, and economic activity" (Gruesz 54). The conflicts between Spanish-French Creoles and Anglo-Americans (the "*Américains*"), with the intrusion of European and Caribbean migrants, are central to the plot to explore white Southerners' singular opposition to African American citizenship. In the latter case, there is more at stake than white superiority but also a contaminated cultural identity (by comparison to *othered* New Orleans) that exposes ideological flaws in Southernness restricted by racial prejudices. The image of U.S. tyranny (read as white power in general) is re-imagined in the novel when Creoles, African slaves, and *gens de coloures* are juxtaposed as victims of impending nationalism and racism.

Despite the fact that his contemporaries felt he was a radical, when addressing the Negro Problem, Cable indeed took a moderate stance, even advocating a separate but equal policy at times:

> Social relations, one will say, are sacred. True, but civil rights are sacred, also. Hence social relations must not impose upon civil rights nor civil rights impose upon social relations. We must have peace. But for peace to be stable we must have justice. Therefore, for peace, we must find that boundary line between social relations and civil rights, from which the one has no warrant ever to push the other; and, for justice, this boundary must remain ever faithfully the same, no matter whose the social relations are on one side or whose the civil rights are on the other. (*Negro Question* 86–87)

The terminology of U.S. invasions into foreign lands is implicit in Cable's idealism to achieve "peaceful" relations between blacks and white Southerners. His diplomatic resolutions appear equitable to all parties. Indeed, Cable was one of the most outspoken white Southerners to present "the freedman's case in equity" during the late nineteenth century. Some historians believe that "a dominated group [e.g. of slaves] has, perforce, a much clearer picture of those who dominate [e.g. slaveholders] than the other way around" (Scott 31), but looking at Cable as a spokesman does offer an opportunity for self-reflection in ways different from a black man or a black woman, for instance, writing about their experiences of being "Southern." My book as a whole examines how black women—in fact and fiction—challenge an oppressive regime and transform Southern cultural standards. In the previous chapter, I examined how a black woman labeled as an outsider can re-claim her regional identity and is empowered by it and, earlier in this chapter, how a representative black man, once empowered by suffrage, relies on fictional black women to cope with regional conflict. As a "good Samaritan," Cable speaks from a position of power to challenge the very authority that empowered him as a white man in a sociopolitical hierarchy.[38] In his subversive response to racial discrimination, segregation, and violence in the region, in *The Grandissimes*, Cable inverts this hierarchy to allow fictional black women to be prominent social actors in the (re-)making of the "new" South.

In recognizing how Cable makes black women serve as an index for race and gender problems, I will consider the vital roles fictional black women play in their community, the narrative structure, and Cable's civil rights campaign. Perhaps only in New Orleans could their actions be justified. As "tricksters," the conjuring they perform demonstrates racial equality, complicates beliefs about blacks' inferiority, and, nevertheless, illustrates the important historical presence of blacks in the South.

"FAMILY TREES"

In *The Grandissimes*, the trope of flawed Southernness identifies the inconsistency between the idea of Southern culture prevalent in traditional literary and historical narratives and the reality of social circumstances. Cultural miscegenation in the novel illustrates how encounters among various groups of people sustain certain elements like their customs, values, and even languages. The novel's miscegenated cultural setting is also perfect for the development of competing identities: Creole vs. American, black vs. white, and, theoretically, displaced if "true" Southerners vs. flawed and then exiled Southerners. In reviewing the first and second set of identities, I will also explain the third set since it provides a context to understand the others. The level of acceptance by the dominant group in a community, as with the first two sets of identities, marks the difference between a displaced and a flawed Southerner.

In the novel, New Orleans in 1803 is just becoming a part of the American South. The Creoles must become assimilated Americans at the expense of destroying parts of their unique European cultural heritage. Contrarily, the Creoles, even liberal ones like the white Honoré, or a "foreigner" like the German immigrant Joseph Frowenfeld, can remain deviant in their actions but are not displaced by them. They may defy social mores that promote racial inequality nevertheless; other ruling white Southerners recognize Honoré and Joseph as full-fledged members of their local community.

As "white" men, they retain their membership privileges because of their race and gender, naturalized power and influence. By the novel's resolution, for instance, both Joseph and Honoré live happily ever after with their Southern belle brides despite the men's staunch liberalism. Thus, Joseph and the white Honoré are *flawed Southerners*. So has Cable been fondly called a "native outsider" and a "Southern heretic" because he was committed to writing about the South and claiming his Southern heritage even though he dissented from then popular opinions about race relations.

In *The Grandissimes*, notions of kinship, race, and region complicate the meaning of "place." The novel's plot concentrates on the rivalry among proud Creole families, the Grandissimes and the De Grapions. The offspring of the Grandissimes vastly outnumber the De Grapions, yet both families are equally reverent of their "white" ancestry in spite of possible blemishes. The related *gens de colouer libre*, for example, are despised though they are important links between the two families. Initially a valuable slave of the De Grapions, Palmyre is bartered to the Grandissimes as a measure of good faith between the families. Agricola Fusilier, the patriarch of the Grandissimes, becomes her guardian. Whereas kinship is determined by blood relationships in the novel, racism excludes black relatives from full membership in both clans.

During the nineteenth century, white Creoles protested any association with blacks, fearing that outsiders (Americans) would perceive them as "half-brother to the black, a sort of mixed breed stripped of blood pride as well as of any claim to social or political preferment. . . . [T]he very suspicion of 'tainted blood' guaranteed a ticket to opprobrium, contempt, and ostracism" (Tregle 173). Hence, the term "Creole" was redefined to include only the "pure-white" French and Spanish descendants, unlike before when the term generally classified all persons native-born without regard to color (i.e. race) or social hierarchy (Tregle 172). When the legacy of criolity was nullified in the assimilation process, free mulattos and blacks were displaced under the new American regime. Palmyre and Honoré, f.m.c., for instance, are immediately assigned to the same social status as slaves and other blacks; they eventually lose their legal rights as well under the two-tier, white/black, caste system in the American South. Agricola's aversion towards these characters reveals this transition in the narrative.

Prior to the outbreak of racial hysteria, during the colonial French occupation of Louisiana, a set of laws called the Code Noir, or the "Black Codes," defined racial classifications to maintain civil order. A three-tier caste system was created: whites, free blacks (usually mixed-race individuals), and slaves.[39] The free people of color generally adopted the attitudes and culture of the white French and Spanish; most of them were also the products of racial miscegenation, an act outlawed by the Black Codes but maintained as a social custom. Free people of color enjoyed "degrees of freedom in conformity with their proximity or separation from the white race" (Dunbar-Nelson 21). The confined social spaces allotted to Cable's mixed-race characters exemplify this racial paradox. For instance, through the doubling of the white Honoré, the protagonist, with his mulatto brother, the author diagnoses the "half-brother" paranoia among Creoles. Cable draws clear lines of racial prejudice and discrimination between the protagonist and his "black" brother; miscegenation is a social problem rather than a legal one in this relationship. That is, Honoré, f.m.c. has some legal privileges as the chief heir of his white father's fortune; he is tolerated but despised. To the Creoles, he is simply "that darkey who has had the impudence to try to make a commercial white gentleman of himself" (295). Furthermore, he appears too weak to pose a legal problem to the community before he murders his uncle Agricola. The darker Honoré's shadowy appearance throughout the novel exemplifies his fragile disposition. Yet, there are superficial reasons why he seems to aggravate the Creoles a great deal more than Palmyre. He is an educated, successful realtor and slaveholder. In spite of his substantial wealth, Honoré, f.m.c. is considered most threatening because he shares the lineal name of his white relatives. In the dim sick-room, where the darker Honoré meets with his white brother, the two eventually settle the family dispute to become business partners, "Grandissimes Brothers." This compromise ignites controversy in the community, with race relations and family disgrace at the core: "Not dat h-use [the white Honoré] de money, but it is dat name w'at 'e give de h-establishmen'—Grandissime Frères! H-only for 'is money we would 'ave catch' dat quadroon gen'leman an' put some tar and fedder. Grandissime Frères!" (277).

As an ex-slave quadroon freed by her white relatives, I think Palmyre la Philosophe's illegitimacy complicates the plot even more than the doubling of the Honorés. Unlike Honoré, f.m.c.'s relationship to the Grandissimes, Palmyre's relationship to the De Grapions is more hidden socially and structurally in the narrative. It is the secret everyone knows but doesn't seem to acknowledge. Alice Moore Dunbar-Nelson offers an insider's view of such racial taboos in New Orleans around the turn of the 19th century: "the glory and the shame of the city were her quadroons and octoroons, apparently constituting two aristocratic circles of society, the one as elegant as the other, the complexions the same, the men the same, the women different in race, but not in color, nor in dress, nor in jewels" (27). Mulatto women apparently were distinctly categorized as "other" by their racialized gender, while mulatto men could become "commercial white gentlemen" without complete censure.[40] In the text, we are only given subtle clues about Palmyre's racial heritage, and her material possessions are few. When Palmyre becomes a legal problem (an attempted murderer), she is exiled from the community, otherwise, until then, the Creoles (except Agricola) tolerate her in social circles. Dr. Keene, a trusted physician and pseudo-social historian, admits that he would "a'most as soon trust that woman [Palmyre] as if she was white" (58). Here gender is used to excuse the problem of race unlike in the case of Honoré, f.m.c.

By virtue of their gender, black women characters sustain intimate contact with whites without them perceiving these black women as a real threat. Consequently, black women become both agents and victims of cultural change. For instance, by labeling Palmyre a "monument of the shame of two races" (symbolic of illicit sexual relationships between white men and black women), Cable projects the *social component* of the South's Negro problem onto the body of Palmyre (134). With emphasis on immorality, this social component is a concern with creating and maintaining a sense of community, that is, regional identity, despite the South's complicated past with slavery. Accordingly, Clemence unifies the diverging plots in her role as slave albeit a rebellious one: "To Clemence the order of society was nothing. . . . She had certain affections toward people and places; but they were not of a consuming sort" (251). Unlike the free quadroons, Clemence is a "slave in form but free in spirit." She acts for Palmyre in Palmyre's revenge scheme against the Grandissimes and, as Honoré f.m.c.'s slave, Clemence serves as "trickster" mediator (and agitator) of conflict between him and the community. She is responsible for bringing Honoré f.m.c. to rescue the slain Doctor Keene after his duel with Sylvestre (267). I will discuss Clemence's role as an informant in greater detail later in the chapter; notably, her public performances and sarcastic wit relieve racial tensions in the narrative. But Clemence and Palmyre are more than simple narrative props.

In *The Grandissimes,* Cable writes as a flawed Southerner when he presents the case of blacks' civil equality implicitly through the actions of his black female characters surviving under conditions of servitude *while they manage to sustain intimate community relations.* Cultural miscegenation makes this possible. It is evident in the language used by black women—especially when voodoo is used as a communicative tool—and in the construction of their regional identities, with an emphasis on their social status. Though they are never completely accepted by whites on terms of equality, both Palmyre and Clemence mediate between the black and white worlds better than either of the major black male figures. Bras-Coupé and Honoré, f.m.c. are against the community and not well integrated into it like the black women. Respectively, as a diabolical, majestic slave warrior and as a refined, rich gentleman, the black men generally pose a threat to white Southerners' social privileges and the community's economic infrastructure.[41] These men are despised most of all because they are civil rights activists in their own right. As they struggle to survive, on the other hand, the fictional black women appear as sympathetic figures even in their aggression.

TWO WOMEN, ONE SOUTH

In an intricate web of identities predicated on race, class, and gender, Palmyre la Philosophe is positioned as the black widow in the narrative.

Whites are frightened by her conjuring deeds, yet Cable makes her vulnerable to "the slavery of caste." Specifically, Palmyre is an object of desire placed under strict limitations. She is set in three different love triangles based on hierarchical conditions of color and caste: between the rebellious African slave Bras-Coupé and the mulatto Honoré; between the white Honoré and his mulatto brother; between the white Honoré and Aurora, his white love interest and Palmyre's half-sister. However, Palmyre cannot fully participate in any of these relationships because of her status as a free woman of color. Although she is legally "free," this status agitated circumstances surrounding her experiences as black, female, and Southern. In particular, it sets her apart from ideologies of womanhood governing white women and female slaves. Like other women in her position, Palmyre is still held up to aspirations of the "ideal" of white women's superiority even as the illegitimate daughter of a white patriarch.[42] In particular, her brief marriage to Bras-Coupé and the mulatto Honoré's marriage proposal are insults to "one who *shared the blood of the De Grapions*" (176) (original emphasis). Moreover, Colonel De Grapion, her alleged father, even threatens to kill "whosoever should give Palmyre to a black man" although she is unaware of such protection (185).

Since it was a common antebellum practice in New Orleans, Palmyre's only option is to participate in plaçage and become a white man's concubine. Plaçage was a system of contractual relationships between white men and women of color in which the suitor provided for his "placée" usually a house and financial support for her and any children born from the union. Other benefits included land and other property inheritance, a good education (for the children), luxurious material possessions, and, most importantly, freedom. Some of these relationships resulted in long-term commitments, while it was also very common that the relationship was dissolved when the man married a white woman. These relationships were once viewed as a form of prostitution but most scholars now agree that they resembled common-law marriages instead (Blassingame 18). [43] Historians trace the development of plaçage to the colonial period when there was a gender imbalance in Louisiana: more women of color (Africans and Native Americans) and white men than black men and white women (Martin 57–64). The increase in interracial sexual liaisons contributed to the rise of the class of free people of color, who became the privileged offspring of European men. As such, free women of color were forbidden by law to marry slaves and white men; suitable arrangements could be made with other free blacks, but plaçage was most desirable to the women involved. When Harriet Martineau, the radical English feminist and travel writer, observed Creole society, she declared that it was a free woman of color's prerogative to reject the hand of a man of her caste in favor of a white man; these women were 'brought up by their mothers to be what they have been, mistresses of white gentlemen' (qtd. in Dunbar-Nelson 22, n.53). Joan M. Martin proclaims that in order to insure the survival of black women and their offspring, plaçage was their "best" alternative (64). Under plaçage, black women were given a sense of security unmatched by offers from any black man in a society ruled by white men.

Cable was well aware of plaçage, but he goes to great lengths to place Palmyre outside of this context. The fact that he (in the voice of Frowenfeld) condemns the practice as a "paltry bait of sham freedom" (196) suggests that Cable wants Palmyre to transcend this kind of moral degradation, can she? First of all, she works for a living as a skilled hairdresser and voodoo priestess. There are few references to payments Palmyre receives, but her monetary value is reflected in the dignity she maintains. To further complicate the issue, Cable gives us only the outline of plaçage, that is, the symbolic relations of the institution but makes no real claims to its legitimacy with Palmyre's situation. For instance, Palmyre's unrequited love for the white Honoré is that of a quadroon desiring to be rescued by her white mate. Even Palmyre's rejection of Honoré, f.m.c. can be attributed to the influence of plaçage. However, Cable does not explore this option with Palmyre as he does with Honoré, f.m.c. Numa Grandissime, the father of the two Honorés, had "forfeited the right to wed" before meeting Agricola's sister, "they all knew how." But in order to resolve family conflicts, Numa "'nobly sacrificed a little sentimental feeling,' as his family defined it, by breaking faith with the mother of" Honoré, f.m.c. when he was just a young boy (108). The black son inherited the bulk of his father's wealth as a fulfillment of a broken promise and proof of his father's sincerity towards his black mother. His inheritance is a blessing and a curse; Honoré f.m.c. is "free in form" yet "a slave in spirit" (196).

The love affair between Numa Grandissime and his black concubine is the closest portrayal of plaçage that we get in *The Grandissimes*. Even though it is romanticized, members of the community acknowledge that such arrangements openly existed, and the Grandissimes talk about plaçage as part of their family's heritage, though they deny the mulatto child. Also, in this story of an interracial love affair, the fate of black women in these arrangements is uncertain. Palmyre has more mysterious origins than Honoré, f.m.c.[44] We do not know, for instance, if Palmyre is actually a product of plaçage or rape. All the allusions to her vulnerability (e.g. standing with "a dagger in hand," as a "monument of shame of two races," "legitimate prey" to all men) place Palmyre in a violent context. It is almost as if she is a stand-in for her mother, or other black women, who were possibly placed in a similar situation. This is slightly different from Cable's portrayal of the Nancanou ladies.[45] They are not endangered physically, but without an official male benefactor they are symbolically vulnerable to sexual exploitation. Their financial recovery rests with the benevolence of the white Honoré and his marriage proposal rescues the women from social ostracism. Palmyre may not receive a financial inheritance, like these women and Honoré, f.m.c., but the ambivalent protection her father tries to provide for her undermines Palmyre's "tragic" status.

Hortense J. Spillers interprets the subjectivity of black women in terms of language construction(s) and places it in the context of slavery. Though I am intrigued by her deconstruction of gender and the abstraction of black femininity (i.e. the embodiment of the "flesh"), I am interested in the concreteness of her argument about familial relationships as it relates to Palmyre's illegitimacy, culturally and legally.[46] Colonel De Grapion's "mocking presence," as Spillers would label it, overshadows Palmyre's absent mother's identity. Ignoring her paternity in the text—as a secret that everyone knows, but does not speak—doubly deprives Palmyre of any source of identity. Altogether, it negates Spillers' "mama's baby, papa's maybe" theoretical, biological equation, in which maternal bonds are clearly defined if paternal claims are not. The family structure here is broken down, leaving a cursed daughter without any antecedents (acknowledged or otherwise). Palmyre does not have a mother to claim her and provide guidance. Her father is too passive to make a difference in her life.

In Spillers' estimate, kinship, defined in a traditional sense, is made irrelevant in slavery especially when it involves miscegenation. The mulatto children of black females are "orphaned" in enslavement due to an intricate set of power relations that determine the offspring's heritage.[47] A child is not "related" to the parent even if blood connections are evident—this goes for the white "father" also—since the mother and child are the property of their master and no familial relations exist for humans defined as chattel. Yet, slave codes stipulated that the child of a female slave should follow in the condition of the mother. With the mother being property herself, this "law of the Mother" renders black motherhood a falsified paradox: "the enslaved must not be permitted to perceive that he or she has any human rights that matter. Certainly if 'kinship' were possible, the property relations would be undermined, since the offspring would then 'belong' to a mother and a father" (Spillers 271). Clemence's role as a black slave mother exemplifies this paradox in the text:

> She remembered her mother. They had been separated in her childhood, in Virginia when it was a province. She remembered, with pride, the price her mother had brought at auction, and remarked, as an additional interesting item, that she had never seen or heard of her since. [Clemence] had had children, assorted colors—had one with her now, ... the others were here and there, some in the Grandissime households or field-gangs, some elsewhere within occasional sight, some dead, some not accounted for. (251)

The pain and suffering caused by the separation between Clemence and her own mother, then again with her own children, blunts her maternal instincts. At least, there is no perceptible emotional connection between her and her only remaining child, the narrator discloses the relationship almost as an afterthought. The severed familial ties make Clemence less human, almost like a puppet; her most striking feature is her voice. Therefore, she becomes an ideal narrative prop to convey Cable's radical views about civil equality.

As it relates to Palmyre's narrative role, Spillers' logic about kinship ties is useful to understanding two things about Palmyre: first, she is not a tragic quadroon and, second, Cable uses this non-stereotype to his advantage. As I've mentioned before, missing from Palmyre's family tree is her mulatto mother. Given the ¼ black ratio of her ancestry, several clues indicate that Palmyre's blackness is traceable through a matrilineal side. Matriarchy is touted in the story of the Creoles, via their Native American ancestry. Despite the emphasis on symbolic motherhood, most mothers are absent from the text, or motherhood is redefined, in the case of Aurora, as a childlike woman, and Clemence, as a slave mother, without any power to claim and protect her children. Black mothers were pivotal figures in the Negro Problem; they were morally responsible for their own families and the entire race.

Spillers maintains that "the destructive loss of the natural mother, whose biological/genetic relationship to the child remains unique and unambiguous, opens the enslaved young to social ambiguity and chaos: the ambiguity of his/her fatherhood and to a structure of other relational elements . . ." (272). Some may conclude that the absence of her mother is a way of alienating Palmyre from her blackness and thus strengthening her bond with whites. This would be a trite plot for the tragic story of a beautiful quadroon and Cable is not fully invested in this sort of melo-drama.[48] Though Palmyre may appear vulnerable to her crush on Hon-oré, she is not pathetic. James Kinney compares her to earlier abolitionist stereotypes of the tragic octoroon due to her beauty and assigned role as a victim, but Palmyre's "refusal to acquiesce" to this fate exonerates her (131). Only in her hopeless desires for the white Honoré, Kinney assumes, does she appear defeated. However, this doesn't make her a "tragic" ste-reotype, it makes her more *human*, considering the history of miscegena-tion and plaçage in New Orleans.

The lax morals of Creole society are almost enough to justify the survival of a mixed-race woman who defies notions of race and caste. Cable relies on scientific theories about heredity in his characterization of Palmyre, which makes it possible to re-claim her as an untragic figure.[49] As a prod-uct of "high Latin ancestry" and "Jaloff African," Palmyre appears to have inherited the dominant traits of both groups to become "a barbaric and magnetic beauty" (60).[50] It appears that Cable also combined genetic theo-ries to depict Palmyre in this way. On the one hand, Darwinian theories of blended inheritance, where the fusion of parental traits occurs to create a new variety, are appropriate in Palmyre's case.[51] She seems to have inher-ited her nobility, strength, pride, passion, and complexion from each side of her family. Though she is often depicted as an erotic savage, she seems closely related to Agricola in her fierceness. After all, they are both depicted as regal felines; he as a lion and she a lioness.

By extension, Francis Galton's "Law of Ancestry" is equally important when considering Palmyre's identity. With "Galtonian fusion," an individual's grandparents contribute to their descendants' genetic makeup (Bramen 218–219). Palmyre's quadroon status depends on the "one-drop" rule, on the basis that one-out-of-four of her immediate ancestors were black. But in a tragic scenario, what normally leads to a "divided self" or a "double consciousness" for the "white Negro" doesn't occur for Palmyre. She achieves equilibrium in her position as a confident, free woman of color. She does not experience any anxiety for having a mixed ancestry, unlike stereotypical tragic mulattos/octoroons.[52] Indeed, Cable's novel highlights her middle status between whites and blacks more than most critics have acknowledged. True, she does not show an "allegiance to the suffering of blacks," as Kinney notes, but she does not embrace all whites either. Instead, we see Palmyre interacting with those of both races in which she has formed reciprocal relations. For instance, her connections to Aurora, Dr. Keene, and Joseph Frowenfeld are based on mutual respect; she is defensive with Agricola and any other white man likely to do her harm. Though she loathes the idea of being the wife of a black man, Bras-Coupé, Palmyre's "feelings were wonderfully knit to the African" (184). Even though she was a slave then, Palmyre had greater influence with her master/mistress and therefore was superior to Bras-Coupé within the context of plantation life. She wanted to manipulate him just as she tries with Clemence to achieve her revenge on Agricola. Palmyre's free status influences her interactions with most blacks in the text: since they are slaves, they service her. Likewise, when Palmyre is a slave she is submissive to her white mistress out of respect and due to the conditions of her enslavement. Yet, even as a slave, her hatred for Agricola is evident. Agricola, in turn, is afraid of her because she has always challenged his racist, white authority (61).

Cable's image of Palmyre as a destructive force can be attributed not only to eugenics but culture as well. Her characterization epitomizes the treatment of black women set at a gender and social disadvantage under the conditions of slavery and institutional racism prevalent in American society. The nineteenth century ideology of "true womanhood," in which "purity, piety, submissiveness, and domesticity are the cardinal virtues," is implicit in the contradictions that set Palmyre at odds with possible love interests (Carby 23).[53] If there is the opportunity for Palmyre to possess the virtues of the "cult" of true womanhood as the daughter of the white Creole aristocracy, fractional blood equations forbid her from completely fulfilling this role. As a youth, Palmyre has "that rarest of gifts" of purity for "one of her tincture" (60), she yearns for domesticity in her love for the white Honoré, and even submits herself, although briefly, to her superiors. Initially, she is the epitome of Victorian femininity. In offsetting this ideology, Cable substitutes Palmyre's piety, the fourth element of "true" womanhood, with the practicing of voodoo, an exchange that only darkens the fair image of her youth and labels her as a seductress once she is an adult.

Heightened sexual tension, for instance, is apparent in the climactic sick-bed scene with Palmyre and Joseph Frowenfeld. As he tries to dress her wounds, Palmyre grabs his hands and begs the apothecary to use his "powers" to make a love match between her and the white Honoré:

> However harmless or healthful Joseph's touch might be to the Philosophe, he felt now that hers, to him, was poisonous. He dared encounter her eyes, her touch, her voice, no longer. The better man in him was suffocating. He scarce had power left to liberate his right hand with his left, to seize his hat and go.
>
> Instantly she rose from her chair, threw herself on her knees in his path, and found command of his language sufficient to cry as she lifted her arms, bared of their drapery:
>
> 'Oh, my God! Don' rif-used me—don' rif-used me!' (201)

This image of her overt sexuality is stereotypical of lustful black slave women (Carby 27). In the controversy that ensues when Joseph Frowenfeld is seen staggering from Palmyre's house (after her servant hits him over the head, assuming Joseph had assaulted her mistress), the apothecary's reputation as a "gentleman" is considered ruined. Since even the Creole elite "consult the voudou horses," as Honoré informs Joseph as a new immigrant to New Orleans, the professional services they provide are common (55). So why does the incident between Joseph and Palmyre appears as a sex scandal in the eyes of the community?[54]

According to K. Sue Jewell, the sultry temptress image of black womanhood is represented by the biblical Jezebel or "the bad-black-girl" type. Jewell describes her as:

> a mulatto or a fair-complexioned African American female, who possesses features that are considered European. Thin lips, long straight hair, slender nose, thin figure . . . conforms more to the [white] American standard of beauty than any of the other [black stereotypical] images. The bad-black-girl is depicted as alluring, sexually arousing and seductive. She fulfills the sex objectification requirement of White womanhood, although she is portrayed as a less naïve, more worldly seductress. (Jewell 46)

This description, although it is a twentieth-century interpretation, could easily be mistaken as the blueprint for Cable's portrayal of Palmyre. At the expense of making her a sympathetic figure, Cable vilifies Palmyre in the process. Primitive images of her feline femininity abound in the text. When describing her sensuality, Cable reduces Palmyre to "a creature that one would want to find chained" (71). She even walks with the grace and pride of a regal, wild cat (71) and, when her passions rage, she is said to be "untamable" (147). As a small child, "her eyes were large and black, and rolled and sparkled if she but turned to answer to her name," which suggests the agility of a tigress on guard perhaps (59). She resembles "a pet leopard" during her bartered time at the Grandissimes' mansion where she matures under the guidance of a kind and superior mistress (146). Palmyre's most impressive quality is her fierce tenacity. Her inability to fulfill her own love relationships is counterbalanced by her desires for revenge.

Palmyre is transformed from a victim to a villain as she conspires against Agricola, the symbol of a conservative, racist white South. Inspired by a Syrian attack against the Roman Empire, her name is deemed "appropriate" for "a woman engaged in futile rebellion against more powerful forces" (Bendixen 30). Yet, the war she wages is necessary regardless of the final outcome. Palmyre's struggles for autonomy and recognition have historical significance like that of the Syrian Queen Zenobia.[55] Agricola becomes Palmyre's archenemy when he ignores the warning against her marriage to Bras-Coupé and Palmyre's own objection to the arrangement (174). To proceed without either her master's consent or her own is a direct violation of the Code Noir, which stipulates that

> the consent of the father and mother of the slave is not necessary; that of the master shall be the only one required . . . [and] all curates [are forbidden] to proceed to effect marriages between slaves without proof of the consent of their masters; and . . . all masters [are forbidden] to force their slaves into any marriage against their will. (Gayarre 538)

Even though she remains infatuated with the white Honoré, Palmyre takes advantage of the ill-fated marriage: she becomes "fifty times the mutineer she had been before—the mutineer who has nothing to lose" (184). Palmyre plans to use Bras-Coupé for her own purposes, to "show his mighty arm how and when to strike" (178). In a drunken fury, however, the black warrior assaults his master, a crime punishable by death under the Code Noir (Gayarre 541).[56] Consequently, he seals his fate and, temporarily, dashes the hopes of Palmyre. "The lesson she would have taught the giant was Insurrection" and not self-destruction (184). Some critics use the legend of Bras-Coupé to support Cable's renegade status as a writer; they consider it to be Cable's attempt to indoctrinate his white readers prior to beginning his official civil rights crusade. They also view this defining moment in the narrative as a framework for understanding the experiences of the other black characters. Bras-Coupé is especially viewed as a terrorist model for Palmyre and Clemence's rebellion (Ladd 67).

"The Story of Bras-Coupé," as told through a series of narrators, resonates in the lives of the fictional audiences. Yet, the importance attached to the story by most critics (then and now) might impede readers' ability to understand the other characters in their own right without this historical context. In the case of Palmyre, her intelligence, radical spirit, and native status place her at odds with the African Bras-Coupé rather than making the two analogous. In other words, critics have let their similarities over-shadow key differences. Robert Allen Alexander, Jr. labels Palmyre a "more lethal threat" to her enemies. Even after the death of Bras-Coupé, who is installed as a martyr, Palmyre "continues as a potent psychological force, haunting the nightmares of her oppressors and compelling them to lash out at those within their grasp . . . [she] is boundless" (Alexander 130–131). To view her experience as an American slave and, later, as a freed black woman in the shadow of a savage African dismisses Cable's creation of a black woman who defies racial *and* gender stereotypes. Subordinating Palmyre to Bras-Coupé does show how Cable works on the legal component of the Negro Problem if we consider Bras-Coupé as representing the disenfranchised Negro (i.e. black man). Palmyre's role as a cultural agent is most apparent in her revenge skims when she tries to eliminate Agricola, the key defender of white supremacy.

Though Palmyre's ambition is symbolized in the majestic body of Bras-Coupé it is realized in Honoré, f.m.c.'s attack on Agricola. Honoré, f.m.c. has his own reasons for wanting to kill Agricola, who had previously assaulted his illegitimate nephew in public. Agricola also ignored the mulatto Honoré's request to marry Palmyre. So his love for and devotion to Palmyre could have also inspired his attack on his uncle, to right the wrongs against both him and her. If not the lovesick suitor, perhaps Palmyre's most effective weapon is her silence. The one command Palmyre obeys that triggers her malevolence for Agricola is when she is forced to accept her interim "master's" decision to allow Agricola's consent to seal the deal for the marriage between her and Bras-Coupé: "And she was silent; and so, sometimes, is fire in the wall" (175). Without the exterior narrator, the details of Palmyre's plans for revenge are suppressed in the narrative despite the actions it incites in others like Clemence. Depending on when and how Palmyre speaks, Cable takes a multifaceted approach to present her mode of communication. First, she uses her body language (e.g. her feline expressions) to influence others. Alexander proclaims that, like Bras-Coupé, Palmyre "speaks most powerfully through her eyes . . . [when used to] effectively subvert the physical and psychological boundaries imposed by their supposed masters" (130). We can also detect Palmyre's affection and respect for others like Aurora and Joseph as reflected through her "large, passionate black eyes." I think it is important to understand exactly what Palmyre tries to communicate to understand the complexity of this character.

Cable makes Palmyre multilingual, which complements the layering of her identity as a slave or freed woman, a victim or villain. Even though she is illiterate, she speaks several native tongues of the slave population in addition to her own Creole French and broken English. She tries to speak the appropriate French with Joseph to impress him though he does not understand it. Likewise, Palmyre appears not to understand his English, but she comprehends his gentle ways, which gain her trust. She is comfortable speaking "plantation French" with Aurora in their intimate relationship. Though they never speak to each other, Agricola often speaks ill of Palmyre, and her constant physical presence challenges him forthrightly. With voodoo as a medium, however, they understand each other well; she uses it to threaten him, and he does not underestimate her abilities. The intrusive narrator may explain the meanings of the various voodoo charms, but Agricola understands them himself even though he refuses to be affected by Palmyre's curses.

When cultural conflicts appear, Cable carefully places an interpreter in the narrative to relieve the tensions. Usually the exterior narrator explains the connections between the characters and events to make the juncture in the historical context seamless. At various times, other characters take this role: Joseph as an English interpreter for Palmyre and Honoré, f.m.c.; Agricola as a reluctant interpreter for Bras-Coupé and willing tutor of Creole culture for Joseph; and Palmyre translates for Bras-Coupé in order to subdue him. A superimposed interpreter appears at a climax in the narrative when Palmyre makes her cruel intentions clear to Joseph and the reader. After Joseph reads the mulatto Honoré's love letter to Palmyre, which also proclaims the white Honoré's affection for another woman, Palmyre rejects the passive suitor and resolves to seek retribution without consequences:

> 'Very well; if I cannot love I can have my revenge.' She took the letter from him and bowed her thanks, still adding, in the same tongue [i.e. her "native patois"], 'There is now no longer anything to prevent.'
> The apothecary understood the dark speech. She meant that, with no hope of Honoré's love, there was no restraining motive to withhold her from wreaking what vengeance she could upon Agricola. But he saw the folly of a debate.
> 'That is all I can do?' asked he.
> '*Oui, merci, Miche*,' she said; then she added, in perfect English, 'butthat is not all *I* can do,' and then—laughed. (292)

With all her might, the message Palmyre usually only conveys with her passionate eyes is announced in black dialect, formal French, and "perfect" English all at once. The readers are forced to suspend disbelief that Palmyre's sublime wickedness makes this complex form of communication possible.

We encounter similar issues when we deal with Clemence as a radical black woman and a two-dimensional character. Dr. Keene declares that she is "a thinker," a careful observer of the societal conditions around her, though she is blind to the matters that affect her most. Clemence always provides Dr. Keene with all the recent gossip of the community. At times, he even tests her propensity for the truth about the South's racial problems. For instance, when Dr. Keene proclaims that "slaves were 'the happiest people under the sun'"(249), Clemence cunningly credits this misconception to white folks trying to validate the racist American caste system for

their own benefit. The quiz continues when another white man in earshot
of their conversation retorts

> 'you niggers don't know when you are happy.'
> 'Dass so, Mawse—*c'est vrai, oui!*' she answered quickly: 'we donno
> no mo'n white folks!'
> The laugh was against him. (250)

Clemence uses slave dialect as a mode of empowerment through a masked
performance of subjugation. Her sarcasm reveals how much black slaves
understood whites due to their intimate relations even though whites generally did not have the same insight about black slaves. Clemence, like
Palmyre, is positioned as a displaced Southerner. She is an American-born
slave from Virginia who assimilates to Creole society. Both Clemence and
Palmyre use language to demonstrate the cultural diversity of New Orleans,
but, in turn, they also use the language(s) to critique this diversity and the
circumstances of race relations in America.

For displaced Southerners, cultural miscegenation allows them to redefine their regional identities in ways that help them to engage in the South's
cultural development. I discuss in the first chapter how Frances Harper
took advantage of her border state Southern heritage to promote her political agenda. In the case of both Clemence and Palmyre's use of language,
the multilingual patterns are evidence of cultural miscegenation. But these
black women are *not* liberals and therefore are not flawed Southerners,
which are also produced by cultural miscegenation under different circumstances. Clemence and Palmyre are not even "Southerners" by traditional
measures: one is a mulatto Creole and the other a *Southern* slave not a
Southerner—the difference being the position of power and autonomy.
Nonetheless, these black women characters bring attention to flaws in an
imagined, pure Southern society: stratified race problems, the maintenance
of a caste system, despite obvious intermixing among blacks and whites of
all classes. This awareness, evident in their language and actions, allows
Palmyre and Clemence to engage in a Southern body politic almost on
terms of equality with white Southerners. They develop a regional "double
consciousness" which enables them to do what Stephanie Foote claims is
possible in a colonized or imperial state like early Louisiana: "The characters' ability to communicate in a variety of languages . . . represents a
necessary ability to speak in public, official discourses (and therefore to
speak as a citizen) as well as an ability to speak from within their own culture" (115). Clemence and Palmyre are aligned with Frowenfeld, the white
Honoré, and even Cable, who are/were Southern white men empowered by
their unpopular rhetoric and behaviors. Clemence is allowed to go only so
far in her indignation before Dr. Keene admonishes her.

Though Clemence is shrewd enough to recognize the social injustice
done to blacks, she is physically little more than a female caricature of the

"happy darkey" slave popularized by plantation fiction. "We know she is a constant singer and laugher" (251) and this "continuous displaying of teeth, in a grin or smile, suggests satisfaction or contentment, which was important to slave owners" (Jewell 41). In contrast, Palmyre displays her "faultless teeth" reluctantly in "a rather hard, yet not repellent smile" (57). Clemence's masking transforms her into a "stereotype plus" like Uncle Julius in Charles Chesnutt's *The Conjure Woman*; they appear content in their subordination to whites, but, in going beyond the stereotype, both Uncle Julius and Clemence are manipulative and conceal bitter recollections of their experiences as slaves. Clemence suffers the loss of her mother, most of her children, and all of her husbands. Her sorrow grows into rage, and it emerges in her sharp wit. In her role as a social commentator, Clemence underestimates her status in the close-knit community. Her pastries are normally accompanied by her peculiar, yet wise sayings. She is literally feeding the Creoles their own dark truths that they otherwise choose not to acknowledge. Her speeches, however, are lodged in the minds of the Creoles and they eventually make Clemence pay for her transgressions with her life.

The lynching scene that places Clemence on trial for attempted murder is memorable if for no other reason than its testimony to the inhumanity of slavery. She endures for hours the excruciating pain caused by the metal animal trap set to catch a suspect in the woods surrounding the Grandissimes' mansion. Though she tries to reason with her captors, Clemence does not receive clemency as her name suggests. She betrays Palmyre, the real culprit, for her own life, but implicates herself in the rebellious scheme: "You musn' b'lieve all dis-yeh nonsense 'bout insurrectionin'; all fool-nigga talk. W'at we want to be insurrectionin' faw? We de happies' people in de God's worl'!" (322). The simplicity of Clemence's dialect is no disguise for the irony of her statements. Palmyre may have instigated plans for a slave insurrection, but similar seditious ideas are often transmitted in Clemence's own "fool-nigga talk." Early on, she explains the problems of the color line in America and even compares it to the conditions in Europe where there was a fixed working class (250). She knows that white Southerners, in particular, perceive the granting of equal rights to blacks as an attempt to undermine their overlying social privileges. Lastly, with the irony in her minstrel performance, Clemence reminds her captive white audience (in this scene and for the post-bellum readers) of their ignorance about the black Southern experience as she does before in the banter with Dr. Keene.

When Clemence realizes that her captors are not sympathetic but remain intent on a suitable punishment, she is defiant to the end:

> Ah! no, mawsteh, you cyan' do dat! It's ag'in de law! I's 'bleeged to have my trial, yit. Oh, no, no! Oh, good God, no! Even if I is a nigga! You cyan' jis' murdeh me hyeh in de woods! *Mo dis la zize!* I tell de

judge on you! You ain' got no mo' biznis to do me so 'an if I was a white 'oman! You dassent tek a white 'oman out'n de Pa'sh Pris'n an' do 'er so! (322) [57]

In Clemence's defense, gender complicates the problem of race (as it does for Palmyre). Joseph Frowenfeld is the first person to adopt this view when he learns of Clemence's capture. He asks Agricola, '[w]ill they treat her exactly as if she were white, and had threatened the life of a slave?' (318). While pleading for her executioners' mercy, Clemence reflects on her own spiritual salvation: "Oh, God 'a' mussy on my wicked ole soul! I aint fitt'n to die! Oh, gen'lemen, I kyan' look God in de face!" (322). Then she curses the lynch mob once: "Oh, gen'lemen, dough yo' kinfolks kyvaeh up yo' tricks now, dey'll dwap f'um undeh you some day!" (323) . . . and again . . ."Oh, yes, deh's a judgmen' day! Den it wont be a bit o' use to you to be white!" (323). In her tirade, Clemence refuses to accept a death sentence without condemning her captors for their own misdeeds. She knows that the Code Noir should protect her, or, better yet, the laws of a just humanity; the value of her life is equal to that of a white person. Her dialect underscores a slave's ability to reason and ventriquilizes the liberal sentiments of Frowenfeld and Cable (as an intrusive narrator). In this way, Clemence, at the level of narrative, links the two plots of revenge and reconciliation. She acts for both Palmyre and Honoré, f.m.c. as their mercenary pawn and hired servant, and as Cable's medium for racial equality. Clemence's curses foreshadow the social upheaval of the Reconstruction era and the revelation African Americans longed for under the oppression of Jim Crow.

This ominous future/present is foreshadowed/realized when Cable dismisses the black female characters. While Clemence is killed for expressing her true feelings about racial injustice, Palmyre is consumed by revenge. If, at times, it seems that Cable tries to correct the tragic image of Palmyre, his efforts nevertheless revert back to common resolves of literary traditions. Everyone in the community knows that Palmyre "has suffered wrongs," but reparations are not made until Honoré, f.m.c. commits suicide and bequeaths her his wealth as a lasting testimony of his unrequited love. With approximately a million dollars inheritance, Palmyre lives comfortably in exile in France after Agricola's death. Outside of death, Cable uses another common alternative in American literature to resolve the miscegenation issue by condemning Palmyre to this physical isolation.[58] As James Kinney argues, she "achieves a kind of salvation, if only a wealthy exile, by the consistency with which she battles the caste system of New Orleans" (131). Reflecting Palmyre's inferior status in Creole society (i.e. the South), her foreign alias "Madame Inconnue," (since "inconnu" means outsider, alien, stranger, etc.) signifies her status as a displaced Southerner. Since Clemence is the only victim of the murderous plot, her death (albeit a violent resolution of the race problem) is symbolic of the regional displacement she experiences as well.

WORKING ON THE NEGRO PROBLEM

The black women radicals in Cable's *The Grandissimes* are not just at odds with the community, they are also in conflict with "the cultural imperatives that governed . . . [these] creations," as Jerry D. Ward suggests is usually the case with any image of fictional black women (186). Moreover, Ward argues that a fictional black woman can represent a collective image and the real experience of an individual simultaneously. His theory of representation merges metaphor with realism taking into account that "the images used in the realization of character involve a sense of time, of history" (Ward 186). To conclude my study of the black women in *The Grandissimes*, I will briefly discuss the construction of gender and Cable's motives for creating black female characters as antagonists of the South.

The novel provides two distinct images of black womanhood with Clemence and Palmyre, even though they are linked by primitive allusions to their humanity. While Palmyre appears to have "a femininity without humanity" (71), Clemence is reduced to a snarling wild animal when she is captured in the woods. Furthermore, these women are positioned as binary opposites in appearance. Palmyre, the exotic beauty, embodies "the majesty of an empress" (136), while Clemence is just a discarded "old hag" or, in her own words, a "po' nigga wench!" (322). Implicit in these images is a class dichotomy that places both women against the prevailing gender ideology in the nineteenth century.

Interesting parallels can be drawn between the cultural imagery of black womanhood and the "true womanhood" construct for elite white women. Both of these ideologies reflect slavery's influence on American cultural standards of beauty. "Black womanhood" differentiates female slaves, while the cult of *true* womanhood is applicable to plantation mistresses in the novel.[59] Comparably, the white definition of femininity contains four virtuous qualities (highlighted by the asterisks) and there are *four* prototypes needed to exhibit the singular concept of black womanhood. The cross-section of a matrix of these attributes would summarily be described as such: mammy and Aunt Jemima are the personifications of domesticity*; likewise, mammy and Aunt Jemima also are the most submissive* stereotypes of black womanhood; mammy is the most pious* prototype, perhaps, because of her maternal nature (i.e. symbolic of the biblical Madonna); unfortunately, purity* is *not* a part of "true" black womanhood at all. Considered in its literal sense as a sexual innuendo, mammy's "purity" is soiled by her numerous pregnancies, which contradicts her piety. Aunt Jemima is condemned to the same fate because she is the identical twin to the mammy figure differing only in her proclivity for cooking. On the other hand, both of these stereotypical women are usually "pure-hearted" at least due to their natural tenderness. Sapphire, another stereotypical black image, resembles mammy and Aunt Jemima in her emotional temperance: "the fierce independence of mammy and the cantankerousness of

Aunt Jemima, in conjunction with a proclivity for being loquacious, head-strong and omniscient, combine to make up Sapphire" (Jewell 45).[60] Sapphire is juxtaposed to the submissive roles assigned to both mammy and Aunt Jemima and, likewise, to white women. Finally, the image of Jezebel contradicts *all* of the qualities deemed virtuous for white women. Her promiscuity prevents any chances of her ever becoming completely domesticated; a family life would restrict her independence. Moreover, she would never submit herself to anyone, unless, of course, for sex. Purity is not in her nature and, like Sapphire, the name "Jezebel" denotes this inherent disposition. Palmyre's Jezebel image may also be seen as the reason why her love for the white Honoré must go unfulfilled.

As a two-dimensional character, Clemence embodies Cable's beliefs in civil equality. In her suffering, she is humanized in the end, and this character projects iconic images of African American womanhood. A direct correlation can be seen between Clemence and the mammy/Aunt Jemima persona. As the dark-complexioned mammy figure, which is most often equated with black women, Clemence performs all the domestic duties required of her: she "breeds" several children of her own, nurses those of her owners, and remains in the submissive station assigned to her. Mammy only voices her discontentment to other blacks or, when situations are relaxed enough around her superiors, she may show some aggression (Jewell 42). The relationship between Clemence and Dr. Keene best illustrates this exchange. The most distinctive features of the mammy image are her "exaggerated" breasts and buttocks even though black domestics are the least sexualized characterizations of African American womanhood (Jewell 40). The mammy/Aunt Jemima prototype is more a maternal role model rather than a sex symbol like the sultry temptress/ Jezebel/ "the bad-black-girl" type that we see in Palmyre (Jewell 40–41). In light of the separation of her own family, Clemence has "the cinders of human feelings" only (251). In this regard, her indifference is perhaps similar to Palmyre. Clemence's culinary skills are like those of Aunt Jemima; Clemence brags about the ginger cakes she sells all over town. These pastries do more than just provide literal access to white public spaces. Selling her cakes is also a critical maneuver that symbolically liberates her.[61] Her domestic sphere is broadened as she participants actively in the civil domain. Clemence may present herself as a groveling sycophant, but her duplicity allows her to engage in lofty conversations about the state of society at times and to criticize daily life among the Creoles in New Orleans.

Cable's sinister portrayal of Palmyre is perhaps partly due to maintaining the conformity of the novel's Creole setting. When he juxtaposes Palmyre to her white half-sister Aurora Nancanou, however, this coupling becomes symbolic on a greater level. The dynamic relationships between white mistresses and their female slaves, as Hazel Carby suggests, only "confirm [black women's] lack of womanly attributes in contrast to the abundance of virtues in their mistresses" (33). Considering how most of the qualities

Cable assigns to Palmyre—aggression, independence, and intellect—are those given primarily to white male characters, the relevance of this parallel is obvious. For each of Palmyre's blemishes, Aurora is portrayed just as the opposite. She is the traditional Southern belle in distress, who eventually is rescued by the white Honoré at the end of the novel. Cable makes him the same love interest for both women, which emphasizes the Palmyre/ Aurora juxtaposition even more. Palmyre, undoubtedly, is Aurora's superior in all attributes, which is evident even in their youth. As a voodoo priestess, however, Palmyre serves ironically a better purpose than if she would have been allowed the privilege of being a pious saint (as is expected of "true" women).

Voodoo serves as Palmyre's tragic flaw even though the tragedy actually occurs for Clemence. Nonetheless, voodoo fetishes allow both characters to challenge their oppressors, or "speak" directly to the Grandissimes, to the white South. All sorts of charms (like the 'bras coupé) are sent to warn the Grandissimes of foreboding danger. Among "African and Afro-Caribbean cultures," according to Barbara Ladd, "the rites [such as the uses of fetishes] associated with voodoo ceremonies were, more often than not, connected with self-government and organized resistance among enslaved people" (61). In *The Grandissimes*, voodoo is a sign of cultural miscegenation, evidence of African, Caribbean, and European relations. It is personified in Palmyre who is likewise the product of racial miscegenation. Cable uses voodoo in the same ways he uses Palmyre to link different racial groups on the basis of a common humanity and to send a political message. The mulatto/a was an important literary figure for the post-Reconstruction South just as it had been to advance the abolitionist cause. For a liberal Southern writer like Cable, it held immense possibilities for trying to resolve the region's race problems. He could show how the South created the mulatto via racial miscegenation and, in turn, how it exposes Southern hypocrisy about race relations. He extends this argument to the broader, hemispheric South given the cross-cultural exchanges in New Orleans, the Caribbean, and Latin America; other places were "Negro problems" were common and being resolved. In its ability to reflect fused cultural values and racial traits, as Palmyre does, "the mulatto actually appears as a most upsetting and subversive character who illuminates the paradoxes of 'race' in America" (Sollors 234).

Cable's editors were against his creation of Palmyre and Clemence as being much more than minor characters. They objected in general to the prominent roles given to blacks and mulattos in the manuscript, but the women were particularly disturbing. Palmyre was thought to be "entirely unbelievable" and "her mere presence was a coarsening of the novel" (Ladd 50). This was equally true for Clemence; they disapproved mostly her sarcasm. "'It is inartistic for [Clemence] to reason so about slavery,'" one editor concluded in a letter to Cable, "'the slave mind is not subjective or ratiocinative, it seems to me, but rather objective'" (qtd. in Ladd 51).

Aurora and Clotide perhaps are more likeable characters because they are so passive. The editors basically thought that too much emphasis on the effects of slavery on contemporary times would distract readers from the novel's reconciliation plot. Cable's intentions were clear and his negotiations with his editors to preserve the authenticity of his narrative included keeping Clemence, at least, mostly intact. After all, she was based on a real slave woman, Cable admits:

> In my childhood I used, at one time, to hear, every morning, a certain black marchande des calas—peddler woman selling rice croquettes— chanting the song [the "Calinda"] as she moved from street to street at the sunrise hour with her broad, shallow, laden basket balanced on her head. ("The Dance in Place Congo" 388)

The Calinda, which was "a vehicle for the white Creole's satire," epitomizes Clemence's characterization as an agent for social change ("Dance" 388). Altogether, Clemence is a product of memory, culture, and racial politics. (Like Chesnutt, Cable imaginatively rewrites historical figures.)

When Cable re-writes Southern history as fiction, black women are indeed brought to the forefront. My book emphasizes the roles of black women in the South, especially when they provide evidence of cultural changes and/or are used as catalysts in these processes. Cultural assumptions about her race and gender compromised the black female's position in Southern society as a slave or a free woman during the nineteenth century. Palmyre, as a free quadroon, is granted agency only by building alliances with members of the ruling class. Her occupation as a voodoo priestess and hairdresser upgrades her social status a little. Clemence, the enslaved cake vendor, on the other hand, is all but excluded from these power dynamics. However, the value of her pastries is immeasurable, considering the freedom she achieves peddling them. Cable owes a debt of gratitude to the real *marchande des calas*, who inspired his creation. In the novel, Clemence receives neither privilege nor rewards for being directly linked to the community as Palmyre is through her white relatives and clientele. The images of these black women at work are significant to the plot and Cable's political message. Some of the first images of black women in *The Grandissimes* are as servants, mute and mysterious. Yet, the appearance of the two most prominent black females, Clemence and Palmyre, disrupts the plot as if to signal the impossibility of a completely homogeneous society based on white superiority.

Cable became infamous for revealing the hypocrisy of conservative white Southerners' attitude about race, especially against blacks being treated as equals when practical social relations were considered. Ironically, a white man like Cable writing about the South's cultural flaws seemed blasphemous during the peak of Southern nationalism, and yet his work has since been almost forgotten. Thus, I will provide one last example of his advocacy of civil rights. In his essay, "The Freedmen's Case in Equity" (1885), Cable argues that whites allowed integration in public accommodations only when blacks were "marked as menials":

> [N]othing is easier to show than that these distinctions on the line of color are really made not from any necessity, but simply for their own sake—to preserve the old arbitrary supremacy of the master class over the menial without regard to the decency or indecency of appearance or manners in either the white individual or the colored . . . Any colored man gains unquestioned admission into innumerable places the moment he appears as the menial attendant of some white person, where he could not cross the threshold in his own right as well-dressed and well-behaved master of himself. *The contrast is even greater in the case of colored women.* There could not be a system which when put into practice would more offensively condemn itself. It does more: it actually creates the confusion it pretends to prevent. (emphasis added) (*The Negro Question* 64–65)

As seen throughout his essay, this passage highlights Cable's class bias in his critique of civil rights. Note how he emphasizes the prejudice against middle class blacks. He provides a story about a genteel black woman being discriminated against and placed in a shabby train car with vile black convicts despite the obvious class differences (*The Negro Question* 67–68). The violation of her civil rights is aligned with Cable's own attitude about codified social privileges. Ironically, Cable's stance here is similar to his charge against racist whites' argument that equates social privilege with civil rights: "They [whites in the South] are merely making the double mistake of first classing as personal social privileges certain common impersonal rights of man, and then turning about and treating them as rights definable by law—which social amenities are not and cannot be" (*The Negro Question* 84). Thus, the complex race relations in the South prevent the effectiveness of a fixed system of oppression. Focusing on the treatment of blacks, Cable, in particular, places emphasis on gender differences in this key political essay, which leads me to consider how he handles the issue of racial equality in his fictional depictions of black women.

Neither Palmyre nor Clemence is fully accepted on terms of equality because they are black in a racist society. As women, their social status is lower. Those that appear least threatening as victims of the caste system apparently offer greater advantages for melodrama and less opportunity for a tainted defense in the court of public opinion. Therefore, in his fiction, Cable allows Southern black female characters to challenge the tyrannical South. Consider Agricola's fear of Palmyre: "he tolerates her even though she does not present herself in the 'strictly menial capacity'" (61). Since *The Grandissimes* was written several years before "The Freedmen's Case in Equity" and other tracts, Cable used his fiction to stimulate audiences' sensibilities; they were likely to condemn his formal political rhetoric, his more radical form of protest. His readers could sympathize with Palmyre's fate as a "tragic mulatto" and even Clemence's horrible fate without undermining the readers' own racial prejudices. Simultaneously, these readers were also enlightened about the plight of the Negro under racial segregation.

We can not overlook how Cable disposes of Clemence and Palmyre from the text despite their effectiveness as literary characters. As Carby acknowledges, some of the stereotypes of black women were also readily used in anti-slavery fiction as well as in pro-slavery works (32). Cable himself confessed of *The Grandissimes'* political significance as being a novel of principle moral fiber. Though his later works would earn him the notoriety of "a negrophile" for ardently declaring the equality of blacks, in *The Grandissimes*, his treatment of black women, in the end, is questionable. Cable not only uses black women to construct a narrative in which Southernness is flawed, but he relegates black women to the margins of his narrative. He finally chooses sectional reconciliation over racial justice when it comes to depicting a South that is exclusive rather than inclusive; he is more concerned with the fate of his white heroines than his black women. Cable builds up tension around these women only to try to resolve the problem by getting rid of the South's racial pariahs. Maybe they are both mainly useful as "a narrative device of mediation," which Carby argues is generally the case with mulatto figures (89). Maybe Cable's vision of the South was limited by liberal preoccupations, which led to his realistic creations, but he anticipated racist white Southerners' prevailing power in the end. After all, Cable, like Charles Chesnutt, condemns his black female characters to the same fate he eventually experienced as a regional outcast.

Cable's inability to incorporate black women completely into the Southern body politic may also be a personal shortcoming of the author, which shows that he did not fully understand the circumstances surrounding the lives of black women. His depictions are remarkable, but his images sometimes appear to be projected from a distance. Take, for instance, his description of Clemence as a minstrel figure; some of the things we are told about her are reported in third-person narration (251). Similarly, Chesnutt also places Aunt Peggy in "a tale within a tale." This narrative technique compromises both Chesnutt's and Cable's first-hand knowledge of conjurers and a cake vendor and their depictions of these women as effective characters beyond my reading. But, Clemence's role as a social commentator encourages readers to learn more about real women like her. The way Cable uses fictional black women to explore racial politics in the South is an incentive to understand black women's roles and responsibilities in constructing their personal identities and in their own sense of place as regional subjects. By examining the experiences of women like the mysterious Marie Laveau (the voodoo queen that likely inspired his creation of Palmyre), Frances E.W. Harper (as I have already done), and Anna Julia Cooper, among countless

other Southern black women, we can better understand regional critiques
of *other Souths*. Cable's disposal of Palmyre and Clemence in *The Grandissimes* appears as an attempt to diminish the threat of black women such
as these who dared to challenge racial oppression in their own right. Cable
does not anticipate Cooper's acerbic response to the Negro Problem in *A
Voice from the South* (1892), which is the focus of my next chapter, and
Chesnutt as a "race man" (like many others) would rather ignore it.

By juxtaposing the problems of gender, race, and politics, Cooper
achieves what Chesnutt and Cable advocates in their civil rights campaign
and depicts in their fiction. She critiques the Negro Problem from the perspective of a displaced subject—in the region and nation at large. Public
debates waged by race men, white liberals, supremacists, and other dema-
gogues centered on black disenfranchisement and civil inequality. Cooper
realizes that the muted response of black women might appear so only when
they are not recognized as active members of the political body. In fact,
those in the club movement at least were busy doing the work of nation-
building starting with their own communities. How these women engage
in the debates is just as important as why they do so at all. They occupy
multiple subject positions in the "natural" juxtaposing to black men, white
men, and white women. Added to these and other "forces," Cooper also
recognizes the advantages and disadvantages of black women positioned
against the multiple dimensions of the Negro Problem—economic, social,
and political implications of unsolvable race dilemmas.

3 New South, New Negro
Anna Julia Cooper's
A Voice from the South

In 2009, the greater public was introduced to Anna Julia Cooper (1858?–1964) on a commemorative U.S. Postal Service stamp for the Black Heritage Series. She is honored for her achievements as an educator, feminist, scholar, and activist. For a black Southern woman, her accomplishments are remarkable for a life that began in slavery and witnessed the modern Civil Rights Movement. The portrait—a middle-aged image of her in profile with a white stiff-necked, Victorian blouse, wispy gray strains of hair shadowed in black and neatly pinned-up in a bun as she faces the bright dawn of a new era—however, belie her 105 years experience of being a black woman in America. The prideful expression gives way to a perfect brow slightly grimaced; she appears staid, priggish, and conventional. Respect *is* what she earned. The stamp is merited in a year when the "Quest for Citizenship in the Americas" is the National Black History theme to celebrate the National Association for the Advancement of Colored People (NAACP) Centennial.

Anna Julia Cooper's struggle for justice and equality predates the founding of the NAACP. In the post-Reconstruction South, Cooper knew well what it meant to be *Southern*, a politicized cultural identity. She experienced the racial and gender consequences of Jim Crow legislation and its developing culture at the turn-of-the-twentieth century. Her seminal text, *A Voice from the South* (1892), identifies the writer as "A Black Woman of the South."[1] It is a brazen call for recognition of the experiences of a doubled-minority status, with justifiable reasons to speak and be heard within the fray of public debates of the Negro Problem. Cooper positions herself not so much against Northerners, but, instead, juxtaposed to white "Southerners" who assumed natural rights to an inherited identity created by slavery and reclaimed after Reconstruction. Southernness, for these white natives, was a privileged-position of power to subjugate African Americans (and other ethnic groups) during the late nineteenth century. It was a premise to argue against *social equality* when the color line is drawn. Cooper therefore appears as a displaced Southerner in her stance against the racist status quo.

Cooper's life as a public intellectual is framed by a regional consciousness that ignites her activism and writing. I see Cooper as a leading spokesperson in her affinity to a region, people, and culture that could try to deny her. She inspired my book's critique of Southernness because she understands the South to be inclusive, geographically and metaphorically, with allowable space for dissension and cohesion among those who work on regional problems that also affect the nation at large. Cooper reminds us that, when facing even the most dismal reality (segregation, discrimination, and violence), we must confront the changing conditions around us. She addresses the Negro Problem, for instance, forcefully and with practicality. Yet, though Cooper's *A Voice from the South* appeared over a decade before *The Souls of Black Folk* and *The Negro Problem* (a collection by "Representative American Negroes") were published in 1903, black men—DuBois, Washington, and Chesnutt—are the voices people listen to more.[2] True, their battle was waged on behalf of the entire race; yet, black men, on a national stage, had more at stake when you consider the legal factors of the Negro Problem as I discuss earlier. Fictional black women, like those I examine previously, function as effective local agents of cultural changes by comparison. The historical black women I profile commit to changing social problems and attitudes against blacks in their activism and writing. As with Frances Harper, Cooper suggests ways of re-writing the South in her contribution to New South literature. Her motives are political as much as personal.[3] Juxtaposed next to the color line at a moment when society was "transitional and unsettled," her marginal social and legal status enabled her intervention. Cooper was a "New Negro" for the New South—black, Southern, and female, educated and independent, communal and antagonistic—multiple and fluid identities; claiming Southerness as an act of alliance with newly consolidating Southern power, an act of alliance with black folks and black intellectuals, and, ultimately, an act of alliance with other women.

In this chapter, I will examine what makes Anna Julia Cooper *Southern* not only by birth but conditioning. Both Cooper and Frances Harper, for instance, appear as displaced Southerners in the context of a slavery-based, imagined communal (i.e. Confederate) identity that is reconstructed as white hegemony by the end of the nineteenth century. Harper, as I have argued, was born free in the border slave state of Maryland and she is inscribed by this marginal status; she illustrates nonetheless how Southernness is not determined by static features of a "place" attached to geographical location nor is it a fixed cultural identity. I will show how Cooper, like Harper, asserts her Southernness (especially against the dominant image of the South) in her work and lived experiences. Both women published their most important works in 1892.[4] So I am concerned partly with how these Southern black writers understood the Negro Problem as a national problem that could undermine their own regional identity. (Cooper, Harper, and Ida B. Wells-Barnett, for instance, are not typically labeled as Southerners in discussions of their work as "race women.") Cooper positions herself against the grain to expose Southern hypocrisy, black male chauvinism, and white women's prejudice. She recognizes how "all the forces which make for our civilization"[5] reconstruct the South and nation, including the role that even flawed Southerners like herself should play.

"ANNIE ONE": SUBJECTIVITY *IN A VOICE FROM THE SOUTH*

We can trace Anna Julia Cooper's origin to Raleigh, North Carolina, an identifiable Southern locale, even if her *Southernness* needs further justification. The title page of *A Voice from the South* identifies the author anonymously as "A Black Woman of the South" not as Anna Julia Cooper as the copyright imprint indicates. The prologue suggests that the "mute" and "voiceless . . . sadly expectant Black Woman" awaits her opportunity to speak about America's race problem from her own lowly perspective. Thus, the reader gathers with each successive essay that the writer intends to introduce us to the politics of identity. Rare details of the author's biography do appear at random in the first part of the book: her early education, her peers and relations, her public life—involvement in civic and social organizations, and her travels in the South and abroad. Cooper reflects on a life lived under pressure and in contest with competing identities, those that define her *Southern* self.

By her own account, Anna ("Annie") Julia was born into slavery during the Civil War around 1858.[6] Her mother Hannah Stanley (1817–1899) and her white father, presumably, Dr. Fabius J. Haywood, produced two other offspring, sons: Rufus Haywood (1836?-1892) and Andrew Haywood (1848–1918). The family tree appears like many illicit relations between white men and black female slaves in the South. Hannah Stanley (Haywood) worked as a domestic for her owners and the children she bore were in name only fathered by her master. Writing later in life about her parents, Cooper vows allegiance to her mother: "My mother was a slave and the finest woman I have ever known . . . I owe [the father] not a sou and [her mother] was always too modest and shamefaced ever to mention him" (Lemert and Bhan 331). Her mother was a role model and advocate for her daughter's career aspirations. Hannah Stanley was a semi-illiterate ex-slave often tutored by her small child. After slavery, her mother's hard work as a domestic supported Annie's early education.

In 1868, Cooper enrolled at St. Augustine Normal School in Raleigh, North Carolina. She was around ten years old when she went to this all-black secondary education institution that also offered college-preparatory courses. Unlike many of her classmates, Cooper worked to support herself until she graduated in 1877. She continued her studies there as at student-teacher until 1881. She had met George A.C. Cooper, a Greek teacher and Episcopalian minister at St. Augustine, and married him also in 1877. Her husband died suddenly in 1879 leaving his young wife a life-long widow; she continued her studies and built an illustrious career though she never remarried.

Cooper moved to Ohio and enrolled in Oberlin College in the fall of 1881. She completed her Bachelor's (1884) and earned her Master's (1887) degrees in Mathematics from Oberlin. Cooper later held administrative positions and taught at Wilberforce University, St. Augustine, Lincoln University (Missouri), and M Street High School / Dunbar High School in Washington, D.C. Cooper's renown as an educator increased during her tenure at the latter institution.[7] Though she did not have children of her own, she had adopted her brother Andrew's five grandchildren by 1915, and supported Andrew's widow (Jane Henderson Haywood), all on a meager teacher's salary. Cooper's dedication to family was matched only by the value of education and a tenacious regard for hard work throughout her life. At sixty-six, she became only the fourth African American woman to earn a Ph.D. (in History), from the Sorbonne, University of Paris. In her own home, she eventually founded the Frelinghuysen University for working adults in 1930 and served as its President, a Professor, and Registrar for more than twenty years. Anna Julia Cooper once acknowledged that in her "struggle for existence [she] could not have told you how the simplest encounter with fate would end" (Lemert and Bhan 331). Surely, she did not anticipate such a meteoric rise up from slavery. Cooper died on February 27, 1964 in Washington, D. C. The extraordinary life she lived spanned the course of one of the most vital periods in American history and, fortunately, the record of her contributions has been preserved.

I limit my focus to her young adulthood during the late nineteenth and early twentieth centuries, the cultural climate in which she wrote *A Voice from the South*, her only book-length project published in her lifetime.[8] It is during this time that we see how the South takes shape in a new era, how Southernness becomes a hegemonized, white political and social power structure as the region's economy is rebuilt: sharecropping replaces slavery and the South's agribusiness tries to "northernize" (though without labor conflicts and immigrant problems), and New South proponents reconfigure Confederate hierarchies and glory in Old South traditions—imagined and material artifacts (Cobb 67–71). Thus, I am interested in Cooper's critiques of race, gender, and regional identification, her lived experiences, claiming the South as *home* and all its people as her kinsmen despite the conflicts she witnessed and endured. We recognize patriarchal whiteness as "Southern" if not the subaltern voice of a black woman, but I contend that our cultural awareness of the South is broaden when we consider the multidimensional ways a black women like Cooper redefines her historical displacement in dominant regional narratives. My work serves, as Vivian May's, to exhume Cooper's politics and theories of subjectivity that are "matric or intersectional" ("By a Black Woman of the South" 127; *Visionary Black Feminist* 94–97). Cooper's agency is achieved because her perceived marginal status places her at an advantage to interrogate dominance. She acts as Frances Harper's Aunt Chloe, speaking "on tother side of her mouth" and, therefore, undermines her opposition's ability to dismiss her in the New South project.

Three crucial identities Cooper claims—black, Southern, and female—
are integrated into her call for social justice, advocacy for education, and
women's rights. We often examine *A Voice of the South* primarily as a
feminist text, a race problem treatise, and/or a black intellectual man-
date to "uplift the race." Her gender, race, and class identity supersede
her regional subjectivity even though she self-identifies as a Southerner
in the book's title as throughout her other writings. Only recently do we
recognize Cooper's insistence to be "both/and" as well as her refusal to
be "either/or" (*Visionary Black Feminist* 95).[9] Re-defining Cooper to
suit our discourses has not preserved her full legacy without interrogating her complex Southernness. What might we gain if we think of her
as a Southern woman making dissenting statements about her "home"?
Her commitment to regional recovery as much as racial progress? Cooper testifies to the atrocities and inequality in the South and its complex
structuring of race, class, gender, and regional identities. So, when reading *A Voice from the South*, varied subject positions from which she
speaks appear.

Cooper's critique of the South intersects with the views of other representative *voices* though she is always conscious of how the black woman
is implicated in the problems at hand. By the late-nineteenth century, critiques of the South's Negro Problem involved an empathetic turn to the
status of black women. While black men were criminalized by the specter
of "Negro domination," a racist ideology with political and sexual implications, the assault on the black woman's body and character was even
more "calamitous" for racial progress. Dr. Alexander Crummell (1819–
1898), an Episcopalian minister, missionary, and scholar, was a leading
black spokesman on these disparaging conditions in the South.[10] In *The
Black Woman of the South: Her Neglects and Her Needs* (1883), Crummell proclaims:

> If you want the civilization of a people to reach the very best elements
> of their being, and then, having reached them, there to abide as an
> indigenous principle, you must imbue the *womanhood* of that people
> with all its elements and qualities. Any movement which passes by the
> female sex is an ephemeral thing. Without them, no true nationality,
> patriotism, religion, cultivation, family life, or true social status is a
> possibility. (111) (original emphasis)[11]

Crummell advocates a domestic model of racial uplift, in which black
women could assume responsibility for the welfare of the family, race, and
nation. Black women, especially in the rural South, were encouraged to
cultivate the home life: to be dexterous housekeepers, to take charge of the
moral training of their children, and to be always decent in appearance and
social behavior. These precepts were justifiable in an era of reform in which
the "race problem" and "a woman question" converged. [12]

In *A Voice from the South*, Cooper responds to Crummell with respect to his status among public intellectuals and black clergy and as a mentor.[13] She proposes a similar call to protect black women in the South using the ideal language of *true* womanhood: delicate and domestic, charming to a fault of appearing naïve (24–25). Her sarcasm is only thinly veiled by her real life experiences. Cooper was without male protection most of her life but she dons the mask of a Southern *lady* in desperate need of rescuing.[14] However, the most troubling image that she evokes is that of a *black Southern lady*, which might have appeared as an oxymoron to the greater public's perception of black women once viewed as salacious wenches in the late nineteenth century.[15] Black women were particularly vulnerable to the reassertion of white supremacy in the South; neither civil law nor social mores kept them from being violated at will by white men.[16] More than propaganda, Cooper espouses an action plan to create benevolent organizations for black women, especially by church missionaries. She delivered her speech "Womanhood A Vital Element in the Regeneration and Progress of a Race" before a gathering of her peers in Washington, D.C. in 1886. Crummell was perhaps in this audience of the all-male clergy who stood condemned. The reaction of the audience is lost in the printed text though the rhetoric is peppered to arouse. She accuses Episcopalians, especially, for failing to become Southern missionaries among the black masses (34–35). Moreover, she rebukes the church for failing to heed Crummell's suggestions to uplift black women in the South. Why then would they listen to her, she asks? The irony here is that Cooper enters the debate not as a mute witness to the human crimes against African Americans. When the case for black women is even more distressing, Cooper is acutely aware that her message should not fall on deaf ears. The feminist speech she delivers becomes the premise of *A Voice from the South*. The tagged signature of the text, "By a Black Woman of the South," is in obeisance to Crummell's earlier text, but the position she claims with due authority (Lemert and Bhan 48).

At the peak of activity during the 1890s "Black Woman's Era," for instance, Cooper was an eloquent and acerbic public speaker on racial and gender inequality. She scrutinized discrimination in the clergy, among white feminists, and her black male peers. In the international arena, she advocated human rights—connecting the conditions of African Americans with others in the Black Diaspora, joining forces with DuBois at the 1900 Pan-African Conference in London (*Visionary Black Feminist* 23). With like-minded black women, Cooper helped to create the National Association of Colored Women (NACW), a platform upon which their nation-building efforts coalesced in 1896. The members of this national club movement organized to eliminate poverty, to provide healthcare and adequate housing, to support working mothers, to provide educational resources and opportunities, and to create safe, sustainable black communities. Cooper was a co-founder of the Colored Women's League (1892) in Washington, D.C., one of over two hundred clubs that formed the NACW.[17] It is during this period as an activist, educator, and Southerner that Cooper wrote *A Voice from the South*.

In the essay, "Woman versus the Indian," Cooper exposes racial prejudice in the national woman's movement lead by such organizations as "Wimodaughsis," whose Southern members resisted forming inter-racial coalitions. Cooper uses a single discriminatory incident against a "cream-colored applicant" to the all-white club to launch a greater critique of intolerance. The conflict arises because of former master-slave relationships and the ideology of social inequality based on this Southern history. Cooper recognizes how Southern white women would rather maintain caste privileges than to accept black women as peers in organizations established to achieve equal rights for all women (87). Thus she offers a corrective to the acronym for wives, mothers, daughters, and sisters by clarifying whiteness in "*Whi*modaughsis" (81–82). Later, Cooper nevertheless identifies with such Southern white women with whom she seemed to have little in common. What I find most intriguing is how Cooper distinguishes her own Southernness in regards to the "Southern woman" in a self-reflective dialogue: "The Black Woman has tried to understand the Southern woman's difficulties; to put herself in her place, and to be as fair, as charitable, and as free from prejudice in judging her antipathies, as she would have others in regard to her own" (100). Cooper's doublespeak reveals a oneness with her opposition, crossing the racial boundaries against which the Southern white woman opposes yet uniting on the basis of class privilege. We get a mirrored image of black and white women sharing a single space, with rectitude, and Cooper capitalizes on her opponent's intellectual inferiority to be the wiser of the subtleties. She presumes, "Now the Southern woman (I may be pardoned, being one myself) was never renowned for her reasoning powers, and it is not surprising that just a little picking will make her logic fall to pieces even here" (108–109). Though whiteness is implicit in identifying the "Southern woman," Cooper is confident in her claims also as a daughter of the South when debating gender and racial equality, and, implicitly, against white patriarchy to which black and white women were subject.

Cooper honed hers skills for debate while attending St. Augustine. Glenda Elizabeth Gilmore outlines Cooper's Southernness as defined by her educational experiences in rural North Carolina. During the 1870s and 1880s, when formal education was instituted throughout the region, white Southerners segregated the sexes, separate curriculums and schools, while most black institutions catered to a united student body. Such tactics would thus prevent black women from identifying with the "cult of southern ladyhood," an ideology lingering from the not so distant past when slave women worked in public spaces and, a generation later, so too would their descendents without "a cloak of chivalry" (Gilmore 36). St. Augustine trained African American students to become teachers especially at newly formed black schools throughout the South. The full liberal arts curriculum included Greek and Latin classes that were offered preferably for males enrolled as theology majors. Cooper became an astute scholar despite the limited options provided for female students; she petitioned to take "gentlemen" courses that were equally suitable for her career aspirations. Cooper recalls being singled out for her ambition by one teacher: "In every one of these classes [organized for the male ministers] I was expected to go, with the sole intent, I thought at the time, of enabling the dear old principal, as he looked from the vacant countenances of his sleepy old class over to where I sat, to get off his solitary pun . . . as he called out 'Any one!' to the effect that '*any* one' then meant '*Annie* one'" (76). Cooper found little encouragement to continue her studies among her male peers. She felt that they relied too much on ideals of true womanhood to prevent the higher education of black women:

> They leave nothing to be desired generally in regard to gallantry and chivalry, but they actually do not seem sometimes to have outgrown that old contemporary of chivalry—the idea that women may stand on pedestals or live in doll houses, (if they happen to have them) but they must not furrow their brows with thought or attempt to help men tug at the great questions of the world. (75)

Black women nevertheless benefited from the coeducational model at St. Augustine. Unlike single-sex institutions for white Southern women, for instance, St. Augustine stimulated black women's rights for equality and sharpened their critiques of race relations. "Once together, [black] men and women openly questioned southern white patriarchal norms" (Gilmore 37). Black women were given a rare chance to become independent thinkers and workers. Education for them was a useful tool compared to the value of education as a mere accessory for many Southern white women. African American women could then enter "a middle space between the spheres into which they might venture on the business of the race" (Gilmore 36).[18]

Though education was mostly responsible for this new concept of black womanhood,[19] certain qualities distinguished the black "lady"—or the "Black Victoria"—from the white original: "First and foremost, [the black woman] was intelligent and well-educated. She displayed a strong community and racial consciousness, often revealed in her work—whether paid or unpaid—within the black community. Self-confident and out-spoken, she was highly esteemed by her community which frequently applauded her as a 'race woman' and role model for young people" (Carlson 62). This black ideology of womanhood did not jeopardize their status as "true women." It appears instead that these black women were able to pledge their commitment to the race *because* they were taught the value of domestic culture and the implications it held for improving their communities. Many of them believed, as did Cooper, that "a race is but a total of families" (29). Shirley J. Carlson explains, "the ideal black woman's domain, then, was both the private and the public spheres. She was wife and mother, but she could also assume other roles, such as school teacher, social activist, businesswoman, among others" (62). When intelligent black women became leaders of the racial uplift movement, these black women were empowered by their club activities and the most important reform work remained in the South.[20]

As a race woman and Southerner, Cooper remained on a "quest for an authoritative subject position requiring, . . . a pragmatic variety of political stances" (Gaines 130). It is disturbing then to see how she can both claim authority as a black woman who suffers from racism by white women and sexism by black men while, at other times, she possibly identifies with white paternalism. This odd re-positioning is evident, Kevin K. Gaines argues, when Cooper aligns with the white merchant class rather than the working poor in disputes about labor supply in the New South economy.[21] This is contradictory since she subscribed to the Hampton Institute model of industrial education for minorities, who, as laborers, were prepared to enter capitalistic power relations on equal footing. Cooper advocates: "the laborer is always worthy of his hire. Should the owner of the land and the capital have the power and the greed to disregard the claims of the man who contributed the labor, and pocket the entire product, he is manifestly a robber whether the jailors can catch him or not" ("Wage-Earners" 201).[22] This theorem is directed especially to aid black women workers. Cooper's rebuttal, in "Women versus the Indians," to the Rev. Anna Shaw (1847–1919), a leading white suffragist and Methodist minister, though justly argues for universal freedom: "It is not the intelligent woman vs. the ignorant woman; nor the white woman vs. the black, the brown, and the red,—it is not even the cause of woman vs. man" (121).

However, Gaines cites Cooper's fear of foreign labor competition, which further exemplifies contested Southerness. European immigrants recruited to the South for the cotton mill and railroad industries stood to gain from the out-migrations of black and white natives to northern industrial areas. These foreigners threaten the class privilege of black conservative intellectuals like Cooper who invested in maintaining a sizable black labor supply, according to Gaines (145–147). She appears then to practice the same bigotry that she derides in *A Voice from the South*. "Like many black writers who sought covenant with white elites," Gaines contends, "Cooper's antiracism was selective, singling out poor whites and immigrant workers and exonerating southern planters, merchants, and bankers, who personified the 'wealth and intelligence' of the region" (133). Rather than condemn her assumed hypocrisy consider what this flawed allegiance to the South illustrates. Foreign immigrants, when brought into the racial politics of the day, explode conventional ideas of Southernness. Who is Southern counts as a labor question (factored into the South's racial problem—foreign immigrants were re-read as new "Negroes" for the potential of exploitation) and whiteness is possibly undermined as the European immigrant population increased.[23] Black Southerners may have had concerns about the capital flow, job competitiveness. Altogether, white industrialists, black intellectuals, and immigrant and black labor-ers were in contest to acquire wealth and social mobility, and, in doing so, they shared a common space (in and outside the labor market), one organized around white supremacy. Similarly, as past conflicts of labor and race privilege reappear today, black and white "Southerners" respond to Latino immigrants with angst or relief, depending on whom you ask. African Americans may feel entitled to their earned place in the official Southern history (i.e. slavery, Jim Crow segregation, and the Civil Rights Movement) and therefore refuse to allow other ethnic minorities to ben-efit from black struggles, or, some African Americans recognize a shared history of oppression with Latinos. White employers today may welcome a new labor source, freeing them from "a historic dependence on black labor." The rise in the Latino population, at the millenium, especially in the South, signals to some white elites that African Americans would "'just have to get used to not being 'The Minority'" (qtd. in Smith, "Place and the Past in the Global South" 695). In the South, white supremacy nevertheless is re-constituted today because of immigration just as it did in the late nineteenth century.

Cooper choose not to identify with Southernness as it solidified with white supremacy, racists and/or conservative whites,[24] neither did she fit the mold of true Southern *lady*hood nor would she yield to black repressive chivalry. Cooper would not betray her loyalty to a black slave mother for the sake of claiming the propriety of her planter class father. Gaines's read-ing alludes to such a paternalistic betrayal in economic terms (150). I find that Cooper stands alone—as *"Annie* one"—to redefine Southernness from an important centralized position beyond that circumscribed by readings of uplift ideology. Her uniqueness was both "political and historical," her theoretical status as a Southern black woman is also juxtaposed to the lived experiences of black men and white women as she addresses in *A Voice from the South*. As I argue in the final section, her work is juxtaposed to masculinist (white and black) texts on the Negro Problem. Even the struc-ture of *A Voice from the South*, according to Karen Baker-Fletcher, sets Cooper's solo act (the first four essays on black womanhood) against a chorus of other voices with "a singing something" in the second half of the book (Lemert 12–14).

A NEW VOICE IN NEW SOUTH LITERATURE AND CULTURE

In *A Voice from the South*, Anna Julia Cooper opens up notions of South-ern identity during a time when notions of Southern identity were being re-codified based on (imagined) memories of antebellum life: "Who we are based on nostalgic notions of who we were." Slavery served as a backdrop for such developments, but black Southerners redefined their cultural iden-tity in opposition to and not in celebration of the past as did many white

Southerners. James C. Cobb and Charles Reagan Wilson, among others, trace the South's modern white identity to the late nineteenth century. We witness then "[t]he creation of a new group identity" when cultural traditions are (re)invented "wherever and whenever 'a rapid transformation of society weakens or destroys the social patterns for which *old* traditions had been designed'" (emphasis added, Cobb 81). [25] The Civil War and Reconstruction destroyed the Confederacy and the dominant cultural identity it bolstered. A generation of white Southerners bemoaned "the Lost Cause" and its attendant consequences: capital wealth from slave property and labor, cotton as a cash crop, and Southern nationalism all destroyed. This Lost Cause generation worshipped the idolatry of the real and symbolic Robert E. Lee and other Confederate soldiers who fought to save their dear ol' South (Cobb 61–63). The romance narratives of regional reconciliation germinated in plantation fiction by Thomas Nelson Page (*In Ole Virginia*, 1887) and Joel Chandler Harris' quaint black folktales (*Uncle Remus: His Songs and His Sayings*, 1880) also appealed to a Northern audience. [26] In response, the writers I profile—Frances Harper, Charles Chesnutt, and George Washington Cable—created realistic fiction to dismantle the cultural myths of the post-bellum South. If the "Lost Cause ethos responded to the emotional, racial, and political needs of many white southerners," an abundance of raw materials and cheap labor aided the economic recovery necessary to rebuilt the region's infrastructure with Northern investments (Cobb 67). Such industrialization would also help to restore white patriarchy (over lower class whites, women, and ethnic minorities) in the New South.

As a Southern dissenter, Cooper writes with a new voice to confront the crisis in the New South. She joined efforts with other African Americans that came-of-age in the inaugural era of black education. Pioneers Booker T. Washington establishes Tuskegee Institute, Mary Church Terrell (1863–1954) and others organize the National Association of Colored Women (NACW), Ida B. Wells-Barnett ignites an international campaign against black lynching, and Arthur A. Schomburg (1874–1938), John E. Bruce (1856–1924), and Carter G. Woodson (1875–1950) create historical societies to preserve black culture. These "first children born out of bondage collectively made a mark on their own time, many before they were thirty," with plenty odds stacked against them (Gebhard and McCaskill 4–5). Behind the "trope of the New Negro" stood individuals whom made real sacrifices and commitments not just to racial progress but confronting America's problems. [27] Gabriel A. Briggs' re-interprets these "New Negroes" as a generation who were determined to modify repressive social systems at home. He argues that the South was not a place too threatening for black sustainability and progress. When Southern blacks witnessed the reassertion of white hegemony in the "unreconstructed" South, writers like Sutton E. Griggs (1872–1933) responded as sociologists concerned about the fate of the race. Griggs imagines in his utopian fiction a place and role for blacks in a *reconstructed* South (a South rehabilitated from the wounds of the Civil War), even as they dealt with the social, economic, and political chaos of the war's aftermath.[28] The literary productivity of Cooper's "nadir" generation was unparalleled until the Harlem Renaissance of the 1920s. They responded to Jim Crow in fiction, essays, plays, speeches, poetry, and novels.[29] In *A Voice from the South*, Cooper rejects the derogatory depictions of blacks in American literature and find sharp realism in white writers'—William Dean Howells (1837–1920), Albion W. Tourgee (1835–1905), and George Washington Cable—protest fiction. She praises Cable's "judicial, convincing, irreproachable" work on the Negro Problem (190–191). With black and white writers, the emphasis on the Negro Problem as a political and literary subject captured the nation's attention. Segregation was the legal solution to problematic race relations but it would not resolve social tensions in the South nor America at large.

Cooper, like other black Southerners, contested views of a unilateral race problem. She saw whiteness as a naturalized social privilege imposed by laws and, thus, a significant factor contributing to the nation's problems: "don't let them argue as if there were no part to be played in life by black men and black women, and as if to become white were the sole specific and panacea for all the ills that flesh is heir to—the universal solvent for all America's irritations" (172). Cooper's argument is grounded in ancient history of world civilizations, those destroyed by tyranny or salvaged by freedom of equality. She proposes thus extreme options for solutions to America's race problem. Here she writes as an U.S. and global citizen not specifically as a Southerner. But, given that "the force of her social activism was local"—the community service programs she created and long-term advocacy for racial, gender, and class equity was waged from her home-base in the District of Columbia where she lived almost her entire life (Lemert 7), Cooper's Southernness is not undermined in her nationalistic discourse nor international activism.[30] By 1888, she had "planted [her] little North Carolina colony on Seventeenth street" where she settled into a new life in the urban South (Lemert and Bhan 310).[31] The feminist clubs she organized and her career as an educator at the M Street / Dunbar High School was mostly in her adopted hometown. Like many African Americans in her generation, Cooper migrated to Northern cities but Washington, D.C. in the 1890s was not as cosmopolitan as today. Its Southernness was apparent in the conferences of the United Daughters of the Confederacy it hosted as late as 1912, the presidency of Woodrow Wilson, a Southerner who screened the 1915 racist epic The *Birth of a Nation*, and the segregated neighborhoods (Cooper's home was in a white-flight district) that outlined the city.[32] New technologies (electricity, cars, train, etc.) did alter the cultural landscape. Cooper even once traveled to Great Britain as an escape from her Southern home:

> It was the good fortune of the Black Woman of the South to spend some
> weeks, not long since, in a land over which floated the Union Jack. The

Stars and Stripes were not the only familiar experiences missed. A uniform, matter-of-fact courtesy, a genial kindliness, quick perception of opportunities for rendering any little manly assistance, a readiness to give information to strangers,—a hospitable, thawing-out atmosphere everywhere—in shops and waiting rooms, on cars and in the streets, actually seemed to her chilled little soul to transform the commonest boor in the service of the public into one of nature's noblemen, and when the old whipped-cur feeling was taken up and analyzed she could hardly tell whether it consisted mostly of self pity for her own wounded sensibilities, or of shame for her country and mortification that her countrymen offered such an unfavorable contrast. (88–89)

Cooper's testimony is tempered by her own vulnerability at times and genteel mannerisms she assumes. The truth of American racism is contrasted with congenial race relations abroad. In these nationalistic contrasts, Cooper argues for solutions in America, induced by studying historical revolutions: "Progressive peace in a nation is the result of conflict; and conflict, such as is healthy, stimulating, and progressive, is produced through the co-existence of a radically opposing or racially different elements" (151). These changes must certainly take effect in the New South experiencing increased European immigration and black agitation: "The community that closes its gates against foreign talent can never hope to advance beyond a certain point. Resolve to keep out foreigners and you keep out progress" (160) and "let us not disparage the factor which the Negro is appointed to contribute to the problem. America needs the Negro for ballast if for nothing else" (173). Cooper concludes with expositions about the contributions African Americans and foreigners make to American industries and culture, thus expanding notions of American multiculturalism and Southerness.

Though social problems did persist, Anna Julia Cooper suggests ways of re-writing the South in *A Voice from the South*. It is her lasting contribution to the development of New South literature. Reading regional literature that addresses the politics of race, as I do, reveals "the Negro problem," a characteristic feature of Southern life and culture during the late nineteenth and early twentieth centuries. This period of hardship, struggle, *and* black survival marked a sociopolitical transition concurrent with the development of African American literature. In this "post-bellum, pre-Harlem" stage, many African American writers address these issues in their works by suggesting practical (and sometimes radical) ways for improving race relations. Through archival research, I have discovered early and, often, rare social documents as well as literary texts that influenced public opinion and defined a culture. Some writers like Cooper tried to provide solutions when conservative Southern apologists, radical black "race leaders," virulent dogmatist, and other public spokesmen could not. Extensive investigation to identify, analyze the narrative structures used to address the Negro Problem and examine the culture of segregation that served as an impetus for the development of this body of protest literature is beyond the scope of this project. My examination of *A Voice from the South* and contributions by Frances Harper, Charles Chesnutt, and George Washington Cable, however, *is* a way to think differently about the South and its fictions. Cooper argues forcefully what roles black women could and did play in reconstructing master narratives of the region. The historical black women I profile in the final chapter offer other testimonials of experiencing regional displacement while yet laying claim to a Southern identity. These black women wrote political autobiographies as cultural narratives about the South to challenge a constructed Southernness based on white supremacy. I focus on how these women position themselves in a chaotic historical moment—during the early days of Jim Crow and American modernization—that not only threatened their physical wellbeing but also undermined their ability to identify with Southernness.

4 'The South *Is* Our Home'
Cultural Narratives of Place and Displacement

> If I had to live in a racial house, it was important, at the least, to rebuild it so that it was not a windowless prison into which I was forced, a thick-walled, impenetrable container from which no cry could be heard, but rather an open house, grounded, yet generous in its supply of windows and doors. Or, at the most, it became imperative for me to transform this house completely.
>
> —Toni Morrison, "Home." *The House that Race Built: Black Americans, U.S. Terrain* (New York: Pantheon Books, 1997: 4)

In telling their life stories, the Southern black women introduced in this chapter fret over their connections to the "white" South while refusing to remain in their place as second-class citizens during the late nineteenth and early twentieth centuries. Black disfranchisement, lynch law/mob rule, "peonage slavery," and the creation of Black Codes to enforce systematic oppression all signified the loss of political advantages African Americans had gained during Reconstruction. Black education, paid labor of the black masses, and the rise of a black middle class only antagonized white Southerners. Such problematic race relations captured the public's attention, bringing what most Americans considered as a regional issue into a national focus as the South's "Negro Problem."

Challenges to these discourses about black communities and individuals have been conventionally understood to be dominated by black men. But there were significant numbers of black women writing within this context, and in this chapter I want to explore how they used the genre of autobiography as political and social commentary. I argue that some black women wrote autobiographies as cultural narratives about the South to challenge a constructed Southernness based on white supremacy. Their writing is a form of activism. Though informed by the uplift ideology, with which scholars are more familiar, these texts also "give voice to oppositional or counterhegemonic ways of knowing that repeatedly invite readers to challenge their own assumptions and level of comfort with the status quo" (Perkins, *Autobiography* xii). To this extent, these narratives share features of later, more radical "political autobiographies" written by black female activists during the Black Power Movement of the 1960s. Similar to the aims of Margo V. Perkins, I therefore draw attention to these early narratives by focusing on how these women position themselves in a chaotic historical moment that not only threatened their physical wellbeing but also undermined their ability to identify with Southernness, a group affiliation whose importance we have not yet recognized. *These women wrote against racial injustices while exposing the potential erasure of their cultural identities.*[1]

Southernness is a complex cultural, regional, and racial idea. It has distinct qualities that give taste to "soul food," rhythm to original music, and vivid imagery to local folklore. The Mason-Dixon Line once determined the geographical limits of "the" South within the continental U.S., while today Southernesss extends even to the Caribbean. Historian Grace Elizabeth Hale contend that white Southerners created a "culture of segregation" for a modern South's distinct social order: the color line that bifurcated the region into "separate and (un)equal" public spaces defined blackness as inferior in opposition to whiteness. Signs for public restrooms indicating "ladies," "gents," and "colored people" for instance, made blackness visible and whiteness more pervasive yet invisible. "As culture, southern segregation made a new collective white identity across lines of gender and class and a new regional distinctiveness." More importantly, this Southern whiteness proved successful for national reconciliation in providing a model of racial order—Southern whiteness and black inferiority—to legitimate white privilege for other Americans as African Americans migrated from the South (Hale 9).

While white supremacy in the Jim Crow South increased black migration to Northern urban areas for decades, those blacks who remained in the region (or identified with the region) however were not recognized as "Southerners" because they were not integrated into the ideal "culture" of the South. Homi K. Bhabha's interrogation of culture illuminates this kind of adverse repercussion to differences:

> The enunciation of cultural difference problematizes the division of past and present, tradition and modernity, at the level of cultural representation and its authoritative address. It is the problem of how, in signifying the present, something comes to be repeated, relocated, and translated in the name of tradition, in the guise of a pastness that is not necessarily a faithful sign of historical memory but a strategy of representing authority in terms of the artifice of the archaic. That iteration negates our sense of the origins of the struggle. It undermines our sense of the homogenizing effects of cultural symbols and icons, by questioning our sense of the authority of cultural synthesis in general. (269)

The postcolonial situation described by Bhabha here is applicable to black subjectivity during the development of a "new" South after the Civil War and Reconstruction. To (re-)define themselves, some black women did so against the self-perceptions of their immediate antagonists, white Southern women. Paradoxically, the social history of the region grounds the identities of these black and white women as Southerners. The "enunciation of cultural difference," however, found in these autobiographies reconstitute a past fixed in the present. What results is a modern hybridity of a black/white *Southern* self, one with a complicated past, renegotiated in the present, and transformed for the future.

Bhabha's argument shows us that the process of forgetting cultural differences contains within itself the very methodology to challenge that forgetting, and in the process, reopen a space for difference in the past as well as in the present. I will use this methodology to introduce voices of regional and cultural difference into how we understand nineteenth-century Southernness by looking at black women's autobiographies. The autobiographies I focus on were published in *The Independent*, a sensationalist weekly journal of the Progressive Era. Ultimately, these rare narratives are important additions to other archival materials that document "the Negro Problem," which remain largely uncollected and understudied.[2] I read these narratives not strictly as propaganda tools but personal interventions into regional politics, considering that the women writers had yet to acquire voting rights. Organized activism—i.e. women's suffrage, the racial uplift movement, and national club movement—influenced some women writers' perspectives of race relations. The short narratives I critique share features with other more familiar black autobiographies. *They are similar to longer book-length autobiographies (e.g. slave narratives, historical memoirs, etc.) in coverage of the subjects' lives though they offer more condensed episodes of experiences.* Formulaic structures are apparent among the series of articles, creating a subcategory of autobiographical writing as "life stories," in this case, brief narratives about "real" ordinary people as "representatives." My sources first seemed to present certain conceptual problems in how they define the South too broadly, which shows how (and perhaps why) Northern readers envisioned a unified South despite its cultural diversity. Whiteness studies that examine how "the" South developed in the modern American imagination via political and economical forces offer new ways of understanding "differences" that segregated black and white Southerners around the turn-of-the-twentieth century. I use such studies to explain how and why certain writers internalized these differences when representing themselves and others. I consider therefore the various workings of race, class, sex, and gender that influenced the autobiographical "I" presented in these cultural narratives.

VOICES OF THE SOUTH

In defense of themselves, these writer-activists were determined to dispel racial myths and gender stereotypes that signified the Negro Problem. They were aware of the pivotal positions in which black women were placed: the irony of being blamed for blacks' ruination and viewed as the solution to the race problem simultaneously.[3] Many black women of this generation became "race women," role models of black womanhood, in order to improve their communities and the black public image. They were intelligent, self-confident, and often outspoken members of the black elite.[4] Even years before Booker T. Washington and W.E.B. DuBois emerged as pivotal black leaders, as I discuss in the previous chapter, educator Anna Julia Cooper and journalist Ida B. Wells-Barnett were celebrated race women *and* Southerners who encountered racism and sexism though prevalent in the South, but not limited to the South alone. They both served as spokespersons for the region often defending other Southern black women and black womanhood in general. Cooper and Wells-Barnett also faced opposition from white men and women as well as black men (White 60–61). Yet, both women were empowered by their activist writings in particular which allowed them to engage in the public debate about Southern race relations that rarely recognized what Cooper sarcastically labeled as the "mute and voiceless . . . [but] sadly expectant Black Woman" (i).[5]

Like Cooper and Wells-Barnett, other black women did make their case for civil equality in the court of public opinion. From 1901 to 1904, a series of articles about the South's "Negro Problem" by black and white women appeared in *The Independent*.[6] Most were Southerners but a couple of Northern women also weigh in with candid observations. These balanced accounts were used to appeal to a national readership engrossed with Southern racial matters. Most of the articles were presented anonymously as a safety precaution, but they include a regional genealogy that helps to construct the writers' identities in the narratives and it bolsters their comments. The women who are identified speak directly to an assumable receptive audience.

The Independent was a radical weekly magazine that widened the public sphere by covering diverse perspectives on controversial issues.[7] Founded in 1848, *The Independent* began as a Protestant-sponsored abolitionist publication. By the turn of the twentieth century, the paper still advocated equality—racial, gender, and class—but with little reference to its prior religious affiliations. To reach a more general audience, the magazine's "political character" by 1900 appears more 'liberal' and 'non-partisan' (Boylan 14). *The Independent* maintained an editorial policy of equal access: any writer, any issue. Women writers were especially welcome contributors. Occasionally, the magazine would feature articles by familiar public figures. The usually anonymous autobiographies or "life stories" of "undistinguished Americans," however, are another unique feature of this publication. The purpose was to 'to make each story the genuine experience of a real person' (qtd. in Katzman and Tuttle xi).[8] "Preferably, the article was actually written by the subject; alternatively, it was compiled from interviews and read back to the subject for approval" to insure authenticity (Boylan 21).

Some scholars validate such editorial practices that insured each account appear accurate, 'truthful, both as to facts and mode of thought' (qtd. in Katzman and Tuttle xii). There were "historical and sociological" motives for collecting these stories. During the second-wave of massive European immigration and increasing mobility of native Americans, the editors were more interested in the real experiences of ordinary individuals to document Americanization in the modern era (Katzman and Tuttle ix–xx). Lead by the reform-minded editor Hamilton Holt from 1897–1921, *The Independent* cared less for cold statistics about the foreign masses or glorified portraits of the rich and famous; it gave more attention to voices of the vulnerable than the powerful. True to its mission statement—"the purpose of *The Independent* is not merely to amuse, not merely to instruct, but to inspire and incite to action" (Boylan 17)—this Progressive Era journal took on the "Negro Problem" in the South.

Arguably, at issue for the public were not problems that merely involved African Americans, but also the failure to recognize and condemn white Southerners' role in creating racialized political and economic problems that affected the nation. The epithet "Silent South" was coined for this reason while the nation waited for the regional problems to dissolve. Those that did speak out had decidedly biased viewpoints. For instance, the Southern writer George Washington Cable, whom I discuss in chapter two, was a staunch white liberal and civil rights advocate for African Americans when conservative and/or racist white Southerners contested the idea of black citizenship. The success of the educated black elite undermined concepts of black inferiority. Although the black masses were generally poor, uneducated, and lacked some resources to improve their lives, many were motivated to do so.[9] Altogether, the concerted efforts for "racial uplift"—improving the social, political, and moral conditions for African Americans—antagonized white supremacy in the South, herein lies the inexcusable "race problem." W.E.B. DuBois and Booker T. Washington made regular contributions on this issue in *The Independent* (Boylan 23–24).[10] Washington's advocacy of industrial self-sufficiency and DuBois's political radicalism polarized black intellectuals when determining solutions to the race problem. Most disturbing is how the racial uplift ideologies that most elite African Americans espoused appear infected by "unconscious internalized racism," according to Kevin K. Gaines, yet another factor of the Negro Problem (6). As an ideology, racial uplift could have dual objectives for the black elite: to illustrate their assumed superiority to the masses and/or to demonstrate their commitment to community service for racial progress (Gaines xv). Dissecting the race problem in all its nuances not surprisingly create fractured perspectives on the issue.

In the race problem sketches, these elements assemble around the idea of Southernness, as culture and identity. The South figures as a place and space for negotiated differences. In her 1901 article, "A Southern Woman's Appeal for Justice," for instance, Amanda Smith Jermand, a black woman from New Orleans, Louisiana, clarifies her status as a Southerner and American citizen:

> [w]hen the Southerner says if we do not like the South let us leave it, I answer him, we do like the South, it is our home, and we shall stay here and continue to ask for civil, not social, equality. (438)

In Jermand's affirmation, regional identity is gendered as male and racialized as white, but her testimony also shows how the South is a contested ideological space as well as a geographical place. Here, this narrative manifests what Toni Morrison describes as "the anxiety of belonging" that is often apparent in discourses on nationhood, especially when race complicates the matter (10). Jermand claims the South as "home" even while recognizing that it is *not* home; she may issue a vocal command for equal rights but not with an assurance that her demands will ever be met. The rival hostility of "the Southerner" suggests the drawing of the color line that exposes the "black side of segregation" and invisible yet visible white power structure in the Jim Crow South. Through various accounts, Jermand describes the experiences of blacks facing discrimination and racial prejudice at the hands white Southerners whether in public transportation or religious worship. More telling of the effects of segregation is how Jermand, like other African Americans, is ostracized from the regional concept of cultural identity. As Hale explains, the racial fissure white Southerners created to signal "absolute blackness and whiteness" (especially with publicly marked spaces) made "racial segregation . . . the central metaphor of the new regional culture" (21–22). By making blackness more visible as an inferior status the power of whiteness was inherent in discriminatory tactics. That the South and Southernness would eventually become synonymous with whiteness was a process ignited by segregation.

Consequently, the South's transformation penetrates the narrative self, causing the writer to (re-)position herself accordingly within the culture of segregation. Jermand initially asserts her class privilege by illustrating distinctions between refined blacks and the vulgar black masses. She wants respectable white Southerners of similar stature to recognize such differences. Black criminals, minstrel stereotypes, and lewd revelers tarnish the reputations of an elite class (Jermand 438). However, Jermand does not consider her role as a racial antagonist too. Of the large population of African Americans in the South, aspiring "New Negroes" presented a more threatening visual and political challenge to white authority. The more successful these blacks were the more pressure white Southerners (regardless of economic status) felt to form a solid front against their racial opposition (Hale 21–22). Jermand likewise writes in a collective consciousness representing the concerns of other black aristocrats while compromising the individual self.[11] In doing so, the biographical "we" or "us" replaces the autobiographical "I" throughout the narrative demonstrating how racism diminishes class privilege.

Almost five years after the landmark 1896 *Plessy vs Ferguson* case, Jermand makes an appeal for justice on behalf of all African Americans dealing with the repercussions of the judicial ruling especially in the South. This legal battle for "separate but equal" public facilities was waged in Jermand's hometown before reaching the U.S. Supreme Court.[12] So, in demanding "civil, not social, equality," she engages in regional and national politics as a black Southerner for the benefit of other African Americans. Her political stance oscillates between a moderate accommodation and militant action: "We ask no social rights. I think it is time these [white] people knew the difference between social and civil rights" (Jermand 439). Before soliciting the aid of white Southern ministers and Christian mothers, Jermand recalls the discrimination particularly suffered by Southern black women in segregated public spaces. Only as the reporter and valid witness of such incidents does Jermand interjects the first-person "I." Yet, by presenting the experiences of others, she relies on the proof of her evidence to support her own class-based plea for equality: "Why cannot I ride in the first-class car when every Southern white woman is allowed to carry her black nurse or maid into a first-class car if she chooses?" (439). This servitude trope about the color line appears frequently in cultural narratives about the race problem.[13] Using it, Jermand identifies with the privilege of the white woman and not working-class black women. What emerges overall is a critique of the actual miscegenated nature of Southerners not just in New Orleans's Creole society.

To address the race problem, exposing the historical and intimate ties among black and white Southerners might appear most effective yet confrontational. In Jermand's appeal, both regional identity and civil rights are at stake. Exactly who are "Southerners"? What makes the South their "home"? Blacks in the South, according to Jermand, had the right to be *Southerners* based on their experiences with slavery. By this pathology, most black Southerners then held "some gruesome attraction to the scene of [their] suffering," as with Charles W. Chesnutt's fictional ex-slaves in *The Conjure Woman*. Likewise, white Southerners, especially ex-slave owners, held on to the privileges of their racial and social class status as benefactors of a predominantly black labor system. In Jermand's narrative, and as Thadious M. Davis argues, the culture and history of the region provides "a major grounding for identity" and, especially, a greater understanding of "'the regionality of the black self'" (Davis 6–7):

> The Southerner boasts this is *a white man's country. I deny it; it is my country as well as his.* The South, especially, is as much *the black man's* as the white man's; for every plantation, town and city shows the work of *his hands.*
>
> A goodly share of the South was bought and cultivated with the proceeds from *the sale of his body.* (Jermand 438) (emphasis added)

> Some of us—and I do not say it with pride—with more of the *Southern white man's blood* in our veins than [N]egro blood, with much of

his tastes, habits, likes and dislikes, receive less of his sympathy . . .
(Jermand 439) (emphasis added)

Jermand recalls also in her tirade black participation in every American
war from the Revolutionary era to the Spanish-American War in 1898. She
uses masculine discourse however to validate claims of black patriotism
and Southern cultural heritage. The black "we" she evokes have traceable
roots in slavery though she sacrifices the body of black women in turn. Jermand neither acknowledges the productive nor reproductive labor of black
female slaves explicitly. To dissemble the sexual abuse of these women in
economic terms, however, is a *selfless* act of protection. Despite the white
man's bravado and the black man's humiliation, Jermand stands proud.
She evades patriarchal control by "creating the appearance of disclosure,
or openness" about herself and other Southern black women, their genuine
thoughts and feelings about the race problem, "while actually remaining
enigmatic" (Hine, "Rape" 183). Protected self-disclosure is an essential
feature of Jermand's narrative that is common in other black and white
Southern women's autobiographies.

All of the Negro Problem autobiographies reveal the women writers'
sensitivity to issues of regional identity and, for black women, of their
possible displacement in the dominant South's cultural narrative. In the
two articles published in 1902, "The Negro Problem: How It Appeals to a
Southern Colored Woman" and "The Negro Problem: How It Appeals to
a Southern White Woman," the anonymous writers begin their narratives
with the first-person affirmative, "I am . . . ," with each writer placing different emphasis on her racial and regional identities, respectively: "I am a
colored woman, wife and mother. I have lived all my life in the South . . ."
(2221) versus "I am a Southern woman, thirty-five years of age, married,
and the mother of one child" (2224). These descriptions reveal more about
the construction of regional identity and culture than about their personal
lives. Note the importance of Southernness to the women's self-perceptions.
Both women are Alabama natives, yet, the "colored" woman uses race as
an identifying marker more than region. With the white woman, there is
no mention of race though whiteness is implied and Southernness becomes
her ethnicity. This phenomenon, as described by Davis, occurs as a result
of "'[s]lavery and a 'slave-based economy' [which] historically provided
a primary means . . . for cultural insiders to justify both self-perception
and social order." Davis contends that the dominant image of the South
excluded racial minorities since "whites in the South became simply 'Southerners' without a racial designation, but blacks in the South became simply
'blacks' without a regional designation" (4). In writing about the Negro
Problem, however, the women underscore their racial and gender experiences of being Southern.

In the 1902 narrative, the white Southern woman speaks from a threatened place of racial and class privilege as she condemns black education,

social equality, and blacks' immorality. She aims her frustration especially at black women: "I, for instance, have never come in contact with but one negro woman whom I believed to be chaste" ("Southern White Woman" 2226). Since she denies the possibility of sexual abuse during slavery, the white woman base her assumption about promiscuous black women on the rate of their illegitimate pregnancies and, especially, on the creation of a large mulatto population as evidence of black women's promiscuity. She even accuses educated black women of being superficial for desiring white men: "Nor does education as a rule increase [black women's] powers of honorable resistance. But on the other hand, it does mightily increase their passion for beauty . . . the comparatively educated black woman is more anxious for mulatto children than her less fastidious and more ignorant sisters" ("Southern White Woman" 2226–2227). The writer assumes that educated black women were eager to acquire certain class privileges as guaranteed by "white" skin. Like many white Southerners, this writer then thinks that education spoils blacks, assuming that it stimulates their political aspirations and sexual desires for equality.[14] For instance, this writer makes no distinction between granting blacks equal rights and allowing individual choice to dictate interracial social relations. The writer assigns blacks gender roles that support a corruption of both civil and social equality: she views educated black men as "contemptible," "dangerous firebrand" race leaders and all black women as whores. In her opinion, blacks' inferiority is best displayed in their roles as servants, with an emphasis on black women. She claims that "[t]here is less danger of contamination from our washerwomen, who are less presumptuous, and so, less offensive" than educated black men, yet the depravity still extends to black female domestics acting as petty thieves ("Southern White Woman" 2225). The Southern white woman accuses them of stealing from white households— food, clothing, etc.—to provide for their own families. Often times black domestics used tactics like "pan-toting" to compensate their low wages (Hunter 132–134). However, the Southern white woman attributes this "racial defect" to blacks' immorality.

Dependent on black domestic service nevertheless, the Southern white household becomes an integrated space while providing a ground for racial differences. Black cooks, maids, nurses, and laundresses (among other domestic employees) consistently crossed the color line in service to Southern whites. The ideal Old South plantation evolved into the modern homes of Southern middle-class whites as they sought to re-create the antebellum racial hierarchy in the New South; white women were the mistresses to black servants once again (Hale 87–88). Tera W. Hunter examines black domestics in the post-bellum urban South to illustrate how they were autonomous paid laborers however. Hunter postulates that the theory about black domestics being potential carries of diseases like tuberculosis was a faulty medical perspective of "the Negro Problem" (195). The diseased metaphor above linking black domestics and black intellectuals does reveal white Southerners' insecurity about the intimate relations they maintained with some blacks despite *de jure* segregation. Writing in 1902, a colored woman explains the irony of Southern white women's reliance on black caretakers for their children even though, in the minds of many white Southerners, "[a] colored woman, however respectable, is lower than the white prostitute" ("Southern Colored Woman" 2222).

The contamination theme is reversed in the Southern black woman's description of black-white domestic relations. Facing housing discrimination, shortly after her marriage, the black woman remembers being offered "an unhealthy pigsty" as the only "colored property" available for purchase ("Southern Colored Woman" 2221). Her family eventually settled in a working-class interracial neighborhood where they remained alienated for years:

> Altho the neighbors speak to us, and occasionally one will send a child to borrow the morning's paper or ask the loan of a pattern, not one woman has ever been inside my house . . . ("Southern Colored Woman" 2222)

This social taboo is inverted when these same Southern white women "go in the houses of [N]egro women who wash or scrub for them, and laugh and talk . . ." Only then does the writer understands how "somehow [her] home is different" ("Southern Colored Woman" 2222). Here the writer exposes her class-consciousness while trying to represent the collective experiences of black women without undermining her subjectivity. In the household of their servants, Southern white women did not compromise their power status as would have been the case if they entered the middle-class black woman's house as a social equal. While segregated public spaces like trains, stores, theaters, and parks were under surveillance, the color line was permeable within the private homes of Southerners.

The Negro Problem narratives contest domestic space primarily as it signifies the racial troubles in the South as a whole. Considering the South's central influence on the nation, however, the realm of domesticity is extended, allowing others to debate the issues. Women from the North and South, for instance, wrote the 1904 race problem autobiographies published in *The Independent*. When the editors seized the opportunity to give these women the platform, they issued the following disclaimer: "We know of no women in the whole South better qualified to write on this painful topic from their various standpoints".[15] The first three—written by a Southern "colored" woman, a Southern white woman, and a Northern white woman transplant to the South—begin with their paternal descent as the daughters of an enterprising ex-slave, Southern gentleman, and liberal Yankee, respectively. The fourth narrative, by Fannie Barrier Williams, recalls her lineage of free blacks living in the North. Unlike the anonymous women, Williams was a well-known social activist and feminist. Her article probably captured the public's attention more than the others since the chief editor Hamilton Holt, openly solicited contributions from celebrities, with particular "strong representation by women" (Boylan 19–20).[16] The editors must have had this goal in mind when they decided to publish Williams' article four months later as a supplement to the first three, given the large amount of replies they had received (See editorial note for "A Northern Negro's Autobiography," p. 91). The editors also felt that Williams' regional perspective was rarely presented in the public forum about the Negro Problem.

As in the previous years, all of the 1904 narratives critique white supremacy in the South and its effect on the lives of women. Their individual experiences influence each woman's perception of the culture of segregation, in particular, the racial drama enacted within Southern homes. Except the Southern white women, all the writers acknowledge that the biggest menace to black womanhood was predatory white men. Southern black women most often came into contact with white men by working as domestics in white households. The conditions of their employment could determine the imminent threat of sexual exploitation by white male employers. Black cooks and nurse maids were more likely "live-in" servants than washerwomen, who therefore maintained a considerable degree of autonomy and safety (Hunter 105–106). As one anonymous Southern black woman recalls, her father vowed to protect the women in his family from sexual harassment and humiliation: "my father came very near losing his life for whipping a white man who insulted my mother." Therefore, the woman's "mother and her children never performed any labor outside of [the] father's and their own homes" ("The Race Problem" 586–587). The proud daughter, in turn, made similar sacrifices to keep her own daughters safe.

In her take on illicit sexual relations between white men and black women, the Southern white woman also writing in 1904 charges black women with the depravity and moral degradation of all African Americans. She declares that

> I sometimes read of virtuous [N]egro women, hear of them, but the idea is absolutely inconceivable to me. I do not deny they exist, but after living in a section all my life that teems with [N]egroes I cannot imagine such a creation as a virtuous black woman. ("Experiences" 593)

Writing as another daughter of the South, this Southern white women purports to know only immoral black women, but her wrath is directed at black female domestics in particular. She regrets hiring two recent college graduates with no exception in "character" than her otherwise illiterate workers; undoubtedly, these "yellow Jezebels" suffered unwarranted abuse because of their complexion ("Experiences" 593). Witnessing a graduation ceremony at a black university offered further proof for the Southern white woman about the impropriety of black women; she claims to have noticed only "four full blooded [N]egroes" fathered by black men. Rather, she proclaims that the hundred or so mulatto graduates she saw were the offspring of black women and white men. Here black women are the accused aggressors in such situations not unlike during slavery. Hazel Carby maintains that stereotypes of black women are based in reality (not just adverse reflections of it), functioning as "a disguise, or mystification, of objective social relations" (22). In the 1902 and 1904 narratives by Southern white women, biracial people are proof of the illicit sex relations between black women and white men that can not be easily ignored. Carby also suggests that characterizing black women as sexually aggressive was a plausible explanation for the sexual intercourse between the master and his female slave given the existing anti-miscegenation laws and customs. Although this defense is indicative of patriarchal commands, white women supported the logic to validate their own positions as societal matriarchs: "[i]t offered a way of making sense of the role that the white woman had to play, of resolving the contradictions that could otherwise shatter the pedestal on which she stood, a stool supported by the institution of slavery" (Carby 31). In their narratives, the Southern white women's repugnance for black women then becomes a manifestation of the white women's repressed sexuality and their perception of competitive sex relations. "Whatever this intimates of the Southern white man's morals," the Southern white woman writing in 1904 does not dare to admit ("Experiences" 594). It does suggest however that miscegenation was a common practice in the South in common places like Southern households.

Homes, in general, symbolize the Southern women's sense of place whether it is a plantation or "a white house with green blinds" like the plantation of a former slave owner. In the 1904 narrative by a Southern black woman, she describes how the first home her mulatto father buys was like his white father's house "in miniature" ("The Race Problem" 586–587). Home ownership represents a lot for her family: freedom from their slave past, financial stability, racial progress, and, in the women's case, protection from the abuses of white men. The irony is that her father's appreciation of home ownership was not just an imitation of Southern whites' class values, but more like an extension of *family* values since his former slave owner was also his father. One social historian perceives the white home as a plausible link between past and present experiences of Southerners living in the segregated South; it shapes their self-perceptions as Southerners within the new racial order. "The white home served as a major site in the production of racial identity precisely because there this racial interdependence [between blacks and whites] was both visible and denied" (Hale 88).

In the case of the 1904 narrative by a Southern white woman, the writer's middle-class identity is based on an idealized Southern past within the confines of a plantation home. She reminisces about her father's gallantry and inherited wealth and privilege to achieve a psychic escape from her own reality in a post-bellum, segregated South. His status as an ex-Confederate soldier fueled her father's ambition during the Lost Cause movement to regain control of his naturalized rights as a white man.[17] As the proud daughter imagines, when her father joined the Ku Klux Klan, he "set about disciplining the [N]egroes into a proper understanding of the Southern gentleman's idea of their freedom, more especially its limitations" ("Experiences" 590). By the time our Southern belle narrator is born in 1869, her father had accomplished all his goals, especially regaining the family estate and establishing a prosperous sharecropping venture.

Although this embellished Southern history produces a caste-conscious idea of Southern identity, the white woman perpetuates this "Confederate myth" without realizing how it also oppresses her (and other Southern white women) as well as African Americans. For instance, she exposes the gender restrictions for aristocratic Southern white women as she describes cultural etiquette befitting a young "lady." Social repression appears in the language she uses to describe her childhood relationships with little black girls: "altho I imagined our companionship free from restraint, I know now that it was really controlled by the instincts and customs of our respective races" ("Experiences" 591). When they played "horse," the white woman claims that she would never switch roles, with the black girls as the horses and her as their driver, not even "for the pleasure of being the wildest colt." But one strong black girl had acted as an untamed "vicious horse," which made a lasting impressing on our narrator. While riding the girl's back, "the effort [to 'tame' her] was an experience [the white woman] coveted." As she remembers, "I would seat myself firmly, clasp my hands tightly in the wool on the back of her head, and wait for the delicious sensation of feeling her take a running, plunging start that invariably landed me over her head somewhere in the grass" ("Experiences" 591). Since she often received bruises from her rough play, the Southern white woman kept this exhilarating experience (almost orgasmic as she remembers it) a secret from her mother. Our narrator was sure that her mother would have not only "punished, but banished" the black girl, which was "a loss [our narrator] refused to contemplate" ("Experiences" 591). As she lives vicariously through her black playmates' actions, the Southern white woman cherishes this moment of (sexual?) freedom from the restrictions placed on her not solely due to race, class, and gender as she points out, but also regional culture.

Looking at the South as "home" in all the 1904 cultural narratives by women from various parts of the nation, the complications of race in America, both then and now, is quite apparent. The history of slavery and the culture of segregation may define "the South" as we know it today. Inherent in our American cultural consciousness, therefore, is the power of whiteness derived from racial conflict within the region.[18] So the South also provides the metaphorical and actual settings to locate and define American racial identities in opposition (Hale 281–282). Consequently, in constructing a Southern self, each of the autobiographies manifests the "anxiety of belonging" that Toni Morrison evokes in the metaphor of a "racial house" in the epigraph for this chapter. The Southern narratives indicate whether or not the women were beneficiaries or victims of the South's racial policy. If when, as a child, the Southern white woman "played 'keeping house,' [she] was the father and the mother of the family, [her black playmates were] the children, subject to the most stringent discipline" ("Experiences" 591). Similarly, childhood experiences even taught the Southern black woman her "place" while "playing house" (at her home) with a white neighbor; the "play dinners" they both enjoyed initially had to remain a secret to the white girl's family. The black girl's bruised psyche was punishment enough as she grew into womanhood fully aware of the psychological effects of racial prejudice ("The Race Problem" 588).

In the case of the two narratives written by Northern women in 1904, the boundaries of ideological regions are permeable and race relations remain static. Their experiences with the race problem make them uncomfortable not just because of discriminatory laws and social customs, but also an awareness of their own "Southernness" complicates their lives. Unaware of the severity of Southern racial prejudice before coming to the South, these women's first-hand experiences reveal more about the South and themselves than either had imagined before living in the region. Born in a Republican state (somewhere in the modern Midwest), the Northern white woman claims to be "free from sectional prejudice" since her family did not even participate in the Civil War and the hardships of pioneer life left little time for the younger generation to revel in "war stories." However, the Northern white woman confesses that popular Southern literature later distorted her view of the South. It had helped "to create interest in and sympathy with the Southern white people, rather than to prolong hostility" after the Civil War ("Observations" 595). Influenced mostly by the romantic images perpetuated in plantation fiction, this newcomer to the South is well aware of the white Southerners' fondness for their black mammies at least.[19] An iconic symbol of the South, "mammies were broad signifiers of whiteness as well as nurturers, protectors, and teachers of manners" to white children. That is, in the "racial house," the authority of black caretakers was always undermined by the power of whiteness. Legally sanctioned treatment of African Americans as inferiors was evident even to young white Southerners (Hale 102). The Northern white woman realizes that white Southerners' sentiment towards the black mammy was forged in a racial paradox. Interestingly, she finds this situational irony applicable to the treatment of women in general:

[T]he Southerner's position on the [N]egro is about the same as his attitude toward woman; he will treat the former with kindness, as he will the latter with adulation, 'in his place.' That 'place' in either case, stripped of the accidental externals which make the one seem menial and the other exalted, means dependence and helpfulness. ("Observations" 596)

Here, as in other cultural narratives published in *The Independent*, white male privilege appears most dominant in the South. The Northern white woman, *as a transplanted Southerner*, therefore goes from observing the race problem to experiencing it. However, she uses the black female body to interrogate the abuses of white patriarchy and the hypocrisy of Southern ethics.

While living in the South, the Northern white woman learned that "truth was indeed stranger than fiction." The goal of her narrative is to set the record straight. For instance, she tries to disprove the charges against black female domestics being thieves, when cited as evidence of their racial immorality. She believes that ignorance causes white Southerners to perpetuate this stereotype since "their lack of experience with white servants makes them ascribe solely to colored women what, unfortunately, is not unknown among white ones of the same class" ("Observations" 597).

As in the narrative by a Northern white woman, Fannie Barrier Williams, in "A Northern Negro's Autobiography" (1904), pleas also for black women to be judged by the content of their character not the color of their skin. She believes that "the colored woman deserves greater credit for what she has done and is doing than blame for what she cannot so soon overcome" (Williams 96). As the wife of a prominent black attorney in Chicago and an active member in local and national women's clubs, Williams' reform work motivated her to try to find employment for Southern black female migrants to the city:

> It is a significant and shameful fact that I am constantly in receipt of letters from the still unprotected colored women of the South, begging me to find employment for their daughters according to their ability, *as domestics or otherwise, to save them from going into the homes of the South as servants*, as there is nothing to save them from dishonor and degradation. (Williams 96) [20] (emphasis added)

Again, the interracial domestic spaces in the South prove most threatening to black women. They flee the South to avoid sexual exploitation. This gendered motive for African American migration is another element of the dominant South's cultural narrative as explored by Farah Jasmine Griffin.[21] Victoria Earle Matthews, one of Williams' club colleagues, founded the White Rose Mission in New York City in 1897 to support black Southern women who arrived with little or no resources to survive (Logan 172–173). As she writes in her narrative, Williams was successful in only a few cases of securing job placement for the new arrivals because most white business owners refused to hire black women despite their superior qualifications. White employers simply did not want to create an interracial work environment, symbolizing the dreaded notion of social equality (Williams 93–94).

Williams' narrative shows just how far black women would go to achieve their independence and how Southern black women became cultural agents to appeal to a national conscience. She explains how white supremacy in the South leads to desperate situations for black women who are unprotected by law or social customs. Even though we do not hear the actual voices of Southern black women in this narrative, they "speak," through their letters to Williams, to the public at large. Her own experiences with Jim Crow are also weaved into the narrative to illustrate the pervasiveness of racial prejudice in and beyond the South. The bigotry she encounters in educational institutions, on transit systems, and within interracial clubs encourages her efforts as activist organizer, speaker, and writer. This "Northern Negro's autobiography," in turn, becomes a biography of a race. Williams was actively involved in the National Association of Colored Women (NACW), a leading organization during the women's club movement of the late-nineteenth and early twentieth centuries. Incorporated in 1896, building on the momentum of local clubs throughout America, the goals of the NACW coalesced with finding solutions to the race problem. Their members participated in various community services, ranging from providing adequate day care for the children of working black mothers to holding political forums addressing the socioeconomic needs of all African Americans. By catering to the needs of black women especially, Williams, Matthews, Anna Julia Cooper, Ida B. Wells-Barnett, and Mary Church Terrell, among hundreds of other clubwomen, took necessary steps to "building a nation," or rather, deconstructing it (White 35–36). As evident in her narrative, Williams relies on the power of political rhetoric to pierce the American social conscience (Logan 98–126).

"HOME"[22]

America's democratic ideology promotes justice and equality, and, as citizens, we must work to secure these liberties. Ultimately, the series of articles published in *The Independent* about America's race problem rely on the freedom of speech to illicit responses that inspire action. By looking at "the Negro Problem" from various perspectives, I show how different factors (e.g. literature, cultural history, and myths) contribute to a national crisis. Through these narratives, I have also traced the development of an ideological "white South" to show how it evolved from slavery and Jim Crow racial policies. As Roberta S. Maguire points out, "the South as a region has so often been a 'white' construction, derived from the fact that the white community has historically been the holder of political and economic power, legally sanctioned for most of the South's past and socially enforced even after such legal sanctions were struck down" ("Anna Julia Cooper" 4). This constructed Southernness does not take into account how blacks in *and* of the South can claim the region as their "home" despite harsh realities. The culture of segregation is equally responsible for blacks and whites' problematic relationship to the South. Regardless of where many black Southerners choose/chose to live, they stay(-ed) connected to the region not only by virtue of their desires to be there but simply because the South is/was their home. Carol Stack's sociological study of urban blacks migrating back to the rural South in the late twentieth century provides an intimate look at how "the image of home is multilayered" for them. These native sons and daughters had to confront their memories of the past in order to return home knowing that it will forever be "a vexed place." Nevertheless, Stack concludes, many African Americans "come home [to the South to] . . . set about appropriating local time and memory and blood and symbols for intimate community purposes of their own" (xv). Likewise, white Americans—especially Southerners, must also first acknowledge and then work to resolve internalized racial trauma produced by the grounds of difference in the South (Hale 281–282). With both groups, such psychological scars give new meaning to the "deep" South. Key to understanding the "Southernness" of my argument in this book is that antagonistic race relations contribute to the shared experiences of being Southern for both black and white natives and non-natives of the South. The race problem autobiographies adhere to traditional forms of writing about the private lives of women when publicized to national audiences. Most importantly, as cultural narratives, these autobiographies illustrate that writing a "true" self without boundaries is the first act of rebuilding the South as a "racial house" transformed from the inside out.

Epilogue

Voices, Bodies, and Texts: Making the Black Woman Visible in New South Literature and Culture

I want my body bathed again by southern suns, my soul reclaimed again from southern land . . .

I want my careless song to strike no minor key; no fiend to stand between my body's southern song—the fusion of the South, my body's song and me.

—"Southern Song" (1942) by Margaret Walker

In this book, I have tried to do what Margaret Walker so eloquently imagines in her poetic vision of the black Southern experience: find a voice of the undeniable Southern self. I decided to listen to the voices of black women singing their Southern songs. Alice Walker, Margaret Walker, Zora Neale Hurston, the women of Jean Toomer's *Cane* (1923), Anna Julia Cooper, and Harriet Jacobs/"Linda Brent" are just a few of the black women that inspired this project. With such prime examples, I knew that other less distinguished "voices" were yet to be discovered and/or acknowledged for their connections and contributions to the South and Southern literature.

The trope of invisibility has been so often used by historians and literary critics to describe and reclaim the identities of black women. I recognize the significance of such recovery efforts by scholars to broaden the canon and/or correct the historical record over the past few decades: Hazel V. Carby, *Reconstructing Womanhood: The Emergence of the Afro-American Woman Novelist* (1987); Angela Y. Davis, *Women, Race, & Class* (1981); Frances Smith Foster, *Written By Herself: Literary Production by African American Women, 1746–1892* (1993); Paula Giddings, *When and Where I Enter: The Impact of Black Women on Race and Sex in America* (1984); Gerda Lerner, *Black Women in White America: A Documentary History* (1973); Deborah Gray White, *Ar'n't I a Woman?: Female Slaves in the Plantation South* (Revised ed.,1999). While my project takes advantage of these developments, I want to suggest, nevertheless, that (re)discovering the black woman is still a matter of looking in the right places. My archival investigation of the Negro Problem began with writers and works that were not all that hidden from public view. What is more pervasive, however, is the idea of Southernness as defined by others within and outside of the region as well as in America's cultural imagination. As Anna Julia Cooper makes clear, black women in the late nineteenth and early twentieth centuries were in a precarious position to influence regional politics and culture when they are recognized as agents of change. My work concludes then with a look at black women as fictional characters and historical figures with an undeniable Southern self, which challenges us to reevaluate our concept of the South and Southernness.

By turning to early writers of dissent, I have found black women writers and fictional characters that challenge(-ed) a pervasive "white South" and, in the process, they become important regional figures. Frances Ellen Watkins Harper, Charles W. Chesnutt, and George Washington Cable recognized the unique status of black women as double minorities and hence their ability to affect culture and society even under the guise of invisibility. All of these writers realized how much the conditions of slavery affected post-bellum black Southerners, with emphasis on the experiences of black women. These writers knew that the Negro Problem would remain unsolved if whites did not recognize their roles in creating and helping to solve it. As writer-activists, Harper, Chesnutt, and Cable were all committed to writing about the South's political issues in their fiction and, as I have shown, their fictional black women convey urgent messages. As regional spokespersons, historical black women wrote about socioeconomic conditions and race relations in the South for a national audience in the pages of *The Independent*. The title of this journal alone is symbolic of the position in which these women were placed to boldly proclaim their self-identity as Southerners. Quite possibly, some of these women, who seem well-educated, could have been responding to popular literary images—such as the mammy and tragic mulatto—because plantation fiction created powerful and convincing images of regional culture with limited representations of real life experiences. These historical women then appear similar to the radical black female characters portrayed in the fiction by the other writers I profile.

Focusing on black women in and of the South allow us to reevaluate "normal" aspects of cultural development as they occur. That is, to understand the appearance of a well-defined, solid Southern identity in the twentieth century (or its evolution in the twenty-first century), we should consider just how much previously ignored or misunderstood social actors and ideologies (e.g. the Negro Problem, the "New Negro," or black womanhood) contributed to a regional identity. We can approach Southernness differently based on cultural histories preserved in literary and political narratives that do not offer justification of the racial status quo of white supremacy but that challenge it. Today, what is labeled as the "U.S. South" is often examined in relation to areas in Latin America and around the world that appear to have social histories and cultures in common (especially those once formed around plantation economies). Ethnic, religious, and linguistic cross-pollination in the past and present have produced Southerners who may look different but share a Southern heritage defined by their "place" in juxtaposition to others'. Global communications, waves of immigration, and commercial imperialism (e.g. Wal-Mart's cheap seduction) have re-mapped the South in the last half of the twentieth century. New Southern Studies, in the twenty-first century, continue to ask what is the "South"? Who or what represents "the" South? *Other* Souths? Why? How? By entering conversations begun by Michael Bibler, I focus on the late nineteenth century for a fresh approach to our current understanding of Southern Studies. I offer a few ways of understanding the South as a geographical place and cultural entity that could lead to more extensive investigations of constructed Southernness. The "black woman" is one response to questions about regional identity, as my project proves, by bringing black women into focus as writers, literary characters, and/or inspiration for fictional depictions of Southerners.

Notes

NOTES TO THE INTRODUCTION

1. My definition of the South is built on the eleven states that seceded to form the Confederacy in 1861, and other areas that were considered "Southern" in the nineteenth century if not today. This South includes Virginia, North Carolina, Tennessee, South Carolina, Georgia, Florida, Alabama, Mississippi, Texas, Arkansas, and Louisiana. I will not analyze work from each state, and recognize that each state had its own particular histories, economies, and ideologies, but these eleven states compose "the South" as it was understood in the world about which I write. The Ohio River and Mason-Dixon Line distinguished the borders between "the South" and "the North"; thus, parts of Kentucky, West Virginia, Maryland, and Delaware were "Southern" since slavery was practiced there.

2. The work of Trudier Harris is exceptional, her early study of fictional black domestics and their relationship to the South and the North. Harris begins with Charles Chesnutt's *The Marrow of Tradition* (1901) as a critical starting point for this type of investigation. See also Virginia Bernhard, et. al., eds. *Hidden Histories of Women in the New South.* Columbia: University of Missouri Press, 1994. J.V. Ridgely's *Nineteenth-Century Southern Literature* (Lexington: University Press of Kentucky, 1980) is a classic text about "The South" as a national problem in the nineteenth century. My work departs from such general studies.

3. Edward L. Ayers, "What We Talk about When We Talk about the South." *All Over the Map: Rethinking American Regions.* Edward L. Ayers, Patricia Nelson Limerick, Stephen Nissenbaum, and Peter S. Onuf, eds. Baltimore: The Johns Hopkins University Press, 1996: 62–82; Michael Kreyling, "Toward 'A New Southern Studies.'" *South Central Review* 22 (Spring 2005): 4–18; Fred Hobson, ed. *South to the Future: An American Region in the Twenty-first Century.* Athens: University of Georgia Press, 2002; Kathryn McKee and Annette Trefzer, "Global Contexts, Local Literatures: The New Southern Studies." *American Literature.* 78.4 (December 2006): 677–690; Barbara Ellen Smith, "Place and the Past in the Global South." *American Literature.* 78.4 (December 2006): 693–695; Jon Smith and Deborah Cohn, eds. *Look Away!: The U.S. South in New World Studies.* Durham: Duke University Press, 2004; "Souths: Global and Local." a special issue of *The Southern Quarterly.* 42.1 (Fall 2003); James L. Peacock, Harry L. Watson, and Carrie R. Matthews, eds. *The American South in a Global World.* Chapel Hill: University of North Carolina Press, 2005.

4. Most of the recent scholarship of this "new" New Southern Studies centers on modern incarnations of Southernness. Few literary scholars address the "embarrassing" episode of Southern antebellum history flawed with defenses of slavery in a predominately unlettered culture. Civil War writings and post-bellum Southern literature (local color, plantation fiction, etc.) are often examined but rarely under the lens of "New Southern Studies." Discussions generated recently on H-Southern Literature listserv about "19th Century Southern Studies and New Southern Studies" by Michael Bibler (University of Manchester) and others post a series of questions to consider as we mine the roots of Southernness.

5. See Michael Perman's *Struggle for Mastery: Disfranchisement in the South, 1888–1908.* Chapel Hill: University of North Carolina Press, 2001.

6. Glenda Elizabeth Gilmore, in *Gender and Jim Crow: Women and the Politics of White Supremacy in North Carolina, 1896–1920*, provides alternative histories of men and women who defy the perceived notions of "public/private spheres."

7. By contrasts, black Southerners' emancipation celebrations oppose the kind of Lost Cause traditions created by Southern whites. According to James C. Cobb, "these ceremonies laid the groundwork for an alternative, African American version of southern identity" (83). These traditions did not much survive however against the pressures of white Southerners' harassment and their own exclusive claims to Southernness in the New South.

NOTES TO CHAPTER 1

1. I draw from various sources on Reconstruction in South Carolina including Eric Foner's *Forever Free: The Story of Emancipation and Reconstruction* (2005) and Willie Lee Rose's "'The Old Allegiance'" and Joel Williamson's "The Meaning of Freedom" in *Reconstruction: An Anthology of Revisionist Writings*, Kenneth M. Stampp and Leon F. Litwack, eds. Baton Rouge: Louisiana State Press, 1969.

2. Harper did not write much about her own life, but others like William Still includes a brief biographical sketch of Harper in his collection of fugitive slave narratives, *The Underground Railroad* (1872), from which I draw most of my information about Harper's life. Frances Smith Foster's "Introduction" in *A Brighter Coming Day: A Frances Ellen Watkins Harper Reader* (1990) and Melba Joyce Boyd's *Discarded Legacy: Politics and Poetics in the Life of Frances E.W. Harper, 1825–1911* (1994) are other sources I used to compile details about Harper's background.

3. See William Loren Katz's editor's introduction in the reprint of *The Underground Railroad* (New York: Arno Press, 1968); Benjamin Quarles, *Black Abolitionists* [1969]. New York: Da Capo Press, 1991. More details about Still's life is found in Sarah Smith Ducksworth's "Forward" in the most recent reprint of *The Underground Railroad* (Medford, NJ: Plexus Publishing, Inc., 2005): ix–xiv.

4. *Poems* (1857), *Moses: A Story of the Nile* (1869, 1889, 1893), *Sketches of a Southern Life* (1872 and 1886), *Idylls of the Bible* (1901), *Atlanta Offering: Poems* (1895), *Martyr of Alabama and Other Poems* (n.p., n.d.; c. 1895), and *Poems* (1895).

5. While I identify Harper as Southern, others label her as an activist "Northerner" writing out of an experience of being free instead of enslaved, writing nationalistic—more so than regional—discourses, poetry, and fiction. See Lyde Cullen Sizer's *The Political Work of Northern Women Writers and the Civil*

War, 1850–1872 (2000) and Carla L. Peterson's *"Doers of the Word": African-American Women Speakers and Writers in the North, 1830–1880* (1995).

6. This poem was also published in the *Weekly Anglo-African* on July 30, 1859.

7. I use Barbara Jeanne Fields, *Slavery and Freedom on the Middle Ground: Maryland during the Nineteenth Century* (New Haven: Yale University Press, 1985) for most of the summary about the state's history. Other references include Leonard P. Curry, *The Free Black in Urban America, 1800–1850: The Shadow of the Dream* (Chicago: University of Chicago Press, 1981) and "Free Blacks in the Urban South: 1800–1850" in *The Southern Quarterly*. 43.2 (Winter 2006): 35–51.

8. For his extensive survey of free blacks in Baltimore, see Curry's *The Free Black in Urban America, 1800–1850* (1981).

9. Elizabeth McHenry examines the development of black literacy from the antebellum era to the present in her book *Forgotten Readers: Recovering the Lost History of African American Literary Societies* (2002). Anna Murray Douglass' illiteracy is better understood in the context of the oral, performative literacy practiced by free blacks who shared information with illiterate "readers" in their communities.

10. Although I view Harper as a displaced Southerner, Hazel Carby, Farah Jasmine Griffin, and especially Dorothy Sterling in her *Speak Out in Thunder Tones* (1973) label Harper a Northern intellectual, a member of the black elite. Similarly, Carla Peterson places Harper among the "freeborn, Northern-rooted, and light-skinned population" found in antebellum cities like Philadelphia, New York, and Boston (8). I examine Harper's hybridity under different conditions than Peterson, who identifies Harper as a member of the heterogeneous black community in the antebellum North: native-born / migrant, freeborn / slave-origin, and literate professional / working class folk. Despite these high / low divisions, urban blacks built self-sufficient communities that might have been "inexplicable to the dominant culture in their disruption of fixed hierarchies and binary oppositions"(Peterson 9–10). Given her critique of the inextricable link between race and region that defines "a Southern self, society, or culture" ("Expanding" 5), even Thadious Davis describes Harper as a "Northern-born free" woman in comparison to Anna J. Cooper, an educated Southern black woman born a slave in Raleigh, North Carolina ("Woman's Art" 26). In this case, slavery seems to be an authentic marker of black Southern identity.

11. Numerous sources include specific references to regional identity, especially as it concerns black Southern women. See Jean Fagan Yellin and Cynthia D. Bond, eds. "Geographical and Regional Discussions" in *The Pen Is Ours* (1991), p. 325 and many other regional references throughout this bibliography under individual authors. During the nineteenth century, the North/South dichotomy divides the black population as much as the insinuating class premise behind the project to "uplift the race."

12. I am grateful to my colleague and friend Rychetta N. Watkins for helping to clarify the realities of African Americans in the South during Reconstruction and under Jim Crow law.

13. At this time, I am uncertain about how many of Harper's letters actually survive. Those selected by Foster to include in the reader, *A Brighter Coming Day*, are the most autobiographical. Most of these letters also appear in William Still's sketch of Harper in *The Underground Railroad*.

14. The "Truth is Stranger than Fiction" letter to William Still that mentions this editorial is reprinted in *A Brighter' Coming Day* (p. 132–133). Still reprints the full editorial in his *Underground Railroad* (p.775–776).

15. For an in-depth discussion of models of black manhood in the South during the late nineteenth-century, see Glenda E. Gilmore, pp. 61–89.
16. The Latin phrase *partus sequitur ventrem* describes the U.S. tradition and law regarding parental relations and property rights during slavery. It dictates that the child follows the condition of the mother (e.g. slave mothers bear slave off-spring and free black women had children who were also born free).
17. In the nineteenth century, Natchez's free black population was limited indeed. I discuss it in relation to free blacks in Baltimore earlier in this chapter. Also, see Edwin Adams Davis and William Ransom Hogan's edition of *William Johnson's Natchez: The Ante-Bellum Diary of a Free Negro* (Baton Rouge: Louisiana State University, 1993).
18. Melba Joyce Boyd has written about Harper's life and career. Boyd examines Harper's poetic sensibilities and how this influenced her political praxis. Boyd's book is a creative experiment that mixes Harper's own "voice" (provided in her writings) with her biographer's narrative. The book "reveals as much about [Boyd's] creative attitude and political and aesthetic motivations as it does about Harper's legacy" (Boyd 26). In her treatment of Harper, Boyd doesn't consider her Southernness as I do in this chapter.
19. See Andrews, "Mark Twain, William Wells Brown, and the Problem of Authority in New South Writing." *Southern Literature and Literary Theory.* Jefferson Humphries, ed. Athens: University of Georgia Press, 1990: 1–21

NOTES TO CHAPTER 2

1. Today, Chesnutt's literary reputation and achievements have exceeded that of his mentor Cable. Chesnutt published his first short stories, "The Goophered Grapevine" (1887) in the *Atlantic Monthly* and "Po' Sandy" (1888) in *The Atlantic* prior to meeting Cable. Their relationship is worth further study beyond the scope of this book. Unfortunately, none of the political articles Chesnutt submitted to the *Century, Forum,* or *North American Review,* among others suggested by Cable, were ever accepted for publication.
2. Cable's main contribution to regional literature is his portraits of Creole culture. His other publications include *Madame Delphine* (1881), *The Creoles of Louisiana* (1884), *Dr. Sevier* (1884), *The Silent South* (1885), *Bonaventure* (1888), *Strange True Stories of Louisiana* (1889), *The Negro Question* (1890), *The Busy Man's Bible* (1891), *A Memory of Roswell Smith* (1892), *John March, Southerner* (1894), *Strong Hearts* (1899), *The Cavalier* (1901), *Bylow Hill* (1902), *Kincaid's Battery* (1908), *Posson Jone' and Pere Raphael* (1909), *Gideon's Band* (1914), *The Amateur Garden* (1914), *The Flower of the Chapdelaines* (1918), and *Lovers of Louisiana* (1918).
3. Cable was concerned about his public reputation as a Southern heretic and did not want it to reflect on the Open Letter Club. So he used William M. Baskervill as a cover for the leadership of the group; the base of operations was at Vanderbilt University in Nashville with Baskervill, a literary scholar and an early supporter of Cable (Turner, *A Biography* 263–265). Cable had relocated to Northampton, Massachusetts by then, which further agitated his detractors who labeled him an outsider.
4. See Beverly Guy-Sheftall's *Daughters of Sorrow: Attitudes Toward Black Women, 1880–1920* (1990).
5. See Cynthia Neverdon-Morton's *Afro-American Women of the South and the Advancement of the Race, 1895–1925.* Knoxville: University of Tennessee Press, 1989.

6. Note Ida B. Wells-Barnett's *Red Record* (1895) and the controversy surrounding the author and her publication(s). She challenged the black-male-rapist thesis of racist whites' reasoning for lynching.

7. The U.S. presence in the Caribbean was magnified by its occupation of Haiti in 1915. American soldiers in Port-au-Prince secured access to Cuba and the Panama Canal as well as safeguarded the country from possible takeover by France or Germany. Haiti was heavily in debt to both countries (*Essays and Speeches*, n. 5, p. 401).

8. A recent collection by Michele Ronnick has unearthed Scarborough's works and legacy and we can better understand his status among public intellectual peers like Chesnutt. See *The Works of William Sanders Scarborough: Black Classist and Race Leader* (New York: Oxford University Press, 2006).

9. See the correspondence between Chesnutt and Cable that detail Chesnutt's frustration with his developing career in *"To Be an Author": Letters of Charles W. Chesnutt, 1889–1905* (1997), pp. 31–35 and 37–41.

10. See "Multitude of Counselors" in *Essays and Speeches*, p.82.

11. Chesnutt's persuasive method is similar to Angelina Grimke's abolitionist campaign; she also appealed to white women for help when her options were limited. As white Southerners, Angelina and her sister Sarah became regional outcasts when they advocated for blacks' racial equality like Cable.

12. Chesnutt's most controversial move was when he suggested absolute assimilation as the ultimate solution to the race problem in America. See his essays "The Future American" series (1900) reprinted in *Charles W. Chesnutt: Essays and Speeches* (1999).

13. Recently, critics have recognized the importance of a female audience to Chesnutt's writing career. See Samina Najmi's "Janet, Polly, and Olivia" which discusses the white female readership of *Marrow of Tradition* (1901). Also, William Gleason's "Voices at the Nadir: Charles Chesnutt and David Bryant Fulton." *American Literary Realism* 24:3 (1992): 22–41 and Stephen Knadler's "Untragic Mulatto: Charles Chesnutt and the Discourse of Whiteness." *American Literary History* 8:3 (1996) 426–448.

14. In August 1915, Chesnutt published an article, "Women's Rights" in *The Crisis* as part of a symposium entitled, "Votes for Women." His advocacy comes rather late compared to other prominent black men's support of female suffrage. See Rosalyn Terborg-Penn's "Black Male Perspectives on the Nineteenth-Century Woman" in *The Afro-American Woman: Struggles and Images* (1978).

15. Although June Stocken recognizes the status of black men, especially educated mulattos, in Chesnutt's scheme, she doesn't connect the cultural politics of assimilation with empowering enfranchisement.

16. This early activism among black women is more widely recognized today. See Cynthia Neverdon-Morton's "The Black Woman's Struggle for Equality in the South, 1895–1925" in *The Afro-American Woman: Struggles and Images*, pp.43–57. Also, Neverdon-Morton's book on this topic, *Afro-American Women of the South and the Advancement of the Race, 1895–1920* (1989), examines how black women promoted educational and social reforms within their local communities.

17. The literature about white Southern manhood is extensive, with competing ideologies of masculinity and power. Gilmore identifies characteristics of naturalized white supremacy in the South as traceable to U.S. imperialism, immigration, urbanization, industrialization, class privilege (planter elite versus common farmer), voting rights, and democratic ideas during the late nineteenth and early twentieth centuries. Among her sources, Gilmore cites Gail Bederman, Harry Brod, Peter N. Stearns, David D. Gilmore, John

W. Cell, C. Vann Woodward, and Bertram Wyatt-Brown for their studies of Southern history and white manhood.

18. See Kipling's "If" in *Rewards and Fairies* (1910). Gilmore cites a later reprint of the poem in Joseph Morris and St. Clair Adams edited *It Can Be Done: Poems of Inspiration* (1921).

19. Kevin K. Gaines examines this ideology at length to expose the inherent class prejudices of the black elite leadership. My concern lies mostly with the movement as a collective response to the Negro Problem and Southern race relations; I do not see racial uplift as an isolated phenomenon from the Negro Problem, but an essential factor in the social equation.

20. This 1892 remark is attributed to Anna Julia Cooper. See Gates "Trope," p. 144.

21. See Chesnutt's "Superstitions and Folk-lore of the South." *Modern Culture* (May 13, 1901): 231–35 (Rptd. in *Charles W. Chesnutt: Essays and Speeches*, p. 155–161).

22. See Sylvia Lyon Render's "Regional Character" in *Charles W. Chesnutt*, p. 51–53.

23. See Chesnutt's "Peonage, or the New Slavery" in *Charles W. Chesnutt: Essays and Speeches*, p 205–208.

24. See Robert B. Stepto's "'The Simple But Intensely Human Inner Life of Slavery': Storytelling, Fiction and the Revision of History in Charles W. Chesnutt's 'Uncle Julius Stories' " in *History and Tradition in Afro-American Culture*, pp. 29–55.

25. Render only views Aunt Peggy as unstereotypical. I try to look at how most conjure women are exceptional.

26. Compare Viney's situation to the tragedy of "Po' Sandy." After being turned into a tree by his wife Tenie, a conjure woman, Sandy is "killed" at the saw-mill before Tenie can change him back to human again. As the site of destruction for symbolic black manhood, the sawmill scene is reminiscent of a lynching.

27. These changes are highlighted in Brodhead's editing of *The Conjure Woman*, p.25–26 and 171.

28. See Susan McFatter's article for a discussion about the revenge tactics of Chesnutt's female characters.

29. By comparison, Cleanth Brooks views Faulkner's southern women as "the goal and the end of action" in Sally Page's *Faulkner's Women: Characterization and Meaning.* "Introduction." p. xi-xx.

30. The middle reference precedes the others since Chesnutt composed "The Goophered Grapevine" over ten years prior to the stories with the other references, "Mars Jeem's Nightmare" and "Hot-Foot Hannibal."

31. The tragedy of the "Po' Sandy" tale is that Tenie and Sandy, her husband, suffer despite her conjure abilities. Yet, ideologically, conjuring—not the act of conjuring—serves as a means to the end of their suffering as slaves. Through Sandy's death and Tenie's nervous breakdown, they both experience literal and psychological freedom. (Tenie's duties are demoted from housekeeper to babysitter.) In the end, Tenie is never the "crazy 'oman" her master thinks. She is overcome by grief instead. The illusion created by conjuring, as with Viney's case, produces contradictory perceptions of Tenie's character.

32. A more in depth analysis is needed to discuss Aunt Peggy's status as a "spinster" figure according to Victorian standards. I will address this issue in more detail in the final chapter, focusing specifically on the characteristics of black womanhood in regards to Southern culture.

33. See Tiffany Duet's "'Do You Not Know that Women Can Make Money?': Women and Labor in Louisiana Literature" in *Songs of the Reconstruction*

South: Building Literary Louisiana, 1865–1945, pp. 49–63. Duet recognizes Palmyre, in George Washington Cable's *The Grandissimes* (1880), as a conjure woman who uses her skills as "more of an avocation than a vocation" since her *real* work as a "hair-dresser" is not detailed in the novel as much. I disagree with this reading and will discuss the significance of Palmyre's voodoo practices to her role in society and novel later in this chapter. Palmyre and Aunt Peggy are very similar characters.

34. According to Pryse, Chesnutt used conjuring to wrestle literary authority from a powerful, racist white establishment. Hurston, unlike Chesnutt, uses conjuring to gain literary authority for black women against patriarchal power (11–12).

35. This confession appears in Cable's essay "My Politics" written in 1888–89. He wrote the piece in response to severe Southern criticism of his liberal views on racial equality, which conservatives attributed to the "Puritan blood in his veins." Cable wanted to clarify his position as a Southern native and garner support of his ideas from other white Southerners. He intended to publish this essay as a preface to his collection *The Silent South* (1889), but he accepted the advice of close friends to have the essay only published posthumously. They thought this essay was too personal and perhaps made Cable even more vulnerable to attacks, critical and physical.

36. For contemporary reviews and other noted criticism on Cable, see Arlin Turner's edition of *Critical Essays on George W. Cable* (1980).

37. The opposite is true for Aunt Peggy in Chesnutt's fiction. Julius assume her spellbinding powers in his storytelling. Bras Coupé is a tragic figure who Cable uses to humanize slaves and illicit a moral response to the race problems of his own times.

38. For references to Cable's parable of the Good Samaritan, see "My Politics" in *The Negro Question*, pp. 14–15.

39. The Black Codes continued to function under Spanish rule of the Louisiana territory. The original laws remained in place until the cession of Louisiana to the U.S. in 1803. After then, variations of these laws still regulated social and legal interactions among the races. Other Southern states later in the nineteenth century would also adopt a set of "black codes" to curtail African Americans' civil rights. We are reminded in the narrative that the "Code Noir" still exists, "but the new one is a mental reservation, not an enactment" (181). For the original 1724 Code Noir, see the work of Charles Gayarre's *Louisiana: Its Colonial History and Romances*, pp. 537–546.

40. Historians have discovered that there were far more successful free men of color business owners than free women of color business owners during the early 1800s and throughout the nineteenth century. It's ironic that most of these free men of color inherited property and access to business opportunities from "their mothers and grandmothers who were placées," free women of color protected and supported by white men. I discuss this plaçage system in greater detail later in the chapter. For accounts about the economic status of free people of color in Louisiana, see Mary Gehman's "Visible Means of Support: Businesses, Professions, and Trades of Free People of Color" in *Creole: The History and Legacy of Louisiana's Free People of Color*, pp. 208–222.

41. Arguably Bras-Coupé is the real insurrectionist while Honoré, f.m.c. is more passive. The mulatto Honoré only strikes out against Agricola (symbolic of conservative, Southern white society) when the mulatto suffers a personal insult. Even then, these scenes illustrate a class bias more than a racial bias. Honoré, f.m.c. refuses to become a black leader to advocate for equal rights for the entire black community. He doesn't want to become a symbolic figure

like Bras-Coupé due to their class differences and their distinct social con-
sciences. Nevertheless, the juxtaposition of a militant black male figure to a
pacifist mulatto are striking prototypes of black leadership with historical
significance considering the binary between W.E.B. DuBois and Booker T.
Washington around the turn-of-the nineteenth century.

42. See Virginia Meacham Gould's *Chained to the Rock of Adversity: To Be
Free, Black, & Female in the Old South* (Athens: University of Georgia
Press, 1998).

43. Sometimes the white male remained a "bachelor" for life and maintained
his relationship with a black woman, who served as his official mistress.
The women that were enslaved were generally set free by their lovers either
before or after these men died. The children were also freed often. With all
the information that is available on plaçage, the following sources were especially useful: *Creole: The History and Legacy of Louisiana's Free People of
Color*. Sybil Kein, ed. (Baton Rouge: LSU Press, 2000); John Blassingame's
Black New Orleans, 1860–1880. (Chicago: University of Chicago Press,
1973); Judith K. Schafer's "'Open and Notorious Concubinage': The Emancipation of Slave Mistresses by Will and the Supreme Court in Antebellum
Louisiana." *Louisiana History* 28.2 (Spring 1987): 165–182.

44. This mysterious allure connects Palmyre to the legendary voodoo priestess
Marie Laveau. There are striking similarities between the two: their occupa-
tions, descriptions of their physical appearances, and their influential powers.
Yet, Cable adamantly denied that Palmyre is a literary incarnation of Laveau.
For more biographical information on the legendary voodoo queen, see Bar-
bara Rosendale Duggal's "Marie Laveau: The Voodoo Queen Repossessed."
Creole: The History and Legacy of Louisiana's Free People of Color. Sybil
Kein, ed. Baton Rouge, Louisiana: Louisiana State University Press, 2000:
157–178.

45. See Howells, William D. *Heroines of Fiction*. New York: Harper & Brothers, 1901: 234–44. The legendary critic praises Cable's leading white female
characters: "These lovely ladies, who are in their way ladies to their finger-
tips, and are as gentle in breeding as they are simple in circumstance" (rptd. in
Arlin Turner's *Critical Essays on George W. Cable*. Boston, Massachusetts:
G. .K. Hall & Co., 1980:124). Aurora and Clotilde are singled out as likable
characters more than Palmyre and Clemence because nineteenth-century literary and cultural standards validate the superiority of white womanhood
and black women are degraded or ignored. I argue that black women were
important figures for Cable however.

46. Spillers' theory of the linguistically determined category of family is applicable here too. When she looks at black motherhood in the context of a
patriarchal society, black women as social subjects become objects in slavery.
This lead to the objectification of women in the black family, making black
culture matrifocal.

47. Spillers actually denies the use of the term "orphan" in the context of American slavery because she draws from the work of Claude Meillassoux on the
internal slave trade in Africa, which is useful to examine the property/kin-
ship dynamic. In the context of a denied black motherhood and the erasure
of a "dual fatherhood"—the black biological father and the white "captor"
father, Spillers views the position of the slave child as something "yet to be
defined" (269). She nevertheless provides enough evidence for the dissolution
of the black family caused by the capitalism of slavery that shows conversely
how black slave children are orphans indeed.

48. See Susan Gillman's discussion of Mark Twain's use of the tragic mulatto
motif in her "The Mulatto, Tragic or Triumphant? The Nineteenth-Century

American Race Melodrama." *The Culture of Sentiment: Race, Gender, and Sentimentality in 19ᵗʰ Century America*. Shirley Samuels, ed. New York and Oxford: Oxford University Press, 1992:221–43.

49. My argument here relies on claims made in Carrie Tirado Bramen's *The Uses of Variety: Modern Americanism and the Quest for National Distinctiveness*. In her fifth chapter, she examines how black feminist writers of the nineteenth-century re-claimed the tragic mulatto by emphasizing the blood connections with the black mother. These writers, Bramen argues, relied on genetic theories, like the one-drop rule of negritude, to show how blackness is a dominant trait that the mulatto protagonist of the sentimental novels embraces. The result is the promotion of a black nationalist agenda, which serves as a model for new American standards of citizenship.

50. In Cable's description of Clemence, primitive savagery is a dominant trait that defines her black heritage (251). It is an example of particulate or "hard" heredity, a genetic theory in which certain traits "do not blend but retain their dominant or recessive character," according to Bramen's study (205).

51. Bramen uses this same logic to discuss Charles Chesnutt's design of the "future American," the individual that is the product of two different races (219–224). The fusion of two extremes and the continued mixing of the races over generations (i.e. "Galtonian fusion") would result in a whole nation of individuals with mixed heritages, a new "variety" of the human species.

52. See Werner Sollors' discussion of "The Six Elements of the 'Tragic Mulatto' Complex" in *Neither Black Nor White*, p. 223–228.

53. See Barbara Welters' classic article, "The Cult of True womanhood: 1820–1860." *American Quarterly*. 18.2 (Summer 1966): 151–174.

54. As many critics have determined, this scene is reminiscent of the biblical story of Joseph and the Egyptian pharaoh's, Potiphar, wife in Genesis: 39.

55. Bendixen refers to two history books about Queen Zenobia's leadership of the city Palmyra that were popular during the nineteenth century: Edward Gibbon's *Decline and Fall of the Roman Empire* and William Ware's bestseller, *Zenobia or the Fall of Palmyra* (1837). Since various other travel narratives also recorded this saga, Palmyre as "Palmyra" could have had a greater appeal than most critics today even realize.

56. See also Sollors' "*Code Noir* and Literature" in *Neither Black Nor White*, pp. 162–187.

57. Henry C. Castellanos records the first public execution of a woman at the old Parish Prison in New Orleans around the mid-nineteenth century. The victim was a black woman named Pauline, who had allegedly beaten her white mistress, a crime punishable by death under the Black Codes. The old prison was supposedly built on former swampland. Cable's "lynching" occurs in the woods with racist white authorities presiding. Castellanos's description of the execution contains other details found in Cable's scene, which seem to authenticate the writer's fiction. See Castellanos' *New Orleans as It Was: Episodes of Louisiana Life* [1895]. Gretna, Louisiana: Pelican, 1990:104.

58. See Sollors' "Endings" in *Neither Black Nor White*, pgs. 336–359.

59. The field of Southern Women's History offers evidence of varied experiences of elite white women and female slaves: Anne Firor Scott's *The Southern Lady: From Pedestal to Politics, 1830–1930* (1970); Catherine Clinton's *The Plantation Mistress: Woman's World in the Old South* (1982); Elizabeth Fox-Genovese's *Within the Plantation Household: Black and White Women in the Old South* (1988); Deborah Gray White's *Ar'n't I a Woman?: Female Slaves in the Plantation South* (1985); Sally G. McMillen's *Southern Women: Black and White in the Old South* (1992); Brenda E. Stevenson's *Life in Black and White: Family and Community in the Slave South* (1996).

The comparisons I make here about cultural ideologies of womanhood outline a general perception of racialized gender identities in American society at large in the nineteenth century.

60. The major difference between Sapphire and the other images is that her emotional tyranny is always directed towards an African American male. Sapphire must also have a "sidekick," usually a mature mammy figure; Sapphire's brown or dark brown complexion is the only other identifying characteristic.

61. In the life of urban slaves like Clemence, there were no clear physical boundaries restricting their mobility as with slaves in rural areas on plantations. However, in *The Grandissimes*, the caste system is fortified still since Clemence, for instance, has to obtain a written "pass" from her master to show street patrollers enforcing the night curfew for blacks. See Blassingame's *Black New Orleans: 1860–1880*.

NOTES TO CHAPTER 3

1. *A Voice from the South* remains today the center of Cooper's canon. Much of her later works have been collected for extensive study in *The Voice of Anna Julia Cooper* (1998). Now more attention is directed at later writings to examine the full extent of Cooper's scholarship (e.g. her dissertation on the French Revolution and slavery, linguistic studies, speeches, critical essays, and journalism) and her life-long commitment to education and activism.

2. W.E.B. DuBois (1868–1963) was born in Great Barrington, Massachusetts, became a Harvard graduate and race leader among the co-founders of the NAACP. I include him with Southerners Booker T. Washington (1856–1915) and Chesnutt as "race men" to underscore their contributions in public debates on the Negro Problem. Among the black intellectuals of her day, Cooper aligns with DuBois' political and educational philosophies more than Washington, but it is her status as a Southerner that is most often de-emphasized as a stimulus for her political agency unlike with her Southern black male contemporaries. See discussions of Cooper, gender politics and black leadership in Kevin Gaines, "The Woman and Labor Questions in Racial Uplift Ideology: Anna Julia Cooper's Voices from the South" in *Uplifting the Race: Black Leadership, Politics and Culture in the Twentieth Century* (1996); Vivian May, *Anna Julia Cooper, Visionary Black Feminist* (21–22); Joy James, "Profeminism and Gender Elites: W.E.B. Du Bois, Anna Julia Cooper, and Ida B. Wells-Barnett" in *Next to the Color Line: Gender, Sexuality, and W.E.B. Du Bois*, Susan Gillman and Alys Eve Weinbaum, eds. Minneapolis, Minnesota: University of Minnesota Press, 2007: 69–95.

3. Johnetta B. Cole and Beverly Guy-Sheftall, "The Personal is Political" in *Gender Talk*, p.1–30.

4. Likewise, another race woman from the South, Ida B. Wells-Barnett publishes *Southern Horrors: Lynch Law in All Its Phases*, igniting her anti-lynching crusade. See Rychetta N. Watkins, "The Southern Roots of Ida B. Wells-Barnett's Revolutionary Activism" in *The Southern Quarterly* 45.3 (Spring 2008): 108–126.

5. I isolate these "forces" to the main opposition (racial and gender) Cooper identifies in her work, or what is implicit in her arguments. Broadly defined, these forces would include economic, political, and social factors, which I also enumerate at times.

6. Cooper's birth year has not been confirmed though this date is what most scholars cite as valid according Louise Daniel Hutchinson's early biography. I cite other details of Cooper's family life mostly from May's biographical sketch which is based on Hutchinson's text and Leona C. Gabel's *From Slavery to the Sorbonne and Beyond: The Life & Writings of Anna J. Cooper* (1982).

7. Founded in 1870, M Street High School was the largest public school for African Americans. It attracted the most talented educators and also produced future black leaders. Many of Cooper's students would later study at Ivy League institutions like Harvard and Brown and prestigious black-schools like Fisk and Howard Universities. The M Street faculty included Jessie Redmon Fauset and Angelina Weld Grimké (contributors of the Renaissance in black literature by the 1920s), Kelly Miller (another renowned educator), and activists-educators Mary Church Terrell and Carter G. Woodson (*Visionary Black Feminist* 18, 24). Cooper's reputation was also tarnished by scandal while at M Street. She was criticized for her educational philosophy—a combined emphasis on liberal arts college-preparatory courses and vocational training, as opposed to Booker T. Washington's influential Tuskegee-model of industrial education. Cooper rejected Jim Crow educational standards for blacks, the use of inferior resources and ineffective pedagogy. With her professional reputation in jeopardy, Cooper was accused of having an illicit affair with John Lowe, a M Street student and her foster child. The charges against her leadership as a principal and teacher, and the immoral accusations were unwarranted. See details to the public campaign against Cooper in May, *Visionary Black Feminist*, p. 24–27.

8. See Cooper's full "Curriculum Vitae" in May's *Visionary Black Feminist, p.* 8–12.

9. May believes Cooper establishes such paradigms, which later black feminists (and women of color) would develop further, in *Visionary Black Feminist*, p.182–183.

10. All references to Crummell's work are from *Civilization and Black Progress: Selected Writings of Alexander Crummell on the South*. J.R. Oldfield, ed. Charlottesville, VA: University Press of Virginia, 1995. Crummell was the exalted mentor of W.E.B. DuBois, who immortalizes him in his *Souls of Black Folk* (1903).

11. Crummell delivered his message about the welfare of Southern black women first before the Freedman's Aid Society of the Methodist Episcopal Church in New Jersey on April 15, 1883. When he later published the speech as a pamphlet, it sold over 500,000 copies. He had planned to establish a benevolent home for "colored women" backed by the proceeds from the sale of his pamphlet. I have not discovered evidence about the establishment of this institution. Crummell's plans might have been similar to Victoria Earle Matthew's White Rose Mission in New York, a shelter for black women migrants from the South. See Terborg-Penn's "Black Male Perspectives on the Nineteenth-Century Woman" in *The Afro-American Woman: Struggles and Images* (Port Washington, N.Y.: Kennikat Press, 1978).

12. Another study supported by the John F. Slater Fund entitled "A Report Concerning the Colored Women of the South" (1896) also presents the status of Southern black women as an important sociological issue.

13. Crummell was a leading member of the American Negro Academy (ANA), an exclusive group for black male intellectuals, in Washington, D.C. Cooper was the only female invited to speak before the membership, and, though she could not become a member, she seemed to support their racial uplift philosophies (Gaines 42). She did engage in other intellectual exercises of

literary circles among her friends—especially Francís and Charlotte Forten Grimké—at their home and her own. "Here was activity, planned and purposeful," she recalls (Lemert and Bhan 311–313).

14. Mary Helen Washington (in the introduction to the Oxford-Schomburg Library edition I use here), Karen Baker-Fletcher ('*A Singing Something*': *Womanist Reflections on Anna Julia Cooper* [New York: Crossroad, 1994]), and Hazel Carby (in *Reconstructing Womanhood*) are among those who are most critical of Cooper's promoting true womanhood as a model in which black women should perform. Classic treatment of the ideology of true womanhood appears in Barbara Welter's 1966 article, "The Cult of True Womanhood: 1820–1860,"in *American Quarterly*. Recent assessments of this ideology are found in *The Journal of Women's History*, volume 14, no. 1 (Spring 2002), edited by Leila J. Rupp, see her introduction, "Women's History in the New Millennium: A Retrospective Analysis of Barbara Welter's 'The Cult of True Womanhood: 1820–1860'" and Mary Louise Roberts' "True Womanhood Revisited," 150–155.

15. Beverly Guy-Sheftall, *Daughters of Sorrow: Attitudes Toward Black Women, 1880–1920*. Brooklyn, NY: Carlson Publishing Inc., 1990.

16. See selections, "A Woman's Lot: Black Women are Sex Objects for White Men" (p.150–163) and "The Rape of Black Women as a Weapon of Terror" (p.173–189) in Gerda Learner's *Black Women in White America: A Documentary History* (New York: Random House, 1972); Also, "White Folks Still on Top" in Dorothy Sterling's *We Are Your Sisters: Black Women in the Nineteenth Century* (New York: W.W. Norton,1984: 344–354).

17. A more comprehensive history of the NACW is found in Deborah Gray White, *Too Heavy a Load: Black Women in Defense of Themselves, 1894–1994* (New York: W.W. Norton, 1996); On Cooper's international activism and her scholarship about French and Haitian politics, see *Visionary Black Feminist*, p. 107–140.

18. Cynthia Neverdon-Morton also connects the social activism of black women in Cooper's generation to their educational backgrounds in the South. In *Afro-American Women of the South and the Advancement of the Race, 1895–1925* (Knoxville: University of Tennessee Press, 1989), Neverdon-Morton profiles several historically black colleges and universities (HBCUs): Hampton Institute (now Hampton University), Tuskegee Institute, Fisk University, Atlanta University (now Clark-Atlanta University), Spelman Seminary (now Spelman College), and Morgan State College. In addition to their regular curriculum, these schools also offered nursing and teacher training programs that allowed female students to pursue professional careers with practical benefits. Meharry Medical College in Nashville and the Atlanta School of Social Work are also profiled in this study. Though most schools established for African Americans during this time were co-educational, the fact that a number of single-sex schools were created especially for black women shows how important black women were to the project of racial uplift. Several all-female schools for black women were established by other black women: Nannie Burroughs' National Training School for Women and Girls (1907) and Mary McCleod Bethune's Daytona Normal and Industrial School for Negro Girls (1904), it latter became Bethune Cookman College for both sexes. Scotia Seminary (North Carolina), Bennett College, and Spelman College were all established for black women by whites. Note also Guy-Sheftall's emphasis on educating black women in *Daughters of Sorrow*, p.130–132.

19. It created greater opportunities for the denigrated black woman to evolve into a sophisticated lady, who embodied all the virtues of True Womanhood. See

Linda M. Perkins' "The Impact of the 'Cult of True Womanhood' on the Education of Black Women" *Journal of Social Issues*. Vol. 39, No. 3 (1983): 17–28.

20. While most scholars focus on the class privilege of these "race women," if we
consider their backgrounds more carefully, many of them were once among
the masses of lower class, uneducated blacks they tried to help. Cooper's
poverty and rise "up from slavery" illustrates this development. Often race
men/women would return to their homes to help others acquire the same
opportunities from which they benefited. Gilmore discusses how educated
blacks became role models to inspire future generations (33–35, 39).

21. If indeed Cooper was affected by the labor strikes and violent class warfare
(e.g. the 1886 Haymarket Square in Chicago or Carnegie Homestead steel
plant in 1892) in the urban North, as Gaines suggests, it stands to reason that
Cooper straddles the picketing line. The industrial North was not the land of
the free for foreign immigrant workers and non-union black migrants. Nor
would the New South be able to avoid such economic conflicts (e.g. without
the intervention of Cooper's middle-class appeasement?) when facing similar groups competing for fair and equal employment. Gaines suggests that
Cooper was against labor strikes and therefore sided with industrial leaders.
Though in the Carnegie steel plant strike, black workers tried to seize the
opportunity (as paid strikebreakers) to replace the striking (white, immigrant) steelworkers (See Painter, *Standing at Armageddon*, p.110–114). Black
labor was easily exploited in the South so Cooper could not fully believe in
"an essential harmony of interests between capital and labor" (Gaines 133).

22. This essay was originally published on August 28, 1899 in *The Southern
Workman and Hampton School Record*, which is available in the University
Archives at Hampton University.

23. David R. Roediger, *The Wages of Whiteness: Race and the Making of the
American Working Class* (1991).

24. As noted in Gaines and elsewhere, Cooper once wrote to W.E.B. DuBois
insisting that even he should refute a pro-Southern defense for Reconstruction in Claude Bowers' *The Tragic Era*. See facsimile of Cooper's letter in
Lemert and Bhan, p. 336.

25. Cobbs cites Eric Hobsbawm, "Introduction," in Eric Hobsbawm and Ter-
ence Ranger, eds, *The Invention of Tradition* (Cambridge, 1983).

26. Fred Arthur Bailey, "Thomas Nelson Page and the Patrician Cult of the Old
South." *International Social Science Review*. 72. 3–4 (1997): 110–121.

27. Henry L. Gates, Jr., "The Trope of a New Negro and the Reconstruction of
the Image of the Black." *Representations* 24 (Fall 1988): 129–155.

28. See my "Introduction" in "'My Southern Home': The Lives and Literature
of 19th-Century Southern Black Writers," a special issue of *The Southern
Quarterly*, 45.3 (Spring 2008): 5–19. Gabriel A. Briggs's article, "*Imperium
In Imperio*: Sutton E. Griggs and the New Negro of the South," appears also
in this edition, p. 153–176.

29. Dickson D. Bruce, Jr. *Black American Writing from the Nadir: The Evo-
lution of a Literary Tradition, 1877–1915*. Baton Rouge: Louisiana State
University Press, 1989. Barbara McCaskill and Caroline Gebhard, eds. *Post-
Bellum, Pre-Harlem: African American Literature and Culture, 1877–1919*.
New York: New York University Press, 2006.

30. See also May on Cooper's community activism, *Visionary Black Feminist*
p.21–22.

31. Cooper built networks with other prominent black Washingtonians like
Francis and Charlotte Forten Grimké.

32. See Hale, *Making Whiteness*, p. 85–86, 242. Cooper's Victorian home fell
into disrepair after her death and years of neglect and vandalism once her last

descendents moved out in recent years. It was purchased in 2005 and the new owners plan to restore it as when Cooper lived there. See Natalie Hopkinson, "Restoring with Respect" in *The Washington Post*. (January 19, 2006): H01.

NOTES TO CHAPTER 4

1. The autobiographies by the writer-activists in Perkins's study—Angela Davis, Elaine Brown, and Assata Shakur—embody their blackness and femininity (essentially, humanity) to interrogate American racial policy. These black women risked their lives because of their political affiliations with "militant" community organizations like The Black Panther Party. While Davis and Brown often had to seek temporary protection from the law (during their young adulthood), Shakur remains in political exile today in Cuba for participating in nationalist struggles at "home."
2. Various archives, private and public, contain rare social documents and literary works produced during the late nineteenth and throughout the twentieth centuries on the Negro Problem. I have identified an extensive listing of legal pamphlets, journal articles, photographic images, fiction, poetry, and political essays and speeches. These sources are labeled under synonymous titles or topics like the "Race Problem," the "Negro Question," and even "The South's Negro/Race Problem."
3. See Alexander Crummell, "The Black Woman of the South: Her Neglects and Her Needs" [1883]. Rptd. in *Civilization and Black Progress: Selected Writings of Alexander Crummell on the South*. J.R. Oldfield, ed. Charlottesville: University Press of Virginia, 1995: 101–113. Also, Elizabeth Christophers Hobson (Kimball) and C.E. Hopkins, A *Report Concerning the Colored Women of the South*. Baltimore, Maryland: Trustees of the John F. Slater Fund, 1896.
4. Fictional representation of this professional class of black women and their less educated counterparts appear in African American literature of this period; images of both types of race women suggests that leadership is not determined by class. See Frances Harper's *Iola Leroy* (1892) and her Aunt Chloe poems in *Sketches of a Southern Life* (1872). Also, Henry Louis Gates, Jr. "The Trope of a New Negro and the Reconstruction of the Image of the Black." Representations. 24 (Fall 1988): 129–155.
5. For a recent critique about how these iconic race women were juxtaposed to DuBoisian patriarchy, see Joy James, "Profeminism and Gender Elites: W.E.B. Du Bois, Anna Julia Cooper, and Ida B. Wells-Barnett" in *Next to the Color Line: Gender, Sexuality, and W.E.B. Du Bois*. Susan Gillman and Alys Eve Weinbaum, eds. Minneapolis, MN: University of Minnesota Press, 2007: 69–95.
6. Other articles also appeared that addresses Southern race relations although I only examine those specifically labeled as "race problem autobiographies" or biographical sketches with specific references to "the Negro Problem" published in *The Independent*. See "The New Slavery in the South—An Autobiography" by a Georgia Negro Peon (February 25, 1904): 409–414 or "A Washerwoman" (November 10, 1904): 1073–76. A more comprehensive look at the writings of black men and women is beyond the scope of this project. My goal is to showcase the literary activism among black women in an age dominated by black male leadership. The autobiographical writings listed above however are useful to interrogate the class dynamics and tensions between black elite and the masses.

7. This was known as the paper's "weathercock function" (Boylan 6–7).
8. By one account, at least eighty "life stories" appeared from 1902–1912. See David M. Katzman and William M. Tuttle, Jr., *Plain Folk: the Life Stories of Undistinguished Americans* (Urbana: University of Illinois Press, 1982); An earlier collection, *The Life Stories of Undistinguished Americans: As Told by Themselves*, edited by Hamilton Holt, was published in 1906 (New York: James Pott & Company).
9. For a contemporary critique of the "black masses" and agency, see Robin D.G. Kelley's *Race Rebels: Culture, Politics, and the Black Working Class*. New York: Free Press, 1995.
10. Led by these two, an assembly of other "representative" black men like Charles W. Chesnutt, Paul Laurence Dunbar, and T. Thomas Fortune also voiced their political opinions in a literary forum. This collection of essays was published in 1903 as *The Negro Problem* (New York: Pott & Company).
11. This emphasis on the individual and the community is a common trait among Southern women autobiographies. See Peggy W. Prenshaw, "'The True Happenings of My Life': Reading Southern Women Autobiographers." *Haunted Bodies: Gender and Southern Texts*. Anne Goodwyn Jones and Susan V. Donaldson, eds. Charlottesville, Virginia: University Press of Virginia, 1997: 443–463. Also, Elizabeth Fox-Genovese, "My Statue, My Self: Autobiographical Writings of Afro-American Women." *Reading Black, Reading Feminist: A Critical Anthology*. Henry L. Gates, ed. New York: Penguin Books, 1990: 176–203.
12. Homer Plessy was a young mulatto shoemaker, chosen to test the merits of Louisiana state laws and customs especially within the transit system. His biracial identity was used to challenge how race is defined on the basis of "civil" if not "social equality."
13. See George Washington Cable writings for example.
14. For a historical discussion on white Southerners' attitudes about black education, see James D. Anderson, "Education and the Race Problem in the New South: The Struggle for Ideological Hegemony." *The Education of Blacks in the South, 1860–1935*. Chapel Hill: University of North Carolina Press, 1988: 79–109.
15. This is a part of the note appended to the 1904 narratives about the Race Problem.
16. Among the famous women contributors were leading social reformers like Jane Addams, Florence Kelly, and Ida B. Wells-Barnett. Emerging literary writers like Charlotte Perkins Gilman also contributed to *The Independent*.
17. See Frank E. Vandiver's discussion of "the Confederate myth" in *Myth and Southern History* Patrick Gerster and Nicholas Cords, eds. (Urbana: University of Illinois Press, 1989), pp. 147–153. Hale also asserts that "'[h]istory' was the first battlefield in the creation of modern Southern whiteness" (49).
18. Hollywood depictions of a romanticized South in legendary films like Gone With the Wind (1939), based on Margaret Mitchell's novel, and D.W. Griffth's Birth of a Nation (1915) as well as the tumultuous Civil Rights Movement of the 1950s-60s encapsulate most Americans' perceptions of the South. See Hale's discussion of "American Whiteness" as a product of Southern cultural history (281–296).
19. She also refers to George Washington Cable's local color fiction as a model for Southern writing and cultural realism; though his sketches of exotic Creole life were popular, they were also at times controversial because of his radical politics. See Cable's *The Grandissimes: A Story of Creole Life* [1880]. New York: Penguin Books, 1988; *The Creoles of Louisiana* [1884].

New York: Garrett Press, Inc., 1970; and *Creoles and Cajuns: Stories of Old Louisiana*. Arlin Turner, ed. Garden City, New York: Doubleday, 1959.

20. For other early bibliographic references about the treatment of young black women in urban areas, see *The Pen Is Ours: A Listing of Writings by and about African-American Women before 1910*. Jean F. Yellin and Cynthia D. Bond, eds. New York: Oxford University Press, 1991: 332.

21. See Farah Jasmine Griffin's cultural study in *"Who set you flowin?": The African-American Migration Narrative*. New York: Oxford University Press, 1995.

22. Subtitled inspired by Toni Morrison's brief cultural narrative about the racial paradox of being Americans. See Morrison's essay, "Home," in *The House That Race Built: Black Americans, U.S. Terrain*. Lubiano Wahneema, ed. New York: Pantheon Books, 1997: 3–12.

Bibliography

Abbott, Ernest Hamlin. "The South and the Negro." *Outlook* (May 21, 1904): 165–168.

Alexander, Robert Allen, Jr. "The Irreducible African: Challenges to Racial Stereotypes in George W. Cable's *The Grandissimes.*" *Songs of the Reconstructing South: Building Literary Louisiana, 1865–1945.* Westport, Connecticut: Greenwood Press, 2002:123–133.

Ammons, Elizabeth. "Frances Ellen Watkins Harper." *Legacy* (Fall 1985): 61–66.

Ammons, Elizabeth and Annette White-Parks, eds. *Tricksterism in Turn-of-the-Century American Literature: A Multicultural Perspective.* Hanover, New Hampshire: University Press of New England, 1994.

Andrews, William L. "Mark Twain, William Wells Brown, and the Problem of Authority in New South Writing." *Southern Literature and Literary Theory.* Jefferson Humphries, ed. Athens: University of Georgia Press, 1990: 1–21.

———. *The Literary Career of Charles W. Chesnutt.* Baton Rouge: Louisiana State University Press, 1980.

———. "The Significance of Charles W. Chesnutt's 'Conjure Stories.' " *The Southern Literary Journal.* 7.1(Fall 1974):78–99.

———. ed., et. al., *The Literature of the American South: A Norton Anthology.* New York: W.W. Norton & Company, 1998.

Anderson, James D. "Education and the Race Problem in the New South: The Struggle for Ideological Hegemony." *The Education of Blacks in the South, 1860–1935.* Chapel Hill: University of North Carolina Press, 1988: 79–109.

Ayers, Edward L. "What We Talk about When We Talk about the South." *All Over the Map: Rethinking American Regions.* Edward L. Ayers, Patricia Nelson Limerick, Stephen Nissenbaum, and Peter S. Onuf, eds. Baltimore: The Johns Hopkins University Press, 1996: 62–82.

Baker, Houston A., Jr. *Turning South Again: Re-thinking Modernism / Re-reading Booker T.* Durham: Duke University Press, 2001.

Baker-Fletcher, Karen. *'A Singing Something': Womanist Reflections on Anna Julia Cooper.* New York: Crossroads, 1994.

Bhabha, Homi K. "Cultural Diversity and Cultural Differences" [1988]. *African American Literary Criticism, 1773–2000.* Hazel Arnett Ervin, ed. New York: Twayne Publishers, 1999: 268–272.

Bailey, Fred Arthur. "Thomas Nelson Page and the Patrician Cult of the Old South." *International Social Science Review.* 72. 3–4 (1997): 110–121.

Bell, Roseann P., et.al. eds. *Sturdy Black Bridges: Visions of Black Women in Literature.* Garden City, New York: Anchor Press/Doubleday, 1979.

Bendixen, Alfred. "Cable's *The Grandissimes*: A Literary Pioneer Confronts the Southern Tradition." *The Grandissimes: Centennial Essays.* Thomas J. Richardson, ed. Jackson: University Press of Mississippi, 1981:23–33.

Bernhard, Virginia, et. al., eds. *Hidden Histories of Women in the New South.* Columbia: University of Missouri Press, 1994.

Blassingame, John. *Black New Orleans, 1860–1880.* Chicago: University of Chicago Press, 1973.

Boles, John B. *Black Southerners, 1619–1869.* Lexington: University Press of Kentucky, 1984.

Boxill, Bernard R., ed. *The Negro Problem* [1903]. Amherst, New York: Humanity Books, 2003.

Boyd, Melba Joyce. *Discarded Legacy: Politics and Poetics in the Life of Frances E.W. Harper, 1825–1911.* Detroit, Michigan: Wayne State University Press, 1994.

Boylan, James R. *An Institution of the Historical Public Sphere: The Independent in the Progressive Era.* Boston: n.p., 1991.

Bramen, Carrie Tirado. "Biracial Fictions and the Mendelist Allegory." *The Uses of Variety: Modern Americanism and the Quest for National Distinctiveness.* Cambridge, Massachusetts: Harvard University Press, 2000: 201–249.

Braxton, Joanne M. *Black Women Writing Autobiography: A Tradition Within a Tradition.* Philadelphia, Pennsylvania: Temple University Press, 1989.

Briggs, Gabriel A. "Imperium In Imperio: Sutton E. Griggs and the New Negro of the South." *The Southern Quarterly.* 45.3 (Spring 2008): 153–176.

Britt, David D. "Chesnutt's Conjure Tales: What You See Is What You Get." *CLA* 15 (1972): 269–83.

Brodhead, Richard. *Cultures of Letters: Scenes of Reading and Writing in Nineteenth-Century America.* Chicago: University of Chicago Press, 1993.

Brown, Charlotte Hawkins. *"Mammy": An Appeal to the Heart of the South.* Boston: Pilgrim Press, 1919.

Brown, Elsa Barkley. "To Catch the Vision of Freedom: Reconstructing Southern Black Women's Political History, 1865–1880." *Unequal Sisters: A Multicultural Reader in U.S. Women's History.* 3rd edition. Vicki L. Ruiz and Ellen Carol Dubois, eds. New York: Routledge, 2000: 124–146.

Brown, Sterling. *The Negro in American Fiction.* New York: Sentry Press, 1969.

Brown, William Wells. *My Southern Home, or The South and Its People* [1880]. New York: Negro Universities Press, 1969.

Bruce, Dickson D. Jr. *Black American Writing from the Nadir: The Evolution of a Literary Tradition, 1877–1915.* Baton Rouge: Louisiana State University Press, 1989.

Cable, George Washington. *The Grandissimes: A Story of Creole Life* [1880]. New York: Penguin Books, 1988.

———. *The Creoles of Louisiana* [1884]. New York: Garrett Press, Inc., 1970.

———. "The Dance in Place Congo" [1886]. *Creoles and Cajuns: Stories of Old Louisiana.* Arlin Turner, ed. Garden City, New York: Doubleday, 1959:366–393.

———. *The Negro Question: A Selection of Writings on Civil Rights in the South.* Arlin Turner, ed. New York: W.W. Norton, 1958.

———. *The Silent South.* New York: Scribner, 1885.

Campbell, Michael L. "The Negro in Cable's *The Grandissimes.*" *Mississippi Quarterly* (Spring 1974): 165–178.

Carby, Hazel V. *Reconstructing Womanhood: The Emergence of the Afro-American Woman Novelist.* New York: Oxford University Press, 1987.

Carlson, Shirley J. "Black Ideals of Womanhood in the Late Victorian Era." *The Journal of Negro History.* 77. 2 (Spring 1992): 61–73

Castellanos, Henry C. *New Orleans as It Was: Episodes of Louisiana Life* [1895]. Gretna, Louisiana, Pelican, 1990.

Chesnutt, Charles W. *The Conjure Woman and Other Conjure Tales* [1899]. Richard H. Brodhead, ed. Durham, North Carolina: Duke University Press, 1993.

————. *The House Behind the Cedars* [1900]. New York: Penguin Books, 1993.

————. *Charles W. Chesnutt: Essays and Speeches.* Eds. Joseph R. McElrath, Jr., et. al. Stanford, CA: Stanford University Press, 1999.

————. *"To Be an Author": Letters of Charles W. Chesnutt, 1889–1905.* Joseph R. McElrath, Jr. and Robert C. Leitz III, eds. New Jersey: Princeton University Press, 1997.

————. *The Journals of Charles W. Chesnutt.* Richard H. Brodhead, ed. Durham: Duke University Press, 1993.

Cole, Johnetta B. and Beverly Guy-Sheftall. *Gender Talk: The Struggle for Women's Equality in African American Communities.* New York: Ballantine, 2003.

Cobb, James C. *Away Down South: A History of Southern Identity.* New York: Oxford, 2005.

Cooper, Anna Julia. *A Voice from the South by a Black Woman of the South.* [1892]. Introd. Mary Helen Washington. New York: Oxford University Press, 1988.

————. "Colored Women as Wage-Earners" [1899]. Reprinted in Shirley Wilson Logan, *"We Are Coming": The Persuasive Discourse of Nineteenth-Century Black Women.* Carbondale, Illinois: Southern Illinois University Press, 1999:200–205.

Crummell, Alexander. "The Black Woman of the South: Her Neglects and Her Needs" [1883]. Rptd. in *Civilization and Black Progress: Selected Writings of Alexander Crummell on the South.* J.R. Oldfield, ed. Charlottesville: University Press of Virginia, 1995: 101–113.

Cullen Sizer, Lyde. *The Political Work of Northern Women Writers and the Civil War, 1850–1872.* Chapel Hill: The University of North Carolina Press, 2000.

Curry, Leonard P. *The Free Black in Urban America, 1800–1850: The Shadow of the Dream.* Chicago: University of Chicago Press, 1981.

————. "Free Blacks in the Urban South: 1800–1850." *The Southern Quarterly.* 43.2 (Winter 2006): 35–51.

Davis, Edwin Adams and William Ransom Hogan, eds. *William Johnson's Natchez: The Ante-Bellum Diary of a Free Negro.* Baton Rouge: Louisiana State University, 1993.

Davis, Angela Y. *Women, Race, & Class.* New York: Random House, 1981.

Davis, Thadious. "Expanding the Limits: The Intersections of Race and Region." *Southern Literary Journal.* 20 (1988): 3–11.

————. "Women's Art and Authorship in the Southern Region: Connections." *The Female Tradition in Southern Literature.* Carol S. Manning, ed. Urbana, IL: University of Illinois Press, 1993:15–36.

————. "Sashaying through the South." *South to the Future: An American Region in the Twenty-first Century.* Fred Hopson, ed. Athens: University of Georgia Press, 2002: 56–86.

Decker, William Merrill. *Epistolary Practices: Letter Writing in America before Telecommunications.* Chapel Hill, NC: University of North Carolina Press, 1998.

Degler, Carl N. "There Was Another South." *Myth and Southern History, Vol. 1: The Old South.* 2nd edition. Patrick Gerster and Nicholas Cords, eds. Urbana: University of Illinois Press, 1989: 121–132.

Dixon, Melvin. "The Teller as Folk Trickster in Chesnutt's *The Conjure Woman.*" *CLA.* 18 (1974):184–197.

Donaldson, Susan V. and Anne Goodwyn Jones. "Haunted Bodies: Rethinking the South through Gender." Introduction. *Haunted Bodies: Gender and Southern Texts.* Susan V. Donaldson and Anne Goodwyn Jones, eds. University Press of Virginia, 1997: 1–19.

Douglass, Frederick. *Narrative of the Life of Frederick Douglass: An American Slave, Written by Himself* [1845]. David W. Blight, ed. New York: Bedford/St. Martin's, 1993.

———. "Letter to Thomas Auld [1848]." Reprinted in *Narrative of the Life of Frederick Douglass: An American Slave, Written by Himself* [1845]. David W. Blight, ed. New York: Bedford/St. Martin's, 1993:134–141.

———. "My Slave Experience in Maryland [1845]." Reprinted in *Narrative of the Life of Frederick Douglass: An American Slave, Written by Himself* [1845]. David W. Blight, ed. New York: Bedford/St. Martin's, 1993:130–134.

Duet, Tiffany. "'Do You Not Know that Women Can Make Money?': Women and Labor in Louisiana Literature." *Songs of the Reconstruction South: Building Literary Louisiana, 1865–1945.* Suzanne Disheroon-Green and Lisa Abney, eds. Greenwood Press: Westport, CT, 2002: 49–63.

Duggal, Barbara Rosendale. "Marie Laveau: The Voodoo Queen Repossessed." *Creole: The History and Legacy of Louisiana's Free People of Color.* Sybil Kein, ed. Baton Rouge: Louisiana State University Press, 2000: 157–178.

Dunbar-Nelson, Alice Moore. "People of Color in Louisiana." *Creole: The History and Legacy of Louisiana's Free People of Color.* Sybil Kein, ed. Baton Rouge, Louisiana: Louisiana State University Press, 2000:3–41.

"Experiences of the Race Problem by a Southern White Woman." *The Independent.* 56 (March 17, 1904): 590–594.

Ferguson, Sally Ann. "Rena Walden: Chesnutt's Failed 'Future American.'" *Southern Literary Journal* 15 (1982): 74–82.

Fields, Barabara Jeanne. *Slavery and Freedom on the Middle Ground: Maryland during the Nineteenth Century.* New Haven: Yale University Press, 1985.

Foner, Eric. *Forever Free: The Story of Emancipation and Reconstruction.* New York: Alfred A. Knopf, 2005.

Foote, Stephanie. *Regional Fictions: Culture and Identity in Nineteenth-Century American Literature.* Madison, Wisconsin: University of Wisconsin Press, 2001.

Foster, Frances Smith. *Written By Herself: Literary Production by African American Women, 1746–1892.* Bloomington: Indiana University Press, 1993.

———. "Introduction." *A Brighter Coming Day: A Frances Ellen Watkins Harper Reader.* Francis Smith Foster, ed. New York: The Feminist Press, 1990: 3–40.

Fox-Genovese, Elizabeth. "Slavery, Race, and the Figure of the Tragic Mulatta: or, The Ghost of Southern History in the Writing of African-American Women." *Haunted Bodies: Gender and Southern Texts.* Susan V. Donaldson and Anne Goodwyn Jones, eds. University Press of Virginia, 1997: 464–491.

———. "My Statue, My Self: Autobiographical Writings of Afro-American Women." *The Private Self: Theory and Practice of Women's Autobiographical Writings.* Shari Benstock, ed. (Chapel Hill: University of North Carolina Press, 1988). Rpt. in *Reading Black, Reading Feminist: A Critical Anthology.* Henry Louis Gates, Jr., ed. New York: Meridian, 1990: 176–203.

Franklin, Jimmie Lewis. "Black Southerners, Shared Experience, and Place: A Reflection. *Journal of Southern History.* Vol. LX, No.1 (February 1994): 3–18.

Fugitive Slave Act. *Documents of American History.* Vol.1. Henry Steele Commager, ed. 7th ed. New York: Meredith Publishing Company, 1963: 321–323.

Gabel, Leona C. *From Slavery to the Sorbonne and Beyond: The Life & Writings of Anna J. Cooper.* Northampton, Massachusetts: Smith College Studies in History, 1982.

Gaines, Kevin K. *Uplifting the Race: Black Leadership, Politics, and Culture in the Twentieth Century.* Chapel Hill, North Carolina: University of North Carolina Press, 1996.

Gage, Frank Wellington. *The Negro Problem in the United States: Its Rise, Development, and Solution* [1892]. Westport, Connecticut: Negro Universities Press, 1970.

Gates, Henry Louis, Jr. "The Trope of a New Negro and the Reconstruction of the Image of the Black." *Representations*. 24 (Fall 1988): 129–155.

Gayarre, Charles. *Louisiana; Its Colonial History and Romance*. New York: Harper & Brothers, 1851: 537–546.

Gebhard, Caroline and Barbara McCaskill. "Introduction." *Post-Bellum, Pre-Harlem: African American Literature and Culture, 1877–1919*. Caroline Gebhard and Barbara McCaskill, eds. New York: New York University Press, 2006: 1–14.

Gehman, Mary. "Visible Means of Support: Businesses, Professions, and Trades of Free People of Color." *Creole: The History and Legacy of Louisiana's Free People of Color*. Sybil Kein, ed. Baton Rouge: Louisiana State University Press, 2000:208–222.

———. *The Free People of Color of New Orleans: An Introduction*. New Orleans, Louisiana: Margaret Media, Inc., 1994.

Gere, Anne Ruggles. "Fashioning American Womanhood(s). *Intimate Practices: Literacy and Cultural Work in U.S. Women's Clubs, 1880–1920*. Urbana: University of Illinois Press, 1997: 134–170.

Gerster, Patrick and Nicholas Cords, eds. *Myth and Southern History, Vol. 1: The Old South*. 2nd edition. Urbana: University of Illinois Press, 1989.

Giddings, Paula. *When and Where I Enter: The Impact of Black Women on Race and Sex in America*. New York: William Morrow and Company, Inc., 1984.

Gillman, Susan. "The Mulatto, Tragic or Triumphant? The Nineteenth-Century American Race Melodrama." *The Culture of Sentiment: Race, Gender, and Sentimentality in 19th Century America*. Shirley Samuels, ed. New York and Oxford: Oxford University Press, 1992:221–43.

Gillman, Susan and Alys Eve Weinbaum. "Introduction: W.E.B. DuBois and the Politics of Juxtaposition." *Next to the Color Line: Gender, Sexuality, and W.E.B. DuBois*. Susan Gillman and Alys Eve Weinbaum, eds. Minneapolis: University of Minnesota Press, 2007: 1–34.

Gilman, Charlotte Perkins. "A Suggestion on the Negro Problem." *American Journal of Sociology*. 14.1 (July 1908): 78–85.

Gilmore, Glenda Elizabeth. *Gender and Jim Crow: Women and the Politics of White Supremacy in North Carolina, 1896–1920*. Chapel Hill: University of North Carolina Press, 1996.

Gould, Virginia Meacham. *Chained to the Rock of Adversity: To Be Free, Black & Female in the Old South*. Athens: University of Georgia Press, 1998.

Gray, Richard. *Southern Aberrations: Writers of the American South and the Problems of Regionalism*. Baton Rouge: Louisiana State University, 2000.

Griffin, Farah Jasmine. "Frances Ellen Watkins Harper in the Reconstruction South." *Sage* (1988): 45–47.

———. *"Who set you flowin?": The African-American Migration Narrative*. New York: Oxford University Press, 1995.

Grimke, Angelina. *An Appeal to the Christian Women of the Southern States*. New York: American Anti-Slavery Society, 1836.

———. *An Appeal to the Women of the Nominally Free States*. New York: W.S. Dorr, 1837.

Gross, Theodore L. "The Negro in the Literature of Reconstruction." *Phylon*. 22.1 (Spring 1961): 5–14.

Gruesz, Kirsten Silva. "Delta Desterrados: Antebelum New Orleans and New World Print Culture." *Look Away!: The U.S. South in New World Studies*. Jon Smith and Deborah Cohn, eds. Durham, North Carolina: Duke University Press, 2004: 52–79.

Guy-Sheftall, Beverly. *Daughters of Sorrow: Attitudes Toward Black Women, 1880–1920*. Brooklyn, NY: Carlson Publishing Inc., 1990.

Hale, Grace Elizabeth. *Making Whiteness: The Culture of Segregation in the South, 1890–1940*. New York: Random House, 1998.

Hall, Gwendolyn Midlo. *Africans in Colonial Louisiana: The Development of Afro-Creole Culture in the Eighteenth Century*. Baton Rouge: Louisiana State University Press, 1992.

Hall, Jacquelyn Dowd and Anne Firor Scott. "Women in the South." *Interpreting Southern History: Historiographical Essays in Honor of Sanford W. Higginbotham*. Eds., John B. Boles and Evelyn Thomas Nolen. Baton Rouge: Louisiana State University Press, 1987: 454–509.

Harper, France E.W. Iola Leroy [1892]. New York: Oxford UP, 1988.

———. *Minnie's Sacrifice, Sowing and Reaping, Trial and Triumph*. Frances Smith Foster, ed. Boston, Massachusetts: Beacon Press, 1994.

———. *Sketches of a Southern Life* [1872]. 3rd edition. Philadelphia: Ferguson Bros. & Co. Printers, 1891.

———. *A Brighter Coming Day: A Frances Ellen Watkins Harper Reader*. Frances Smith Foster, ed. New York: The Feminist Press, 1990.

Harris, Trudier. *From Mammies to Militants: Domestics in Black American Literature*. Philadelphia: Temple University Press, 1982.

Hemenway, Robert. "The Functions of Folklore in Charles Chesnutt's *The Conjure Woman*." *Journal of the Folklore Institute*. 13 (1976):283–309.

Hewitt, Nancy A. "Taking the True Woman Hostage." *Journal of Women's History*. 14.1 (Spring 2002): 156–162.

Higginbotham, Evelyn Brooks. "African-American Women's History and the Metalanguage of Race." *Signs* 17 (Winter 1992): 251–74.

Hill, Patricia. "Frances W. Harper's Aunt Chloe Poems from *Sketches of Southern Life*: Antithesis to the Plantation Literary Tradition." *Mississippi Quarterly* 34.4 (Fall 1981): 403–413.

Hine, Darlene Clark. "Lifting the Veil, Shattering the Silence: Black Women's History in Slavery and Freedom." *Hinesight*. Brooklyn, NY: Carlson Publishing, 1994: 3–26.

———. "Rape and the Inner Lives of Southern Black Women: Thoughts on the Culture of Dissemblance." *Southern Women: Histories and Identities*. Eds., Virginia Bernhard, et. al. Columbia: University of Missouri Press, 1992: 177–189.

Hobson, Elizabeth Christophers (Kimball) and C.E. Hopkins. *A Report Concerning the Colored Women of the South*. Baltimore, Maryland: Trustees of the John F. Slater Fund, 1896.

Hobson, Fred, ed. *South to the Future: An American Region in the Twenty-first Century*. Athens: University of Georgia Press, 2002.

Hodes, Martha. *White Women, Black Men: Illicit Sex in the 19th-Century South*. New Haven: Yale University Press, 1997.

Holt, Hamilton. *The Life Stories of Undistinguished Americans as Told by Themselves* [1906]. Expanded Edition. Introduction by Werner Sollars. New York: Routledge, 2000.

Hopkinson, Natalie "Restoring with Respect: In LeDroit Park, a Pioneering Educator's House Begins Its Journey Back to Glory." *The Washington Post*. (January 19, 2006): H01.

Hunter, Tera W. *To 'Joy My Freedom: Southern Black Women's Lives and Labors after the Civil War*. Cambridge, Massachusetts: Harvard University Press, 1997.

Hutchinson, Louise Daniel. *Anna J. Cooper: A Voice from the South*. Washington, D.C.: Smithsonian Institution Press, 1981.

James, Joy. "Profeminism and Gender Elites: W.E.B. Du Bois, Anna Julia Cooper, and Ida B. Wells-Barnett." *Next to the Color Line: Gender, Sexuality, and W.E.B. Du Bois*. Susan Gillman and Alys Eve Weinbaum, eds. Minneapolis, Minnesota: University of Minnesota Press, 2007: 69–95.

Jefferson, Olive Ruth. "The Southern Negro Women." *The Chautauquan*. 18.1 (October 1893) 91–94.

Jermand, Amanda Smith. "A Southern Woman's Appeal for Justice." *The Independent*. 53 (February 21, 1901): 438–440.

Jewell, K. Sue. *From Mammy to Miss America and Beyond: Cultural Images and the Shaping of U.S. Social Policy*. New York: Routledge, 1993.

Johnson, Sherita L. "Introduction." special issue. "'My Southern Home': The Lives and Literature of 19th century Southern Black Writers. *The Southern Quarterly*. 45.3 (Spring 2008): 5–9.

———. "'In the Sunny South': Reconstructing Frances Harper as Southern." special issue, "'My Southern Home': The Lives and Literature of 19th century Southern Black Writers. *The Southern Quarterly*. 45.3 (Spring 2008): 70–87.

Katzman, David M. and William M. Tuttle, Jr., eds. *Plain Folk: The Life Stories of Undistinguished Americans*. Urbana, Illinois: University of Illinois Press, 1982.

Kein, Sybil, ed. *Creole: The History and Legacy of Louisiana's Free People of Color*. Baton Rouge: LSU Press, 2000.

Kinney, James. *Amalgamation!: Race, Sex, and Rhetoric in the Nineteenth-Century American Novel*. Westport, Connecticut: Greenwood Press, 1985.

Kreyling, Michael. *Inventing Southern Literature*. Jackson: Mississippi University Press, 1998.

———."Toward 'A New Southern Studies.'" *South Central Review* 22 (Spring 2005): 4–18.

Ladd, Barbara. "George W. Cable and American Nationalism." *Nationalism and the Color Line in George W. Cable, Mark Twain, and William Faulkner*. Baton Rouge, LA: Louisiana State University Press, 1996: 37–84.

Lemert, Charles. "Anna Julia Cooper: The Colored Woman's Office." *The Voice of Anna Julia Cooper*. Ed. Charles Lemert and Esme Bhan. Lanham, MD: Rowman & Littlefield, 1998: 1–43.

Lemert, Charles and Esme Bhan, eds. *The Voice of Anna Julia Cooper*. Lanham, MD: Rowman & Littlefield, 1998.

Lerner, Gerda, ed. *Black Women in White America: A Documentary History*. New York: Vintage Books, 1973.

Leslie, Kent Anderson. *Woman of Color, Daughter of Privilege: Amanda America Dickson, 1849–1893*. Athens: University of Georgia Press, 1995.

Litwack, Leon F. *Trouble in Mind: Black Southerners in the Age of Jim Crow*. New York: Vintage Books, 1998.

Loewenberg, Bert James and Ruth Bogin, eds. *Black Women in Nineteenth-Century American Life: Their Words, Their Thoughts, Their Feelings*. University Park: Pennsylvania State University Press, 1976.

Logan, Shirley Wilson. *"We Are Coming": The Persuasive Discourse of Nineteenth-Century Black Women*. Carbondale: Southern Illinois University Press, 1999.

Maguire, Roberta S. "Anna Julia Cooper in and of the South." *Society for the Study of Southern Literature (SSSL) Newsletter*. 37.2 (May 2004): 4–5. May 27, 2004. http://www.uark.edu/ua/sssl/>. Path: Current and Recent Newsletters; Spring 2004.

———. "Kate Chopin and Anna Julia Cooper: Critiquing Kentucky and the South. *Southern Literary Journal*. 35.1 (Fall 2002): 123–137.

Martin, Joan M. "Placage and the Louisiana *Gens de Couleur Libre*: How Race and Sex Defined the Lifestyles of Free Women of Color." *Creole: The History and Legacy of Louisiana's Free People of Color*. Sybil Kein, ed. Baton Rouge: Louisiana State University Press, 2000: 57–70.

Mason, Julian D. "Charles W. Chesnutt as Southern Author." *Mississippi Quarterly* 20.2 (Spring 1967): 77–89.

Matthews, Victoria Earle. "The Value of Race Literature" [1895]. *The Massachusetts Review.* 27 (Summer 1986): 169–191.

———. "Aunt Lindy: A Story Founded on Real Life" [1893]. *Revolutionary Tales: African-American Women's Short Stories, From the First Story to the Present.* Bill Mullen, ed. New York: Dell Publishing, 1995:13–19.

———. "Some of the Dangers Confronting Southern Girls in the North" [1898]. Rptd. in *"We Are Coming": The Persuasive Discourse of Nineteenth-Century Black Women.* By Shirley Wilson Logan. Carbondale: Southern Illinois University Press, 1999:215–220.

May, Vivian M. *Anna Julia Cooper, Visionary Black Feminist: A Critical Introduction.* New York: Routledge, 2007.

———. "'By a Black Woman of the South': Race, Place, and Gender in the Work of Anna Julia Cooper." *The Southern Quarterly.* 45.3 (Spring 2008):127–152.

McCaskill, Barbara and Caroline Gebhard, eds. *Post-Bellum, Pre-Harlem: African American Literature and Culture, 1877–1919.* New York: New York University Press, 2006.

McFatter, Susan. "From Revenge to Resolution: The (R)Evolution of Female Characters in Chesnutt's Fiction." *CLA* (December 1998): 194–211.

McKay, Nellie Y. "The Souls of Black Women Folk in the Writings of W.E.B. DuBois." *Reading Black, Reading Feminist: A Critical Anthology.* Henry Louis Gates, Jr., ed. New York: Meridian, 1990: 227–243.

McKee, Kathryn and Annette Trefzer. "Global Contexts, Local Literatures: The New Southern Studies."*American Literature.* 78.4 (December 2006):677–690.

McPherson, James Alan. "A Region Not Home: The View From Exile." *The Prevailing South: Life and Politics in a Changing Culture.* Dudley Clendinen, ed. Atlanta: Longstreet Press, 1988: 194–209.

Mixon, Wayne. "The Unfulfilled Dream: Charles W. Chesnutt and the New South Movement." *Southern Humanities Review.* 10 (July 1976): 23–33.

Morrison, Toni. "Home." *The House that Race Built: Black Americans, U.S. Terrain.* Lubiano Wahneema, ed. New York: Pantheon Books, 1997: 3–12.

Mossell, Mrs. N.F. *The Work of the Afro-American Woman* [1894]. New York: Oxford University Press, 1988.

Murdy, Anne-Elizabeth. *Teach the Nation: Public School, Racial Uplift, and Women's Writing in the 1890s.* New York: Routledge, 2003.

Najmi, Samina. "Janet, Polly, and Olivia: Constructs of Blackness and White Femininity in Charles Chesnutt's *The Marrow of Tradition.*" *Southern Literary Journal.* 32.1 (Fall 1999): 1–19.

The Negro Problem: A Series of Articles by Representative American Negroes of Today [1903]. New York: Arno Press, 1969.

"The Negro Problem: How It Appeals to a Southern Colored Woman." *The Independent.* 54 (September 18, 1902): 2221–2224.

"The Negro Problem: How It Appeals to a Southern White Woman." *The Independent.* 54 (September 18, 1902): 2224–2228.

Neverdon-Morton, Cynthia. *Afro-American Women of the South and the Advancement of the Race, 1895–1925.* Knoxville: University of Tennessee Press, 1989.

"Observations of the Southern Race Feeling by a Northern Woman." *The Independent.* 56 (March 17, 1904): 594–599.

Orrick, Lucy Semmes. "Along the Color Line." *National Magazine* [Boston]. (November 1904): 172–177.

Painter, Nell Irvin. *Standing at Armageddon: The United States, 1877–1919.* New York: W.W. Norton & Co., 1987.

————. *Southern History Across the Color Line.* Chapel Hill: University of North Carolina 2002.

Page, Thomas Nelson. *The Negro: The Southerner's Problem* [1904]. Reprint. New York Johnson Reprint Corporation, 1970.

Payne, Ladell. *Black Novelists and The Southern Literary Tradition.* Athens: Univ. of Georgia Press, 1981.

Peacock, James L., Harry L. Watson, and Carrie R. Matthews, eds. *The American South in a Global World.* Chapel Hill: University of North Carolina Press, 2005.

Perkins, Linda M. "The Impact of the 'Cult of True Womanhood' on the Education of Black Woman." *Journal of Social Issues.* 39.3 (1983): 17–28.

Perkins, Margo V. *Autobiography as Activism: Three Black Women of the Sixties.* Jackson, Mississippi: University Press of Mississippi, 2000.

Perman, Michael. *Struggle for Mastery: Disfranchisement in the South, 1888–1908.* Chapel Hill: University of North Carolina Press, 2001.

Perry, Carolyn and Mary Louise Weaks, eds. *The History of Southern Women's Literature.* Baton Rouge: Louisiana State University Press, 2002.

Peterson, Carla L. *"Doers of the Word": African-American Women Speakers and Writers in the North (1830–1880).* New York: Oxford University Press, 1995.

Prenshaw, Peggy W. "'The True Happenings of My Life': Reading Southern Women Autobiographers." *Haunted Bodies: Gender and Southern Texts.* Anne Goodwyn Jones and Susan V. Donaldson, eds. Charlottesville, Virginia: University Press of Virginia, 1997: 443–463.

Pryse, Marjorie. "Zora Neale Hurston, Alice Walker, and the 'Ancient Power' of Black Women." Introduction. *Conjuring: Black Women, Fiction, and Literary Tradition.* Eds. Marjorie Pryse and Hortense J. Spillers. Bloomington: Indiana University Press, 1985: 1–24.

"The Race Problem—An Autobiography by A Southern Colored Woman." *The Independent.* 56 (March 17, 1904): 586–589.

Reed, John Shelton. "The South: What Is It? Where Is It?" *My Tears Spoiled My Aim and Other Reflections on Southern Culture.* (n.p.: University of Missouri Press, 1993). Rpt. in *The South in Perspective: An Anthology of Southern Literature.* Edward Francisco, Robert Vaughan, and Linda Francisco, eds. Upper Saddle River, New Jersey: Prentice Hall, 2001:1241–1259.

————. *One South: An Ethnic Approach to Regional Culture.* Baton Rouge: Louisiana State University Press, 1982.

Render, Sylvia Lyon. *Charles W. Chesnutt.* Boston: Twayne Publishers, 1980.

Richardson, Thomas J., ed. *The Grandissimes: Centennial Essays.* Jackson: University Press of Mississippi, 1981.

Ridgely, J.V. *Nineteenth-Century Southern Literature.* Lexington: University Press of Kentucky, 1980.

Roberts, Mary Louise. "True Womanhood Revisited." *Journal of Women's History.* 14.1 (Spring 2002): 150–155.

Robinson, Angelo Rich. "Race, Place, and Space: Remaking Whiteness in the Post-Reconstruction South." *Southern Literary Journal.* 35.1 (Fall 2002): 97–107.

Rose, Willie Lee. "'The Old Allegiance'" [1964]. Reprinted in *Reconstruction: An Anthology of Revisionist Writings.* Kenneth M. Stampp and Leon F. Litwack, eds. Baton Rouge: Louisiana State University Press, 1969: 175–192.

Rosen, Hannah. "'Not That Sort of Women': Race, Gender, and Sexual Violence during the Memphis Riot of 1866." *Sex, Love, Race: Crossing Boundaries in North American History.* Ed., Martha Hodes. New York: New York University Press, 1999: 267–293.

Scarborough, Prof. W. S. "The Negro in Fiction as Portrayer and Portrayed." *The Southern Workman.* (September 1899): 358–361.

Scott, Anne Firor. "Women in the South: History as Fiction, Fiction as History." *Rewriting the South: History and Fiction*. Lothar Honnighausen and Valeria Gennaro Lerda, eds. Tubingen, Germany: Francke Verlag, 1993: 22–34.

Schafer, Judith K. "'Open and Notorious Concubinage': The Emancipation of Slave Mistresses by Will and the Supreme Court in Antebellum Louisiana." *Louisiana History* 28.2 (Spring 1987): 165–182.

Selinger, Eric. "Aunts, Uncles, Audience: Gender and Genre in Charles Chesnutt's *The Conjure Woman*." *Black American Literature Forum*. 25.4 (Winter 1991):665–688.

Sellers, Charles Grier, ed. *The Southerner as American*. Chapel Hill: University of North Carolina Press, 1960.

Sieg, Vera, ed. *The Negro Problem: A Bibliography*. Madison, Wisconsin: Wisconsin Free Library Commission, 1908.

Sollors,Werner. *Neither Black Nor White, Yet Both: Thematic Explorations of Interracial Literature*. Cambridge, Massachusetts: Harvard University Press, 1997.

"Souths: Global and Local." Special issue of *The Southern Quarterly*. 42.1 (Fall 2003).

Smith, Barbara Ellen. "Place and the Past in the Global South." *American Literature*. 78.4 (December 2006): 693–695.

Smith, Jon and Deborah Cohn, eds. *Look Away!: The U.S. South in New World Studies*. Durham: Duke University Press, 2004.

Spillers, Hortense J. "Mama's Baby, Papa's Maybe: An American Grammar Book" [1987]. *African American Literary Theory: A Reader*. Winston Napier, ed. New York: New York University Press, 2000: 257–279.

Stack, Carol. *Call to Home: African Americans Reclaim the Rural South*. New York: Basic Books, 1996.

Stepto, Robert B. "'The Simple But Intensely Human Inner Life of Slavery': Storytelling, Fiction and the Revision of History in Charles W. Chesnutt's 'Uncle Julius Stories'. " *History and Tradition in Afro-American Culture*. Gunter Lenz, ed. Frankfurt: Campus, 1984: 29–55.

Sterling, Dorothy, ed. *We Are Your Sisters: Black Women in the Nineteenth Century*. New York: W.W. Norton & Co., 1984.

———. *Speak Out in Thunder Tones: Letters and Other Writings by Black Northerners, 1787–1865*. Garden City, New York: Doubleday, 1973.

Still, William. *The Underground Railroad*. Philadelphia: Porter & Coates Publishers, 1872.

Stocken, June. "Charles Waddell Chesnutt and the Solution to the Race Problem." *Negro American Literature Forum* 3.2 (Summer 1969): 52–56.

Tate, Claudia. *Domestic Allegories of Political Desire: the Black Heroine's Text at the Turn of the Century*. New York: Oxford University Press, 1992.

Terborg-Penn, Rosalyn and Sharon Harley, eds. *The Afro-American Woman: Struggles and Images*. Port Washington, New York: Kennikat Press, 1978.

Thurber, Cheryl. "The Development of the Mammy Image and Mythology." *Southern Women: Histories and Identities*. Eds., Virginia Bernhard, et. al. Columbia: University of Missouri Press, 1992: 87–108.

Tindall, George B. "Mythology: A New Frontier in Southern History." *Myth and Southern History, Vol. 1: The Old South*. 2nd edition. Patrick Gerster and Nicholas Cords, eds. Urbana: University of Illinois Press, 1989:1–15.

Tregle, Joseph G., Jr. "Creoles and Americans." *Creole New Orleans: Race and Americanization*. Arnold R. Hirsch and Joseph Logsdon, eds. Baton Rouge: Louisiana State University, 1992:131–185.

Turner, Arlin. *George W. Cable: A Biography*. Durham, North Carolina: Duke University Press, 1956.

————, ed. *Critical Essays on George W. Cable.* Boston, Massachusetts: G.K. Hall & Co., 1980.

Wadelington, Charles W. and Richard F. Knapp. *Charlotte Hawkins Brown and Palmer Memorial Institute: What One Young African American Woman Could Do.* Chapel Hill: University of North Carolina Press, 1999.

Wade-Gayles, Gloria. "Black Women Journalists in the South, 1880–1905: An Approach to the Study of Black Women's History." *Callaloo* (February-October 1981): 138–152.

Walker, Alice. "In Search of Our Mothers' Garden: The Legacy of Southern Black Women" [1974]. *Norton Anthology of African American Literature.* New York: Norton, 1997: 2380–2387.

Ward, Jerry D. "Bridges and Deep Water." *Sturdy Black Bridges: Visions of Black Women in Literature.* Roseanne P. Bell, Bettye J. Parker, and Beverly Guy-Sheftall, eds. Garden City, New York: Anchor Press/Doubleday, 1979:184–190.

Washington, Mary Helen. Introduction. *A Voice from the South, By a Black Woman of the South.* By Anna Julia Cooper. New York: Oxford University Press, 1988: xxix-xxxi.

Watkins, Rychetta N. "The Southern Roots of Ida B. Wells-Barnett's Revolutionary Activism." *The Southern Quarterly.* 45.3 (Spring 2008): 108–126.

Watson, Thomas E. "The Negro Question in the South." *The Arena.* B.O. Flower, ed. Boston: Arena Publishing Co., 1892.

Welter, Barbara. "The Cult of True Womanhood: 1820–1860." *American Quarterly.* 18.2 (Summer 1966): 151–174.

White, Deborah Gray. *Ar'n't I a Woman?: Female Slaves in the Plantation South.* Revised edition. New York: W.W. Norton & Co., 1999.

————. *To Heavy a Load: Black Women in Defense of Themselves, 1894–1994.* New York: W.W. Norton, 1999.

Williams, Fannie Barrier. "A Northern Negro's Autobiography." *The Independent.* 57 (July 14, 1904): 91–96.

Williamson, Joel. "The Meaning of Freedom" [1965]. Reprinted in *Reconstruction: An Anthology of Revisionist Writings.* Kenneth M. Stampp and Leon F. Litwack, eds. Baton Rouge: Louisiana State University Press, 1969: 193–219.

Wilson, Charles Reagan. "The Invention of Southern Tradition: The Writing and Ritualization of Southern History, 1880–1940." *Rewriting the South: History and Fiction.* Lothar Honnighausen and Valeria Gennaro Lerda, eds. Tubingen, Germany: Francke Verlag, 1993: 3–21.

Wynes, Charles E., ed. *Forgotten Voices: Dissenting Southerners in an Age of Conformity.* Baton Rouge: Louisiana State University, 1967.

Yaeger, Patricia. *Dirt and Desire: Reconstructing Southern Women's Writing, 1930-1990.* Chicago: University of Chicago Press, 2000.

Yellin, Jean Fagan and Cynthia D. Bond, comp. *The Pen Is Ours: A Listing of Writings by and about African-American Women before 1910.* New York: Oxford University Press, 1991.

Index

A

Alabama, 26, 28–29, 31,118
Andrews, William L., 11, 42
autobiographies (on race problems),
114–127

B

Bhabha, Homi K., 112,113
Black Codes (also *Code Noir*), 47, 58,
75, 80, 84, 89, 111, 137n39
black mammies, 30, 32–34, 43, 53,
90–91, 120, 124, 129 Aunt
Chloe Fleet, 30, 32–34, 43, 61
Clemence, 53, 77, 80–81, 86–89,
90, 91, 92, 93 other domestic
workers, 119–120, 121, 125
Brown, William Wells, 11

C

Cable, George Washington, 3, 4, 6, 7,
9, 43, 44, 45–48, 49, 51, 52–55,
57, 70–96, 107, 108, 110, 115,
129 *Grandissimes, The*, 7, 52,
70–72, 74–96 *Negro Question,
The*, 45, 46, 47, 73, 94 *Silent
South, The*, 45
Carby, Hazel V., 20–21, 122, 128
Cary, Mary Ann Shadd, 11, 24
Chesnutt, Charles Waddell, 3, 4, 6, 7,
8–9, 12, 39, 44, 45–48, 49–60,
62–70, 88, 95,107, 110,117,
129 *Conjure Woman, The*,
7, 48, 49, 56, 57, 59, 63, 65,
66–70, 88, 117 *House Behind
the Cedars, The*, 39, 45, 56, 63
Church Terrell, Mary, 21, 52, 61, 107
Cobb, James C., 132n7, 5, 29, 107
Colored Women's League, 52, 102

conjure /-ing, conjuration (also voodoo),
6, 44, 48–53, 63–64, 65–70, 74,
77, 78, 82, 83, 86, 92
Cooper, Anna Julia, 1, 2–3, 4, 6, 7–8,
9, 21, 23, 43, 52, 61, 62, 95,
96, 97–110, 128, 129 *Voice
from the South, A*, 1, 3, 6, 96,
97–110
Creoles, 35, 37–38, 39, 45, 46, 47, 52,
72–73, 74, 75–76, 78–79, 81,
83, 88
Crummell, Alexander, 101–102

D

Davis, Thadious M., 21, 39, 117, 118
disenfranchisement. *See* voting / voting
rights
Dixon, Thomas, 5, 61
Douglass, Frederick, 11, 16, 19, 20, 41
Douglass, Anna Murry, 19, 133n9
DuBois, W.E.B., 57, 62, 98, 102, 114,
115 *Souls of Black Folk, The*,
57, 98
Dunbar / M Street School, 100, 108,
141n7
Dunbar, Paul Laurence, 57, 62

F

Foner, Eric, 22, 132n1
Foster, Frances Smith, 20–21, 23, 28,
128
Fugitive Slave Law, 13, 20, 35, 36, 58

G

Gates, Henry Louis, Jr., 11, 12, 22, 48,
62, 66
Georgia, 26
Grimké, Charlotte Forten, 10, 41

H

Harper, Frances Ellen Watkins, 3, 4, 6–7, 8, 10–16, 19–44, 61, 95, 98, 107, 129 *Iola Leroy,* 12, 14, 15, 34, 35–41, 43, *Sketches of a Southern Life,* 12, 14, 15, 30–34, 61
Harris, Joel Chandler, 5, 30, 65, 107

I

Independent, The, 47, 113–126, 129

J

Jacobs, Harriet, 10, 21, 128
Jermand, Amanda Smith, 115–118

K

Keckley, Elizabeth, 10
Kennedy, John Pendleton, 5

L

Louisiana (New Orleans), 9, 37, 39, 45, 46–47, 48, 52, 72–73, 74, 75, 76, 78, 81, 83, 87, 89, 92, 116, 117

M

Maryland, 6, 13, 14–20, 25, 26, 29, 35, 36, 41, 36, 98 Baltimore, 6, 13, 14, 15, 16, 17, 18, 19, 25, 26,
Matthews, Victoria Earle, 61, 125
miscegenation, 6, 35, 37, 39, 40, 46, 55, 74, 75–76, 77, 78–79, 80, 81, 82, 83, 87, 89, 92, 99, 119, 121–122
Mississippi (Natchez and Vicksburg), 38, 39, 43
Morrison, Toni, 111, 116, 123

N

National Association for the Advancement of Colored People (NAACP), 97
National Association for Colored Women (NACW), 61, 62, 102, 126
Negro Problem, The (book), 57, 98
New Negro, 22–23, 51, 62, 64, 66, 69, 70, 98, 107, 116, 129
North Carolina, 31, 46, 48, 57, 99, 103–104

P

Page, Thomas Nelson, 3, 5, 30, 43, 65, 107
Philadelphia (Pennsylvania), 13, 24
plaçage, 78–79, 81, 138n43
Plantation Literature, 12, 30, 40, 107
Plessy vs. Ferguson, 117
Port Royal Experiment (South Carolina), 10

S

Scarborough, William S., 56–57
South, as southeastern U.S., 5, 131n1 global South (definitions of), 2, 56, 72–73, 92, 129–130, 131n3 New South (definitions of), 5, 9
South Carolina, 26, 27–28
Spillers, Hortense J., 80, 81
Still, William, 13, 14–15, 23, 24, 26, 41
suffrage. *See* voting / voting rights

T

tragic mulatto, 35, 37, 38, 53, 66, 81, 82, 89, 95, 129
Truth, Sojourner, 10
Tuskegee Women's Club, 52

U

Underground Railroad, as abolitionist movement, 13–14, 24
Underground Railroad, The (book), 23
U.S. Constitution 14th and 15th amendments, 4, 54, 56, 57, 58, 59, 60

V

voodoo. *See* conjure / -ing, conjuration
voting / voting rights, 4, 22, 27, 28, 31–33, 52, 54, 55, 57–58, 59, 60, 61, 62, 71, 72, 113

W

Washington, Booker T., 3, 23, 57, 98, 107, 114, 115
Watkins, William, Rev., 13, 19
Wells-Barnett, Ida B., 21, 41, 52, 98, 107, 114
Williams, Fannie B., 62, 120–121, 125–126